(M)othering
Labeled Children

BILINGUAL EDUCATION & BILINGUALISM

Series Editors: **Nancy H. Hornberger** (*University of Pennsylvania, USA*) and **Wayne E. Wright** (*Purdue University, USA*)

Bilingual Education and Bilingualism is an international, multidisciplinary series publishing research on the philosophy, politics, policy, provision and practice of language planning, Indigenous and minority language education, multilingualism, multiculturalism, biliteracy, bilingualism and bilingual education. The series aims to mirror current debates and discussions. New proposals for single-authored, multiple-authored, or edited books in the series are warmly welcomed, in any of the following categories or others authors may propose: overview or introductory texts; course readers or general reference texts; focus books on particular multilingual education program types; school-based case studies; national case studies; collected cases with a clear programmatic or conceptual theme; and professional education manuals.

All books in this series are externally peer-reviewed.

Full details of all the books in this series and of all our other publications can be found on http://www.multilingual-matters.com, or by writing to Multilingual Matters, St Nicholas House, 31-34 High Street, Bristol BS1 2AW, UK.

BILINGUAL EDUCATION & BILINGUALISM: 131

(M)othering Labeled Children

Bilingualism and Disability in the Lives of Latinx Mothers

María Cioè-Peña

MULTILINGUAL MATTERS
Bristol • Blue Ridge Summit

DOI https://doi.org/10.21832/CIOE1289

Names: Cioè-Peña, María - author.

Title: (M)othering Labeled Children: Bilingualism and Disability in the Lives of Latinx Mothers/María Cioè-Peña.

Description: Blue Ridge Summit; Bristol: Multilingual Matters, [2021] | Series: Bilingual Education & Bilingualism: 131 | Based on the author's dissertation (doctoral)—Graduate Center, City University of New York, 2019. | Includes bibliographical references and index. | Summary: "This book explores the experiences and identities of minoritized Latinx mothers who are raising a child who is labeled as both an emergent bilingual and dis/abled. It showcases relationships between families and schools and reveals the ways in which school-based decisions regarding disability, language and academic placement impact family dynamics"—Provided by publisher.

Identifiers: LCCN 2020055992 (print) | LCCN 2020055993 (ebook) | ISBN 9781800411272 (Paperback) | ISBN 9781800411289 (Hardback) | ISBN 9781800411296 (PDF) | ISBN 9781800411302 (ePub) | ISBN 9781800411319 (Kindle Edition)

Subjects: LCSH: Special education—New York (State)—New York. | Children with disabilities—Education—New York (State)—New York. | Education, Bilingual—New York (State)—New York. | Discrimination in education. | Communication in families—United States—Case studies. | Hispanic American mothers—New York (State)—New York—Case studies.

Classification: LCC LC3983.N7 C56 2021 (print) | LCC LC3983.N7 (ebook) | DDC 371.9109747/1—dc23 LC record available at https://lccn.loc.gov/2020055992

LC ebook record available at https://lccn.loc.gov/2020055993

British Library Cataloguing in Publication Data
A catalogue entry for this book is available from the British Library.

ISBN-13: 978-1-80041-128-9 (hbk)
ISBN-13: 978-1-80041-127-2 (pbk)

Multilingual Matters
UK: St Nicholas House, 31-34 High Street, Bristol BS1 2AW, UK.
USA: NBN, Blue Ridge Summit, PA, USA.

Website: www.multilingual-matters.com
Twitter: Multi_Ling_Mat
Facebook: https://www.facebook.com/multilingualmatters
Blog: www.channelviewpublications.wordpress.com

The policy of Multilingual Matters/Channel View Publications is to use papers that are natural, renewable and recyclable products, made from wood grown in sustainable forests. In the manufacturing process of our books, and to further support our policy, preference is given to printers that have FSC and PEFC Chain of Custody certification. The FSC and/or PEFC logos will appear on those books where full certification has been granted to the printer concerned.

Typeset by Deanta Global Publishing Services, Chennai, India
Printed and bound in the UK by the CPI Books Group Ltd.
Printed and bound in the US by NBN.

To all immigrant mothers who continue to journey far from home in the hope that their children will have more than they did. Thank you for taking on the challenges that you do; your sacrifices may not be recognized in real time, but their impact is indisputable.

her dreams become their dreams, the life of an immigrant is hard.
but she prays to god that her kids will become and receive everything she never got.

—unknown

Contents

Acknowledgements ix

The Able Bendiciones of Latina Mothers: A Foreword xi
Ofelia García

Preface: A Note on Positionality xiv

**Part 1: The Social Constructions of Motherhood: Poverty,
Monolingualism and Disability (by Proxy)**

1 Why Mothers? Why *These* Mothers? 3

2 'They don't care, they don't understand, they're in denial':
   Constructions of Mothers as Others 13

3 Other People's Stories 33

4 Setting the Stage: An Introduction to the Mothers and the
   Significance of a Place and Time 43

5 At Home with the Testimonialistas 53

Part 2: Testimonios: Mothers Speak

6 Mothering With, Through and Alongside Dis/ability Labels 67

7 Broken Promise: The Security of Bilingualism for the
   Future and the Ambiguity of Bilingualism in the Present 89

8 Teacher? Student? Both: Mothers as Language Brokers 106

9 Bending Roles: Resisting Exclusion, Creating Paths
   for Engagement 118

10 Broken Spirits: Challenges Faced by MoEBLADs 130

11 Motherhood as Purpose 143

**Part 3: Making Room for Mothers: Visions of
    Radical Possibilities**

12   Repairing Broken Systems   159

13   Moving Forward Together   175

     Making Personal, Professional and Global Connections:
     An Afterword   178
     David J. Connor

     Index   184

Acknowledgements

I am who I am today because of...

my mother, thank you for the (tough and gentle) love and for the countless sacrifices.

Emiliano & Aurelia. You are the center of my world, thank you for making me the center of yours. *Mucho y Siempe.*

Eric. You have pushed me to grow in ways I could have never imagined. Thank you for serving as a sounding board, first and last reader, editor, and, most importantly, frequent destroyer of doubt.

los 'Hernandez', especialmente Hilaritza, Candybelle, Anabelle, Melvin, Diogenes, Hector, Maria Elizabeth, mis tias Deisy y Altagracia, mis tios Melido, Jose, y Armando, gracias por las bolas a la universidad, las firmas en los prestamos de estudios, por el apoyo, aliento, entendimiento y amor. ¡Hoy se bebe!

the Cioes who have showed me the magic of intergenerational love and the importance of lazy days on the beach.

the many great teachers I have had throughout my years as a student at PS. 169, JHS 138 – Dewey in NYC, Brooklyn School for Global Studies, SUNY-Cortland, Long Island University – Brooklyn and, finally, at the CUNY-Graduate Center. Thank you for every word assigned and every bit of feedback offered. Above all, thank you for not only quenching my thirst for information but for *encouraging* it.

every person who worked at or with PS 24K from 2007-2013; special shout out to the fifth grade and third grade planning teams of 2007-2013, Thank you for holding space for me, for sharing your wisdom and for cheering me on even after I left.

Steve Shreefter, a dear friend and mentor. Steve, you showed me that a pedagogical identity that is centered on truth, inquiry and social justice is not only possible but necessary. Thank you. While you did not live to see me on this journey, I have carried your memory with me every step of the way.

Cecelia Traugh, Ofelia García, David Connor, Celia Oyler, Maite Sánchez, Katia Goldfarb and Jaime Grinberg, to name a few. There are no words to thank you for your time, advice, support, generosity, kindness, and, and…. I dedicate my teaching career to carving out paths for those to come, in the same way you did for me.

my students and their families, the mothers in this book and their families. Thank you for trusting me, for letting me into your homes, and for sharing such precious parts of your life. I am forever humbled.

The Institute for Descriptive Inquiry (IDI) and IDI friends whom I only get to see for a week or two every summer but who bring such riches to my life as a teacher, a parent and a human being. I am eternally grateful for all of the reading, writing and questioning that we've shared.

my GC communities and friends, especially cohort 13, CUNY-NYSIEB, Alisa, Emily and Tom, we could've just been classmates or coworkers but our shared commitment to radical possibilities in and out of schools has made us family. Thank you for showing me what a healthy and supportive community can look like in the academy.

my colleagues at MSU, especially in Educational Foundations, thank you for welcoming me with open arms and for making me feel a part of the group from day one.

A sincere and heartfelt thank you to Home Room and the village of scholarly women who supported me each step of the way as friends, writing partners, readers, therapists, accountability buddies and mock audiences. I had never known the wonder of (intellectual) sisterhood until I met you.

Kelly, Christian, Abby, Adrielle, Kate, Heather, Aletha, Rebecca and Liz, … [insert funny GIF].

Toni Morrison, Kate DiCamillo (author of *The Tale of Despereaux*), and Kevin Boyle (author of *Arc of Justice*), none of whom I've ever met but whose writing drew me in, provided safe haven and nurtured me in ways that traditional fictional writing can never compare.

of the immigrant women, many of them mothers, who make my life as a scholar possible by caring for my children and my home. Thank you.

those who came before me. Thank you for opening doors, windows and, in many cases, for making cracks in the ceiling.

The Able Bendiciones of Latina Mothers: A Foreword

While reading María Cioè-Peña's manuscript in order to write this Foreword, I found myself crying. The testimonios of these immigrant monolingual Spanish-speaking Latinx mothers made me feel deeply – sometimes sadness, sometimes anger, most of the time admiration for their unwavering support of their children, children who have been labeled as disabled and as English language learners by a school system. In these pages, Cioè-Peña makes us listen to these mothers, and in so doing, she cracks all the myths that have been built around poor immigrant mothers as ignorant, unengaged, uncaring.

For me, education needs to be a conversation with people whose existence is valued. But in this book, Cioè-Peña makes obvious that the education system has considered these mothers and their children as non-existent, unknowing and damaged. School educators have not held any meaningful conversations with these mothers who are themselves educators too, of their children at home. This is perhaps the first lesson contained in this book – that these mothers exist and that they are mothering their children, not as disabled and monolingual, but as able bendiciones, as very capable bilingual blessings.

In the Preface, Cioè-Peña tells us that she has been like a 'museum curator'. In establishing a true conversation with these mothers as equals, Cioè-Peña brings to life pieces of the mothers and their children that have been made invisible. Rooted in the Latin *curare* of the word *curator*, María approaches this study with pastoral care, caring for the mothers, their children and also her readers. With the ability gained from years of involvement in descriptive inquiry processes, Cioè-Peña shares these mothers' testimonios in ways that bring out our emotions. But in so doing, they heal us, curándonos of the fragmented visions of bilingual dis/abled children and their mothers. Reading this book becomes a catharsis, as we shed notions that educational professionals and scholars have often given us about these children and these mothers. These mothers and their children re-exist through their accounts.

This is not a book about mothers, but a book *with* mothers. In many ways, Cioè-Peña inverts the relationship that has always put so-called professionals first, silencing those who are receiving services, especially if they are mothers of racialized bilingual poor children. Cioè-Peña starts elsewhere. By putting these mothers and their children at the center, she changes the locus of enunciation of who tells the story of their children.

Schools are quick to categorize and label. Some children are labeled as disabled, others as English language learners. But what happens when children are labeled as both? The inability of schools to consider the whole child results in not supporting children holistically. Cioè-Peña describes how when many of these children are placed in classrooms for disabled children, they are then often taken out of bilingual classrooms, robbing them of opportunities to use their bilingualism constructively. Education systems refuse to see the whole child. By taking up the mothers' visions, this book rebuilds these children, reconstituting what has been deconstituted and made destitute – their humanity.

In contrast to the education systems that categorize them, these mothers see their children holistically, beyond singularities of vision. They see them as diferentes, but not as disabled; they see them simply as having very little problemitas. They recognize the emotional and physical toll that mothering a disabled child takes, and they recognize the vacío and emptiness of being in abusive spousal relationships. But these mothers are fierce about their children coming first, about moving heaven and earth for them.

These mothers' testimonios reinforce the importance of bilingualism for their children and families. Spanish is important for the mothers' lives for reasons that go beyond those given in the scholarly literature. Yes, they tell us, Spanish for identity is important, and even for the opportunities it might provide in the future. But most important for these mothers is the role that Spanish plays in their lives as undocumented Latinas. They fear deportation, and they want their children to speak Spanish in case they are forced to live in a Spanish-speaking country in the future. In the present, they want to ensure that their children can speak to their other siblings, other children who are living in their countries of origin. Spanish is not simply for the heart, or for future possibilities; it is important for the lives of these mothers in the present.

Cioè-Peña's book takes us for a spin. Not only does she invert the relationship of authority in the act of educar, giving mothers, and not simply professional educators, their rightful place. She also makes clear that the act of educating is *reciprocal*, that is, children do not just learn from adults; adults learn from children. And the act of educar *extends* beyond the walls of the school and the home *to the community* and is done *in community*. These acts of *reciprocal and extended community education* are especially evident in the mothers' testimonios as they share their mothering experiences with language. The mothers teach their children to read and write Spanish, something the schools are not doing. Beyond the home, the mothers take their children to community activities such as Spanish language catechism. At the same time, these Spanish-speaking mothers educan their children as they work through schoolwork and tareas in English. We find the mothers often asking their children for help in these endeavors, asking them, for example, whether what they're saying is the way it is said in English. We see the mothers finding help not only for their children, but also for themselves – from tutors for their children that cost them dearly, from the translator on the phone as they work with their children, from their other children, from these children themselves. The mothers are quick to recognize that their children help them as they help them, and that they are learning *with* the children.

The mothers' act of educar is not reduced to language. They see education as more expansive. They teach their children to develop caring relationships with others and with God, as well as self-care. In fact, these mothers feel that their children are limited only by labels of disability that cloud the lenses of professional educators. Their vision of their children is that they are the same as all others; the children are limited only by school practices.

Important lessons about motherhood, disability, bilingualism and undocumented status are learned here through the mothers' testimonios. In particular, these accounts speak to teachers of children labeled as disabled and English language learners. They provide them with a different lens, a motherhood lens of care and unconditional love which shifts these children's deficiencies to strengths and possibilities. The mothers' testimonios move our labels, as we are led to really see the children with their abilities and their dynamic bilingual use. The mothers' descriptions of themselves and their children question so-called expert knowledge, and they remind us to look closely at the children in their fullness as they act. These testimonios substitute absences by plenitudes, disabilities by abilities, limited English by competent bilingualism; they spark possibilities, as we see these children emerge as able bendiciones for all.

Ofelia García
The Graduate Center
City University of New York

Preface: A Note on Positionality

Throughout this book, you will find that I have included endnotes where I describe the choices I made, particularly in relation to language use and terminology. I do this in part because as a researcher I see my role more akin to museum curator than art critic. My influence is palpable throughout the book (e.g. in the structural choices I made, the ways in which I frame and group ideas and stories), but what I really want to do is to showcase the subject of the book: Mothers. Still, I start this book by sharing my story, the story of how I came to this work, to this country, to this research. I do this in Chapter 1. Here, I explain why.

My story is an important place to start for multiple reasons: my life experiences are what led me to the fields of bilingual education and special education. As an educator I have had the privilege of experiencing schooling from the stance of both a student and a teacher, from the lens of a daughter and a mother. More importantly still, I start with my story in recognition that we are in a moment in history when 'who you are' and 'who the world makes you out to be' need to be reconciled. It is important to share who I am in order for you, as a reader, to understand the women to whom this book is dedicated, the women whose stories fill the pages you are holding. It is important to understand that I arrived to this research from a place of longing, of emptiness – even if that was not evident to me when I started my doctoral journey or even when I first wrote the dissertation that would eventually result in this book – of wanting to see my mother's efforts, my sister's efforts as a young mother, my efforts as a racialized mother, every immigrant mother's efforts, every Black, indigenous, mother of color in the United States' efforts to be represented from a place of strength and appreciation. I do this in stark contrast to what my educational background conditioned me to believe: that mothers like mine, Black and Brown immigrants who didn't learn English fast enough, who were poor and working class, were empty vessels in need of filling. Over the years, mothers who are racialized as Black, indigenous, people of color, have been framed as welfare queens, and more recently, as public charges (Hancock, 2003; Weber, 2020). This book aims to chip away at those labels, to show the ways in which labels are mounted upon mothers as a way to devalue their contributions, as a way to rationalize the violence that is enacted upon them.

I start this book by telling you about who I am because it is essential to understanding why I chose to study, not what happens to children in schools but rather how what happens in schools reverberates through the home. Much of the academic scholarship that is written about mothers, Latinx mothers in particular, focuses on the ways in which schools can better support them and/or how schools can ensure that they are adequately equipped to support their children. All of this is written from a Western lens, a lens that evaluates Latinx mothers' contributions in relation to those of white mothers, which explains why another common lineage of education scholarship and research is grounded in explaining the cultural dynamics of Latinx families. Still, very little of this work is aimed at finding ways to make space for mothers' funds of knowledge, to make space for them, to ensure that their voices are heard. Most of it is aimed at explaining away their forced absence or to maximize the hidden labor that a school can extract from them. That is the literature that I consumed as a graduate student when working on my master's in science of education, when I was a classroom teacher and when I started my doctoral journey. I swam and waded through those waters long enough to realize that the voices that were missing from those readings were those of the mothers themselves.

In recent years, there has been an increasing push for scholars to state their positionality, to talk about who they are in relation to their work (Lin, 2015; Manohar et al., 2017). In part, this is done to ensure credibility, to ensure that the presentation of the data accounts for researcher bias. With that in mind, it would be easier and less cumbersome to simply write a positionality statement, one that informed you of my relationship to these groups: I am an immigrant, I grew up in the same neighborhood that these mothers are raising their children in, I was a teacher in a local community school, I attended the same church as some of them, we share a common language and, very significantly, we are all mothers. Perhaps it is for this reason that the mothers were so open with me, perhaps my presence and trustworthiness within the community allowed them to feel safe sharing their life with me. However, these points of communal convergence do not absolve me of bias because they also cloud the fact that we have distinct immigrant experiences because unlike many, if not all, of the mothers in this book, I navigate the world as a formally educated, middle class, multilingual, Black Latina who immigrated to the United States through chain migration in a distinctly different time; a time when nationalism wasn't as palpable, at least not to me. I am a mother who, while racialized and pathologized, also has access to spaces of overwhelming privilege. More importantly, this focus on my positionality erases their agency, their own sense of urgency to tell their story, their basic and human need to be heard. I share my story because who I am now is not who I always was, but who I am now is most certainly a product of all of the mothering and nurturing that I have received from traditionally devalued and discounted women.

I start with my story because who I am is embedded in every page you will turn; in every word you will read. I start with my story because, although unconsciously, when you saw my name on the cover of this book, you made assumptions about who I am and why I do this work. In this way, I also share my story because who you are will influence how you receive it. Ultimately, I share my story as an invitation to you: to be open to what you will read, to think about your positionality, to think about how you have upheld systems that devalue and discount mothers. I share my story because too often we allow numbers, titles and degrees to erase human lives. I share my story because part of me wanted to forget it, part of me wanted to fall into the American fold. I share my story, which is really the story of how I was mothered and how I mothered othered people's children, because without it, this book would not exist.

References

Hancock, A.-M. (2003) Contemporary welfare reform and the public identity of the 'welfare queen'. *Race, Gender & Class* 10 (1), 31–59.

Lin, A.M.Y. (2015) Researcher positionality. In F.M. Hult and D.C. Johnson (eds) *Research Methods in Language Policy and Planning* (pp. 21–32). Chichester: John Wiley & Sons Ltd. https://doi.org/10.1002/9781118340349.ch3

Manohar, N., Liamputtong, P., Bhole, S. and Arora, A. (2017) Researcher positionality in cross-cultural and sensitive research. In P. Liamputtong (ed.) *Handbook of Research Methods in Health Social Sciences* (pp. 1–15). Singapore: Springer. https://doi.org/10.1007/978-981-10-2779-6_35-1

Weber, M.C. (2020) Of immigration, public charges, disability discrimination, and, of all things, hobby lobby. *Arizona State Law Journal* 52, 245.

Part 1

The Social Constructions of Motherhood: Poverty, Monolingualism and Disability (by Proxy)

1 Why Mothers?
Why *These* Mothers?

With what price we pay for the glory of motherhood.

Isadora Duncan

When you are a mother, you are never really alone in your thoughts. A mother always has to think twice, once for herself and once for her child.

Sophia Loren

'She broke the bread into two fragments and gave them to the children, who ate with avidity. 'She hath kept none for herself', grumbled the Sergeant. 'Because she is not hungry', said a soldier. 'Because she is a mother', said the Sergeant.

Victor Hugo

As an immigrant child growing up in a single-parent home, I knew the importance of academic success. My mother moved to the United States in 1990 with two young daughters and one suitcase. Having finished only elementary school, the result of growing up in a patriarchal society in which all education is monetized, she viewed moving to the United States as the best way to secure a better future for herself and her two daughters. Once here, she dealt with the harsh realities of New York winters and endless cycles of unemployment, underemployment and a need for social services such as Medicaid, food stamps, welfare and housing choice vouchers, more commonly known as Section 8. However much the reality of life in the United States detracted from its imagined vision, the brunt of the move was softened by the fact that my mother had a large extended family here, which she could turn to for support, and a documented immigrant status, which allowed her to access all of the aforementioned social services. Even though we were poor, we were connected: to our community, our family and the government.

Nonetheless, the fact that my mother was predominantly Spanish-speaking and possessed limited literacy meant that even though I was only seven years old when we arrived, she needed my help in order to access information, fill out paperwork and navigate life in an English-only environment. I was fortunate in that I was able to participate in bilingual education programs from second through eighth grade. This opportunity allowed me to be not only bilingual but also biliterate, which was of great use to my family. Although I resented how much my mother called upon my bilingualism as a child, I know that it was a necessary part of my family's survival.

When I went to college, the expectation was that my sister, six years my junior, would take over as linguistic ambassador in my household, but that would never happen. Early in her elementary school career, my sister was identified as a struggling learner. In response, the school placed her in English-only classes. As a result of this decision, she would only develop oral bilingualism in the home. This meant that my sister's linguistic fluidity could help her sustain cultural and social connections, but not navigate between the Spanish-only world my mother lived in and the English-only world she needed to access. Rather than possessing the *broken* English (Lindemann & Moran, 2017) that is often attributed to emergent bilingual immigrants, my sister reflected another possibility, that of someone with *broken* Spanish (Otheguy & Stern, 2011).

This range of linguistic practices created another fracture in my household; one in which my mother represented the Spanish-mostly world, my sister the English-mostly world and I as the 'bilingual' was supposed to be the glue that held it all together. These labels placed on our language practices led to a lot of tension in my home: my mother would fault my sister for her inability to 'dominar el español', my sister would shame my mother for her inability to learn English after decades living in the United States and I was resented by both for my ability to seemingly move between these two worlds with great ease. In this way, we were also broken. We internalized the demands that North American life had placed on our mouths and our brains; we then made those demands of each other without recognizing the ways in which our linguistic practices were controlled by language policies that were beyond our control.

From Bilingual Daughter to Bilingual Teacher

Throughout my childhood, my mother preached about the importance of an education and the value of being bilingual. While it was my role to help her navigate the English-only world, I also knew the lengths she went to in order to ensure that her needs did not interfere with my success in school. Still, I was witness to her never-ending balancing act as breadwinner and nurturer, and as such I was privy to some of the sacrifices, and many of the battles, she endured. Yet, when I became a teacher, the experiences of mothers like mine seemed absent from the discourse. Spanish-speaking immigrant mothers like mine were often discussed by teachers and administrators in terms of their needs or their faults rather than their actual lived-experiences. Assumptions were made about their intentions and their capacity to engage with their children's academic lives. Often times, these mothers were described in terms of their brokenness. I found this issue to be particularly true when the mothers who were being discussed were those who were raising children who were also labeled as dis/abled (LAD),[1] a categorization that often contributed to children being viewed as broken as well. As a novice teacher, I also struggled to understand how teachers and administrators could view decisions around language of instruction as purely academic, when I knew from experience that there would be a significant impact on the home. However, I would soon realize that in the lives of children with disabilities, the home language is often viewed as a hindrance rather than a support.

Who is Isolated in Our Pursuit for Inclusion?

In January 2011, I was working as a bilingual special education teacher within an elementary school mixed-grade self-contained[2] class when the New York City Department of Education (NYCDOE), under the leadership of Cathleen Black, began to implement what was considered to be a great equalizer with regard to students receiving special education services: a special education reform policy titled 'Shared Pathways to Success' (SPtS). Shared Pathways to Success intended to create more inclusive learning spaces[3] for most, if not all, public school children. One of the greatest changes that came about because of this reform was the provision that students receiving special education services had the right to be educated in their local community school. No longer could schools turn away children solely on the basis that they did not have the appropriate setting needed to educate that child. On the one hand, this provision meant that schools that had previously filled classrooms with children from around the city/district with similar programming needs, now had numerous vacancies (Walcott, 2012). On the other hand, community schools had to educate students whose needs and individual education plans (IEPs) they were ill-equipped to meet (Alvarez, 2012).

This policy would greatly influence the trajectory of my career as a teacher and a scholar. While the changes under SPtS were promoted by NYCDOE representatives, superintendents and administrators as necessary for the academic success and integration of students with dis/abilities, it often seemed as if the decisions made in its wake regarding student placement and classroom structures were haphazard and poorly executed. The administrators enacting them seemed more concerned with compliance than with the needs of the students whose educational experiences the policy was meant to improve. The impact the policy had on my school, my practice and my students was palpable. During the subsequent three years, students, families and teachers within my school were shuffled from one program to another. The first year, I watched as bilingual special education classrooms were shut down and students were moved to monolingual inclusion[4] classes or bilingual mainstream. The following year, teachers and families would express frustration over the new placements but were left with no alternative and little voice. By the third year, a resigned calm had fallen over the school community, a community that was already collapsing under the weight of external reviews that stemmed from statewide and national expectations. These expectations often did not take into account the diverse population the school was serving.

During this time, I would be moved around from teaching in general education settings to experimental inclusion settings. All the while, I felt as if students' needs were not being met and teachers' concerns were being ignored. Special education teachers who raised their voices of concern were seen as just wanting to keep students segregated or failing to set high expectations. By the end of 2012, I knew that something was amiss, but I did not understand why. Years after that initial experience, I arrived at the point where I recognized that the faults with SPtS, and other policies like it, lie not in its desire to include but rather in who remains excluded, both in its production and enactment. The lack of consideration for students who have intersectional identities, that is, identities that consist of multiple minoritized features such as race, language and dis/ability, presents an issue for all policies and practices that aim to meet the needs of one subgroup without considering the varying identity markers children possess both inside and outside of school (Annamma, 2017; Annamma & Morrison, 2018; Annamma & Winn, 2019). This whitewashing of intersectional identities also results in the additional failure to understand how academic decisions impact student's home lives. One critical reason for this might be that while the perspectives of educators are often taken into consideration, the voices of parents – in particular mothers – continue to be absent. This dearth of maternal voices is rather concerning given the prominent role that mothers have in the development of children, both in and out of school.

Mothering at the Margins

Parental involvement in the United States has been identified as a defining marker in academic achievement (Burke, 2013; de Apodaca et al., 2015; Gonzalez et al., 2013). Yet, most of the discourse regarding parents and schools is written about them without including their voice or their stories (Ferlazzo & Hammond, 2009; Goodall, 2017, 2018; Hornby, 2011; Jeynes, 2010; Jeynes, 2018; Morgan, 2016). Additionally, when most people think and talk about parental involvement, it is in a very specific shape and form. The current framing of parental involvement is grounded in First World, White, middle-class values[5]:

participation in school activities, supporting students with homework, reading to them, offering academic guidance, etc. This definition, however, is in many ways in disagreement with the experiences of families who do not identify as White and/or middle class and for whom this lack of identification also results in varying levels of interactions within schools (Aceves, 2014; Ijalba, 2015; Reiman *et al.*, 2010; Wolfe & Durán, 2013). These interactions are often viewed through a deficit perspective[6] that views minoritized parents as *broken* because they lack, among other things, the knowledge, capacity and agency needed to be effective educational participants and advocates for their children. These deficits are magnified when one takes into account the gender politics, immigration status and linguistic practices of parents who speak languages other than English, as is the case of Spanish-speaking Latinx[7] mothers.

While both parents have a central role in the raising of their child, regardless of who is present or absent,[8] the role of mothers in Latinx child-rearing is vast. In talking about motherhood within Mexican-American society, Durand (2010) wrote that

> mothers have been described as the primary socialization agent responsible for maintaining cultural beliefs and values, and structuring the family environment to support and maintain those values (Valdés 1996). Women's status rises when they become mothers, due to the belief among Mexican–Americans that maternal love is greater and more sacred than spousal love (Falicov 2005). [...] Given the centrality of the mother–child relationship in Mexican families, it stands to reason that mothers play key roles in children's development, socialization, and earliest school experiences. As immigrant and transnational Latina mothers strive to mother their children in the US, however, they must do so in the context of a capitalistic, patriarchal, and increasingly racialized, anti-immigrant society, whereby Latina women occupy the lowest rung in the labor market, and might be considered one of the most marginalized groups in the US (Villenas and Moreno 2001). (Durand, 2010: 257–258)

While this summation of motherhood is grounded in the national identity possessed by Mexican mothers, these values and challenges are no less applicable to Latinx mothers whose transnational experiences originate in different nations. This is particularly true when looking at the patterns that are replicated by immigrant mothers in the United States who are regularly tasked as the primary, and often sole, caregiver for their children. As such, these women are 'key figures in their children's early development and learning' and responsible for every aspect of child-rearing including education (Durand, 2010: 261). Mothers of children with disabilities have the added risk of being held responsible for the disability, either by themselves or their families and their communities (Maestas & Erickson, 1992; Salas-Provance *et al.*, 2002).

A Desire to Center Mothers

It was these experiences, both with the literature and with my profession, that piqued my interest in studying mothers, particularly the mothers of emergent bilingual children who were also identified, by the school, as having a disability. I was interested in knowing the stories behind the faces that I had encountered over the course of my career as a bilingual special education teacher. I wanted to know about the hopes and dreams that these mothers carried with them as they dropped their children off at school. I was curious to know the values, perspectives and ideologies mothers held about bilingualism and dis/abilities and how, if at all, were those reflected in their lives at home and at school. Thus, in 2016–2017, I sought them out: Spanish-speaking Latinx mothers raising children who had been identified as English language learners and as students with disabilities. (Side note: Moving forward, I will refer to these children as emergent bilinguals labeled as dis/abled [EBLADs] rather than 'English language learners with dis/abilities' or 'English language learners with special education needs' in order to dismantle the double deficit model that is produced by combining the term 'English language learner', which fails to acknowledge the linguistic resources that a student brings, with the terms 'with disabilities' or 'special education needs', which negate the social and structural power dynamics that are at play, making dis/ability a result of individual failure rather than systemic inequality. Thus, by using the term 'EBLAD', I attempt to acknowledge a student's full linguistic potential as well as emphasizing the imposing nature of labeling and categorizing children.)

After some time, I narrowed my scope to mothers from Sunset Park, the community where I had been raised and where I had worked as a teacher. In time, I found 40 mothers, mothers I had never met before but who, for some reason, chose to talk to me. In the end, I focused on the experiences of 10 mothers, and it is those 10 mothers and their experiences that carry this book.

The experiences of Spanish-speaking mothers of EBLADs vary greatly from those of typically developing children. There is also significant variability within this subgroup with the experiences of mothers with children in English-only special education settings varying greatly from those with children in bilingual special education settings. In order to provide a multifaceted description of these mothers' experiences, this book will present the experiences not only of mothers whose children are in English-only settings, but also of mothers whose children are in bilingual settings. There are mothers raising children who are in a 'more restrictive setting' known as bilingual special education (12:1:1) and there are mothers raising students who are in a 'less restrictive setting' known as integrated co-teaching (ICT) – English-only ICTs and bilingual ICTs. The hope is that by bringing the voices and experiences of

Spanish-speaking Latinx mothers in a myriad of settings to the forefront, they will be at the center of future policy and educational considerations both for their individual children and for bilingual children labeled as dis/abled as a whole.

My Intentions

This book aims not only to include the experiences of immigrant, monolingual Spanish-speaking Latinx women, but also to shift the narrative from one that views them through deficit lenses: broken English, broken children, broken households, parts of broken systems, to one that acknowledges the ways in which they support their children's academic growth through means that are not in keeping with traditional values but are no less meaningful. While these mothers and their children are constructed as broken because of their linguistic practices, socioeconomic position, disability labels and immigration status, the stories featured in this book will highlight the ways in which mothers tirelessly work toward making their children feel, and be seen as, whole.

Ultimately, I hope this book helps us as educators to move away from fragmented, additive models of viewing children; models that position EBLADs as 'special education students' and/or 'bilingual education students' and toward an intersectional understanding that recognizes the interrelatedness of labels like 'English language learners' and 'students with disabilities'. We need to take up intersectional understandings that recognize that language is often used as a marker for disability and that disability is used as exclusionary criteria to multilingualism (Cioè-Peña, 2020a). We must take up an intersectional framework that understands that a child's relationship to their family does not end when they enter a school building and that a school's influence does not dissipate on a child's walk home. An intersectional stance is critical to understanding the ways in which labels work to essentialize student needs while erasing their humanity and their communal belonging. For this reason, we must also approach disability as a representation of human diversity and not as a failure of the individual. We need to take up intersectional frameworks that recognize the ways in which current systems fail to recognize this diversity as simply difference while simultaneously creating harm (Annamma *et al.*, 2013). An intersectional framework is needed to understand how the commodification of bilingualism, exchanging perceptions of bilingualism as deficit for bilingualism as advantage, has left students with disabilities behind (Cioè-Peña, 2017b, 2017c, 2020a, 2020b), has moved language from the specter of human right to meritorious reward (Skutnabb-Kangas, 2005). Bilingual education and special education have deep roots in social justice; both projects arose in an effort to make space for the disenfranchised (Cioè-Peña, 2017a). Yet, these same spaces, which were created to meet the needs of diverse learners so that they could fully participate in a democratic society and so that they could learn alongside their peers, have resulted in tiered systems of schooling and have, in the end, morphed into systems of exclusion. As such, we need to accept the fact that these labels have done nothing beyond othering the children to whom they are ascribed. As educators, we must accept that our current systems do not serve our children, our families nor our visions of inclusive and democratic schools. If we continue to use labels as exclusionary criteria to general education and inclusionary criteria into bilingual education, special education, gifted and talented programs, then we will continue to replicate the tiered systems of oppression that we say we stand against.

Notes

(1) The term 'LAD' is used in lieu of the stand-alone 'dis/abled' or the qualifier 'with dis/abilities' in order to acknowledge the fact that dis/abilities are not inherent to an individual but rather the product of categorizations enacted by external evaluators such as educators, psychologist and medical professionals. As such, the term LAD also brings forth the understanding that 'all dis/ability categories, whether physical, cognitive, or sensory, are [...] subjective' (Annamma *et al.*, 2013). Great effort has been taken to ensure that the language used here and throughout is inclusive. However, terms referring to 'students with disabilities' or 'disabled students' may appear when a text is quoted or cited.
(2) *Self-contained*: A special education classroom setting where students with dis/abilities learn alongside other students with dis/abilities exclusively. This setting is also reflective of a smaller student to teacher ratio than that found in traditional general education and inclusive education classrooms.
(3) These are settings where students with dis/abilities learn alongside their non-disabled peers for most, if not all, of the school day. Also known as 'inclusive classrooms', 'integrated co-teaching classes', 'integrated classes' and ICTs.
(4) The instructional practice of educating students labeled as dis/abled alongside their non-dis/abled peers.
(5) The term 'value' is used to discuss the ideas, factors and features that an individual identifies as important to them. These values are then used to guide their decision-making with regard to the way in which they lead their life.
(6) The term 'perspective' refers to the lenses through which individuals understand the world around them.
(7) The term 'Latinx' is used as a way of 'embracing the intersection between cultural identity and gender' by shifting from a masculine identifier, Latino, to a term that is inclusive of those who live within and outside the gender binary (Licea as quoted by Reichard, 2015).
(8) While it can be argued that an absent parent has no role in the raising of a child, that absence does contribute to the environment in which a child is raised, be that through the emotional loss that is experienced or the added work and stress that is placed upon the remaining single-parent (Lahaie *et al.*, 2009).

References

Aceves, T.C. (2014) Supporting Latino families in special education through community agency–school partnerships. *Multicultural Education* 21 (3/4), 45–50.
Alvarez, C. (2012, September 27) Special ed reform should raise red flags. United Federation of Teachers (UFT). https://doi.org/10.1080/09687599.2018.1509768

Annamma, S. (2017) Not enough: Critiques of Devos and expansive notions of justice. *International Journal of Qualitative Studies in Education* 30 (10), 1047–1052. https://doi.org/10.1080/09518398.2017.1312608

Annamma, S. and Morrison, D. (2018) DisCrit classroom ecology: Using praxis to dismantle dysfunctional education ecologies. *Teaching and Teacher Education* 73, 70–80. https://doi.org/10.1016/j.tate.2018.03.008

Annamma, S.A. and Winn, M. (2019) Transforming our mission: Animating teacher education through intersectional justice. *Theory Into Practice* 58 (4), 318–327. https://doi.org/10.1080/00405841.2019.1626618

Annamma, S.A., Connor, D. and Ferri, B. (2013) Dis/ability critical race studies (DisCrit): Theorizing at the intersections of race and dis/ability. *Race Ethnicity and Education* 16 (1), 1–31. https://doi.org/10.1080/13613324.2012.730511

Burke, M.M. (2013) Improving parental involvement training special education advocates. *Journal of Disability Policy Studies* 23 (4), 225–234. https://doi.org/10.1177/1044207311424910

Cioè-Peña, M. (2017a) Disability, bilingualism and what it means to be normal. *Journal of Bilingual Education Research & Instruction* 19 (1), 138–160.

Cioè-Peña, M. (2017b) Who is excluded from inclusion? Points of union and division in bilingual and special education. *Theory, Research, and Action in Urban Education* V (1). See https://blmtraue.commons.gc.cuny.edu/2017/02/24/who-is-excluded-from-inclusion-points-of-union-and-division-in-bilingual-and-special-education/ (accessed 14 January 2021).

Cioè-Peña, M. (2017c) The intersectional gap: How bilingual students in the United States are excluded from inclusion. *International Journal of Inclusive Education* 21 (9), 906–919. https://doi.org/10.1080/13603116.2017.1296032

Cioè-Peña, M. (2020a) Raciolinguistics and the education of emergent bilinguals labeled as disabled. *The Urban Review*. https://doi.org/10.1007/s11256-020-00581-z

Cioè-Peña, M. (2020b) Bilingualism for students with disabilities, deficit or advantage?: Perspectives of Latinx mothers. *Bilingual Research Journal* 0 (0), 1–14. https://doi.org/10.1080/15235882.2020.1799884

de Apodaca, R.F., Gentling, D.G., Steinhaus, J.K. and Rosenberg, E.A. (2015) Parental involvement as a mediator of academic performance among special education middle school students. *School Community Journal* 25 (2), 35–54.

Durand, T.M. (2010) Latina mothers' cultural beliefs about their children, parental roles, and education: Implications for effective and empowering home–school partnerships. *The Urban Review* 43 (2), 255–278. https://doi.org/10.1007/s11256-010-0167-5

Ferlazzo, L. and Hammond, L.A. (2009) *Building Parent Engagement in Schools*. Santa Barbara, CA: ABC-CLIO/Libraries Unlimited.

Gonzalez, L., Borders, L.D., Hines, E., Villalba, J. and Henderson, A. (2013) Parental involvement in children's education: Considerations for school counselors working with Latino immigrant families. *Professional School Counseling* 16 (3), 185–193. https://doi.org/10.5330/PSC.n.2013-16.183

Goodall, J. (2017) *Narrowing the Achievement Gap: Parental Engagement with Children's Learning*. Abingdon: Routledge.

Goodall, J. (2018) Learning-centred parental engagement: Freire reimagined. *Educational Review* 70 (5), 603–621. https://doi.org/10.1080/00131911.2017.1358697

Hornby, G. (2011) *Parental Involvement in Childhood Education: Building Effective School-Family Partnerships*. New York: Springer Science & Business Media.

Ijalba, E. (2015) Understanding parental engagement in Hispanic mothers of children with autism spectrum disorder: Application of a process-model of cultural competence. *Journal of Multilingual Education Research* 6 (1), 91–110. http://fordham.bepress.com/jmer/vol6/iss1/6

Jeynes, W. (2010) *Parental Involvement and Academic Success*. New York: Routledge.

Jeynes, W.H. (2018) A practical model for school leaders to encourage parental involvement and parental engagement. *School Leadership & Management* 38 (2), 147–163. https://doi.org/10.1080/13632434.2018.1434767

Lahaie, C., Hayes, J.A., Piper, T.M. and Heymann, J. (2009) Work and family divided across borders: The impact of parental migration on Mexican children in transnational families. *Community, Work & Family* 12 (3), 299–312. https://doi.org/10.1080/13668800902966315

Lindemann, S. and Moran, K. (2017) The role of the descriptor 'broken English' in ideologies about nonnative speech. *Language in Society* 46 (5), 649–669. https://doi.org/10.1017/S0047404517000616

Maestas, A.G. and Erickson, J.G. (1992) Mexican immigrant mothers' beliefs about disabilities. *American Journal of Speech-Language Pathology* 1 (4), 5–10. https://doi.org/10.1044/1058-0360.0104.05

Morgan, N.S. (2016) *Engaging Families in Schools: Practical Strategies to Improve Parental Involvement*. New York: Routledge.

Otheguy, R. and Stern, N. (2011) On so-called Spanglish. *International Journal of Bilingualism* 15 (1), 85–100. https://doi.org/10.1177/1367006910379298

Reichard, R. (2015) Why we say Latinx: Trans & gender non-conforming people explain. *Latina*, 29 August. See http://www.latina.com/lifestyle/our-issues/why-we-say-latinx-trans-gender-non-conforming-people-explain (accessed 25 March 2016).

Reiman, J.W., Beck, L., Coppola, T. and Engiles, A. (2010) *Parents' Experiences with the IEP Process: Considerations for Improving Practice*. Eugene, OR: Center for Appropriate Dispute Resolution in Special Education (CADRE). http://eric.ed.gov/?id=ED512611

Salas-Provance, M.B., Erickson, J.G. and Reed, J. (2002) Disabilities as viewed by four generations of one Hispanic family. *American Journal of Speech-Language Pathology* 11, 151–162.

Skutnabb-Kangas, T. (2005) Language policy and linguistic human rights. In T. Ricento (ed.) *An Introduction to Language Policy: Theory and Method* (pp. 273–291). Malden, MA: Blackwell.

Walcott, D.M. (2012) Special Education Reform Reference Guide: School Year 2012–13. New York City Department of Education. See https://www.classsizematters.org/wp-content/uploads/2012/06/DOE-SPED_Reference_Guide_051612_IEPRevision-22.pdf

Wolfe, K. and Durán, L.K. (2013) Culturally and linguistically diverse parents' perceptions of the IEP process. *Multiple Voices for Ethnically Diverse Exceptional Learners* 13 (2), 4–18.

2 'They don't care, they don't understand, they're in denial': Constructions of Mothers as Others

Latinx mothers of emergent bilinguals labeled as dis/abled (MoEBLADs) lead lives that are often bounded by the oppressive nature of a lower socioeconomic status. This leaves them at the mercy of stereotyping and discriminatory practices, both of which result in a lack of agency and a subsequent lack of advocacy on behalf of their children (Aceves, 2014; Cohen, 2013; Montelongo, 2015; Rodriguez *et al.*, 2013; Wolfe & Durán, 2013). According to Cohen (2013), Latinx mothers are unaware of the barriers that they face, be they socioeconomic, racial or linguistic. They also tend to be uneducated at higher rates than other MoEBLADs and may be unaware of the resources available to them. Undocumented Latinx MoEBLADs are a particularly disadvantaged and vulnerable group; their documentation status places them at high risk for abuse (Asad & Rosen, 2019; Garcini *et al.*, 2016; Gonzales, 2016; Ramirez & Monk, 2017; Zadnik *et al.*, 2016) and, as this book will show, their children's disability labels and overwhelming placement in English-only programs restrict their mobility. Studies also show that Latinx mothers participate in fewer individual education plan (IEP) meetings than Euro-American mothers, have a harder time understanding the IEP/special education process and lack the confidence to communicate their needs (Aceves, 2014; Montelongo, 2015; Rodriguez *et al.*, 2013; Wolfe & Durán, 2013). Additionally, according to Wolfe and Durán (2013), Spanish-speaking MoEBLADs participate in fewer IEP meetings than their English-speaking counterparts.

Although they are often disenfranchised, Latinx MoEBLADs are overwhelmingly aware of the disconnect between their values and the schools' values. MoEBLADs express frustration with schools that do not respect their cultural values and do not value their voices (Ijalba, 2015a). MoEBLADs also express a desire to be more involved, while feeling ill-informed and wanting the school to provide them with more information and support (Aceves, 2014; Lalvani, 2015; Wolfe & Durán, 2013). MoEBLADs also express feelings of dissatisfaction with schools and school agents, a sentiment that has not changed since the 1980s (Cohen,

2013; Wolfe & Durán, 2013). This is particularly true in relation to the disjointed linguistic practices of the families and the schools. MoEBLADs are often presented in two lights: either as meek and respectful or as dissatisfied yet resilient. According to Cohen (2013), those who voice their dissatisfaction say that it stems from poor communication, language barriers and experiences in which they have been subject to discrimination. These feelings are supported by Montelongo's (2015) findings in which mothers shared that they were aware of the bias against them, while also expressing feelings of frustration with the lack of cultural considerations on the part of the schools. For these mothers, advocating for their children did not feel like a right so much as 'a fight' or 'a struggle' (Montelongo, 2015). Alternatively, those who can engage sometimes choose to remain quiet out of fear that their interjections will disrupt the process, thus delaying their child's access to support (Montelongo, 2015).

In an effort to alleviate this tension between mothers and schools, researchers make recommendations as to how that knowledge can be transferred to the mothers – through training, the use of interpreters, introductions to community organizations, etc. (Aceves, 2014; Ijalba, 2015b; Rodriguez *et al.*, 2013). However, this focus on teaching/training the mothers as a way to impart knowledge rather than asking them to share their knowledge fails to see mothers as equal partners who are experts on their children. Instead, it positions mothers as being in need of an education, which can then influence the way that teachers and other people in positions of power approach them. Additionally, this focus on information distribution is based on the premise that the reason why mothers do not participate is because they do not know how or even that they can, while ignoring the fact that schools position themselves as the experts and as such do not readily welcome discourse that originates in, or results in, opposition.

The existing power dynamic between schools and mothers allows schools to define parental involvement and, as such, set the standard for high or low levels of involvement within a very rigid framework. This framework measures involvement by keeping track of how often mothers are physically present at the school and how vocal they are once they are there (Vandergrift & Greene, 1992).

What is exemplified by these findings is that a great deal of the data gathered about mothers focuses on what is missing in/from their lives without much consideration for why something is missing or without contemplation that perhaps that which is missing was taken, subsequently failing to ask by whom and for what reasons? In other words, much of the discourse centers on what mothers lack: agency, education, English, engagement, without enough discussion as to which forces impede these women's access to education, agency, community and participation, and to what ends. As this book will show, often the explanation lies in how their ways of being are categorized and pathologized and the ensuing labels they and their children are given.

In order to shift the ways we engage with MoEBLADs, we must first change the ways in which we think and talk about them. Rather than constructing them as broken, empty vessels needing to be fixed and then filled, we need to recognize MoEBLADs as knowledge-rich yet resource-poor women who fall prey to multiple systems of oppression and are at the mercy of social systems they cannot access.

Beyond Singular Dimensions

I approached my study and this book, centering MoEBLADs, with a multifaceted theoretical framework building on the concept of inter-sectionality established by Kimberly Crenshaw. An intersectional frame-work posits that 'inequities are never the result of single, distinct factors. Rather, they are the outcome of intersections of different social locations, power relations and experiences' (Hankivsky, 2014: 2). As such, the theoretical framework for this book extended Crenshaw's theory beyond race, gender and class to include the role of language and dis/ability on an individual or family's subjectivity.

A multifaceted theoretical approach is needed to understand these mothers because no single theory would be effective at capturing the lived experiences of people with intersectional identities. An intersectional framework is not only crucial to research, but it is also the unifying/cen-tral lens by which outcomes and findings can be understood.

Intersectionality: The sum of all parts

Crenshaw's theory of intersectionality is necessary in order to under-stand the experiences of the multidimensional women who took part in the study that this book is based on – they are mothers, wives and individu-als – but they are also subject to their children's positionalities as well. In order to fully see and understand these women as multidimensional people with complicated narratives, one must first acknowledge the multiple social, political and personal labels they take up and are assigned.

Coined by Kimberly Crenshaw in 1989 and rooted in black feminist thought, intersectionality is a way to bring to light the complexity of women of color's (WoC) experiences in the United States.[1] For Cren-shaw, WoC's experiences are often absorbed by activists (and social justice movements) that advocate on behalf of race or gender, but not both. Ultimately, these disjointed approaches never address the very par-ticular issues WoC contend with, issues that reside at the nexus of race and gender. Ultimately, intersectionality is 'the notion that subjectivity is constituted by mutually reinforcing vectors of race, gender, class, and sexuality' (Nash, 2008: 2). In short, intersectionality is the ideology that an individual's experiences are not the result, nor reflective, of any sin-gular demographic factor such as their gender alone but also their race, their social class and sexuality.

In her tenet text 'Mapping the Margins: Intersectionality, Identity Politics, and Violence against Women of Color', Crenshaw briefly weaves in other issues WoC must contend with: more specifically, the way a woman's immigration status, her cultural beliefs/practices and her ability to communicate in English contribute to her continued exposure to violence. However, the core focal group of this framework was (and in many ways continues to be) Black women. As such, whereas Crenshaw presents issues that WoC experience with regard to language (particularly in accessing resources), she never acknowledges that English and monolingualism are representative of Black culture as well. As such, women who have limited English capacity are part of a community of WoC who have additional struggles that are not represented by the intersections of race, gender and class alone.[2] Nonetheless, Crenshaw's framework is incredibly valuable in capturing and valuing 'multiple and conflicting experiences of subordination and power' (McCall, 2005: 1780).

Crenshaw's work continues to be relevant within present-day discourse as people continue to be categorized and find themselves opposing oppressive forces at every turn. The women in this book are subject to multiple subordinate categories: women, Latinx, uneducated/undereducated, immigrants, undocumented, Spanish speaking, monolinguals, dis/abled by proxy[3] and poor. Even as movements fighting for social justice, like those behind #BlackLivesMatter and #EqualPayForEqualWork, continue to strive for improvements for individuals who are minoritized by a hegemonic system, it is important to note that they often present a single story narrative[4] that often reduces or erases the experiences of individuals holding intersectional identities.[5] Given its current (and ongoing) fight for equal and civil rights for all, it is no wonder that intersectionality has moved down from the ivory tower and into the mainstream as activists, researchers and theorists continue to challenge and extend the work of intersectionality beyond the identity markers Crenshaw first posited. Thus, in my study I sought to center not only the educational labels that children had imposed upon them but also the societal markers that these families, especially the mothers, had to carry with them: Latinx immigrants, poor/working-class women, mothers to children *with* disabilities. It was important to look at all of these facets in order to fully understand the mothers' experiences and in order to fully understand the systems with which they were contending. This is exactly what Crenshaw did when she looked at the intersection of gender and race. She looked not at the impact of each singular marker but at the amalgamation and the collective impact that those identities had on the women she represented. Thus, I would fail to fully understand these women if I did not consider their experiences both as mothers and as women, as Spanish monolinguals and as Latinas, as individuals but also as a collective.

Reflective of its longevity, clarity and universality, Crenshaw's theoretical framework on intersectionality continues to have a particularly strong presence within academia – especially within the social sciences – as many researchers attempt to bring awareness to particular niche and minoritized communities. As such, other scholars and activists have made efforts to expand intersectionality beyond theory and into practice by placing it at the forefront of mainstream discourse around discrimination and systemic oppression (Brah & Phoenix, 2013; Davis, 2008; Hancock, 2007; Nash, 2008; Reeves, 2015; Shields, 2008; Smooth, 2011). Additionally, a few researchers such as Annamma, Blanchett, Connor, Harry, Ferri and Klingner have made explicit efforts to conduct research around the intersection of race, class, dis/ability, culture and language. However, for many of these researchers the focus is dis/ability first, race second. Language is often left competing for third, and in many instances gender is completely absent from the discourse. This hegemonic structuring of identity markers is not in keeping with Crenshaw's theory which argues that these factors all deserve equal importance because they are so intricately intertwined in a woman's overall narrative that distinguishing which one is more impactful to her overall experience is not only arbitrary but also harmful. Additionally, the removal of the role of gender contributes to the continued silencing of women. Lastly, much of the current educational research that is grounded in intersectionality, whether the theory is named or not, focuses on the ways in which oppressive factors impact the child's experiences rather than how they impact the mothers' experience in relation to their ability to be (and be seen as) an effective advocate for their child. In doing so, the feminine/feminist component is effectively removed from the discourse. By centering the experiences of the mothers, this book attempts to stay true to Crenshaw's theory by giving equal importance to language, dis/ability and gender with an understanding that, depending on the situation, one of these identity markers may be more prominent and, as such, more impactful to the experience of the participant. However, as will be evident in Part 2 of the book, it is incredibly difficult to parse out what experiences relate to issues of only gender/motherhood, only language and/or only dis/ability. Additionally, I make no claims to present these mothers in their entirety; I do, however, make an attempt to begin to show them in their complexity.

Intersectionality shapes not only the lens with which researchers approach the lived experiences of women, but also the methods with which those experiences are gathered and framed. As such, intersectionality was not used in this project as a way to sustain ideologies that frame the participants as oppressed and subordinate, but rather to show 'The potential for both multiple and conflicting experiences of subordination and power', thus highlighting the numerous facets of oppression participants must contend with in order to advocate for their children and themselves (McCall, 2005: 1780). An intersectional perspective is not meant to further diminish a woman's worth, but rather to indicate her will and drive in the face of so much opposition (Yuval-Davis, 2006). Additionally, while the study focused on the women's roles and identity as mothers, it became evident throughout the data collection process that their subjectivities as women, as Latinxs, as learners, as wives and as daughters are also present. This makes an intersectional framework necessary for understanding not only the way external labels impact a woman's ability to move through the world, but also the way in which her interpersonal labels free her up and/or weigh her down.

As previously mentioned, in order to fully understand the stories or experiences of the Latinx women in this book, a focus on gender and/or race is not sufficient. As such, we move on to the next anchor of this framework: Tove Skutnabb-Kangas' theory on linguistic human rights (LHR).

Labeling language, silencing people

LHR are language rights that are so basic that they are necessary for a dignified life. Essentially, they are the linguistic rights one must be guaranteed in order to be/feel human. Skutnabb-Kangas' work on LHR dates back to the early 1990s when she first proclaimed that individuals have a right to access the world they inhabit in the language/s they possess. Skutnabb-Kangas' asserts that LHR should be

a universal declaration [that] guarantee at an *individual* level that, in relation to

The mother tongue(s)[6,7] **everybody can**
- identify with their mother tongue(s) and have this identification accepted and respected by others,
- learn the mother tongue(s) fully, orally and in writing (which presupposes that minorities are educated through the medium of their mother tongue(s)).
- use the mother tongue in most official situations (including schools);

Other languages, that everybody whose mother tongue is not an official language in the country where s/he is resident, can
- become bilingual (or trilingual, if s/he has 2 mother tongues) in the mother tongue(s) and (one of) the official language(s) (according to her own choice);

The relationship between languages,
- any change of mother tongue is voluntary, not imposed

(Skutnabb-Kangas, 1994: 361)

Skutnabb-Kangas (1994: 361) also warns that 'if these rights are not guaranteed, deprivation of the mother tongue may follow'. Skutnabb-Kangas' work on LHR was rather novel too because it introduced a multidisciplinary approach to the sociolinguistic topic of language education by incorporating the legality of language access into the discourse of how people use languages as well as why and how languages are abandoned or, better yet, actively killed.

This vocalization of LHR aims to create an understanding of how some (if not all) language rights are in fact human rights. LHR are based on (and in some instances critical of) the language rights and human rights declarations made by the United Nations. By creating a legal understanding of linguistic practices, Skutnabb-Kangas shifts home language education out of the dismissible realm of 'wants' and 'niceties' to the authoritative platform of rights and duties. Embedded in Skutnabb-Kangas' (2005) work is an understanding of how language policies within government and within schools contribute, both passively and actively, to linguistic genocide.[8] While the focus of much of Skutnabb-Kangas' writing is the active destruction of languages, with particular attention given to the plight of the Kurdish people, her work also explores the covert ways in which many countries attempt to change the use of a minoritized citizen's mother tongue, be that through a lack of promotion of the home language in education and/or official government business or by asserting that mother tongue education is too costly or counter to the goals of assimilation within the nation state (Skutnabb-Kangas, 1994, 1997, 2002). This assertion of the covert ways in which nations deny the conservation of a mother tongue is critical to understanding the current state of home language education in the United States.

While there is some home language education access within the United States through the promotion of bilingual education, more often than not home languages are used only temporarily and as a scaffold for English language acquisition in the education of minoritized children (National Center for Education Statistics, 2016). In most cases, linguistically, racially and ethnically minoritized children are subject to English-only education; this is even more true for students who are labeled as dis/abled. This reductionist approach to language education is reflective of the United States' poor alignment to the Hague Recommendations[9] regarding '[mother tongue medium] education for all or most national/immigrant minorities in state schools, even if it is transitional' (Skutnabb-Kangas, 2002: 143). It is so poor in fact that it 'outright [denies] the existence of at least some national [and immigrant] minorities' (Skutnabb-Kangas, 2002: 143).

Given its assimilationist history[10] and the current resurgence of nationalism[11] within the United States, it is not surprising to see incidents of systemic violence against immigrant communities take aim at the use of languages other than English by minoritized people. The first and most visible attempt at silencing Spanish speakers in particular came hours after the Trump administration took office and removed the capacity for Spanish translation from the White House's official website. As a result of this erasure, Spanish-literate citizens (documented or not, immigrant and US born), who encompass the largest non-English-speaking community in the United States, were denied access to the most basic level of civic engagement (Zeigler & Camarota, 2016). Other attempts at silencing speakers of other languages have been outright violent.[12] The effects of this type of violence are not limited to the United States. English is increasingly viewed as the lingua franca of the world, even though it is not the most populous language (Gu *et al.*, 2014; Jenkins, 2013, 2015; Jenkins & Leung, 2013; O'Regan, 2014; Simons & Fennig, 2017). So strong is this effect that even nations like Mexico, whose citizens are often the target of monoglossic language policies in the United States, have increased their desire to educate their citizens in English even as the United States actively denies their US-based citizens access to Spanish language development.[13]

Skutnabb-Kangas' work on LHR is critical to countering the current social and political perspectives that regard the linguistic diversity of immigrants and minoritized people as interfering with the cohesiveness of the United States. While the United States does not have an official language, the strong association between American identity and English dominance is reflected in the Pew Research Center's findings that to the United States public 'language matters more to national identity than birthplace' (Stokes, 2017). According to Pew, over 90% of those surveyed stated that 'it is [somewhat or] very important to speak the dominant language to be considered truly a national of' the United States, a number far greater than the 45% who believe that sharing national customs and traditions is very important to national identity (Stokes, 2017).[14] This sentiment of English only/English first is so intense that it permeates the linguistic practices found within immigrant homes. Many of the mothers whose stories are presented in this book made claims that ascribed English as *the* language belonging to their US-born children, regardless of the family's linguistic capacity or cultural identity.

While Skutnabb-Kangas' description of LHR is deeply rooted in the maintenance and survival of indigenous and minority languages internationally, her perspective on educational LHR can be used to understand the way that language policies and practices in US schools impact ethnically, linguistically and politically minoritized families and, as a result, subsequently shape individual and community language practices. Whereas there are few states and situations in which *de jure* denial of LHR exists within the United States, there are plenty of *de facto* ways in which EBLAD students and their families are denied access to the full use of their own language, in both the acquisition and use of said language. Skutnabb-Kangas' concept of *linguistic genocide* can be used to understand the nature of destructive *de facto* language policies and measures that are enacted by schools and experienced by minoritized people. These policies can apply to, but are not limited to practices such as providing homework assignments in only the dominant language, not making bilingual program options available to all students, counseling families out of bilingual settings, offering special education services only in the dominant language and failing to provide qualified interpreters (Fish, 2008; Harry, 2008; Ramirez, 2003; Turney & Kao, 2009). Skutnabb-Kangas' work on LHR is critical to unearthing the way that mothers approach and value the use of Spanish within the household, as well as their understanding of the role English plays in the academic and social lives of their children. Additionally, my experiences as an immigrant, as a teacher and as a researcher are heavily influenced by my relationship to my mother tongue and my belief that access to an education in one's own maternal language is not only a privilege but an inalienable right.

What is a disability?: From medical diagnosis to sorting mechanism

The third theoretical anchor of this book addresses the framing of dis/ability. As such this final section will discuss the social construction model (SCM) of dis/ability, which serves as the theoretical grounding for the field of disability studies (DS).

DS[15] is a multidisciplinary field that is rooted in the belief that dis/ability is socially constructed. As a result, people with dis/abilities[16] are the victims of oppression and discrimination on the basis of a perceived, rather than legitimate, deficit (Baglieri *et al.*, 2011). Whereas the formal field of DS is relatively young, the ideas that it represents date back to the 1960s when dis/ability activists began to challenge the ways in which people with dis/abilities were formally and systemically ostracized from society. From this activism arose the philosophy that 'disability was an idea, not a thing', which was supported by the understanding that dis/abilities were context dependent (Baglieri *et al.*, 2011: 270). An oft-cited historical example of a context-dependent dis/ability relates to deafness. Deafness can be isolating for an individual within mainstream society where communication is primarily based on oral language. As a result, the Deaf are placed at a disadvantage, thus creating a context-based dis/ability. However, in communities like the one that existed in Martha's Vineyard where a substantial part of the population was deaf and where a general communication system consisted of sign and oral language, a deaf individual had no limitations. Thus, the dis/ability was non-existent (Groce, 1985; Scheer & Groce, 1988).

The SCM, similarly to social interpretation(s) and the minority (group) model[17] of dis/ability, is intended to counter the medical model of dis/abilities which perceives a dis/ability[18] as an 'inherent inferiority, a pathology to cure, or an undesirable trait to eliminate' rather than a representation of human variance (Garland-Thomson, 2005). This lens of dis/ability as socially constructed is not to be perceived as an equivocation that to be dis/abled is not to be disadvantaged, but rather to place the fault on society's inability to make room for all types of people rather than on an individual's inability to conform to a set of arbitrary standards that denote a person as *normal* or *abnormal*. While this may seem like a foreign or complex concept to understand, one just has to take a moment to consider the ways in which race is also socially constructed. In this example, race and racial hegemony, like dis/ability and normalcy,[19] would be viewed as socially constructed in that a person of dark phenotype is born at a disadvantage not because they have an inherent deficit but because of the way society has constructed Blackness. The applications of socially constructed deficits and subsequent perceptions of inferiority and discrimination that exist can be applied to a myriad of discourses including but not limited to class, gender and age. Scholars who uphold the SCM view the construction of dis/ability as deficit and the mistreatment of people with dis/abilities as equally baseless and unjust.

The SCM allows for the dismantling of hegemonic systems that are constructed on the basis that *normal* is better and expected while perceiving anything else as not only less valuable but extremely undesirable. The SCM also allows for critiques of segregationist ideals that advocate for separate and unequal social spaces under the guise of treatment or remediation. Instead, the SCM highlights the fact that these settings do not benefit the individual labeled as dis/abled but rather serve to sustain hegemonic divisions of power and ideals of normalcy. The SCM aims to create counter-narratives that reduce stigmatization and improve the lives of people with dis/abilities by attempting to change the way society views difference and by acknowledging equal value and humanity to people with dis/abilities (Harris, 2001). This is done by engaging in research that is reflective of the lived experiences of people with dis/abilities, that views people with dis/abilities as informed participants and/or co-investigators and that questions/challenges labeling and societal structures that place some individuals in the role of outsiders (Connor *et al.*, 2008; Garland-Thomson, 2005; Taylor, 2006). DS research originates from an understanding that people are different without reducing those differences to deficiencies and without attributing a lesser value to the individual. Neither DS nor the SCM attempts to erase the term 'dis/ability' because they also recognize that while dis/abilities may be stigmatizing to some, there are countless individuals who identify as dis/abled with a sense of pride and autonomy – who do not wish to erase their difference, and only wish to be treated as would any other person without a minoritizing[20] label (Brown, 2003; Darling & Heckert, 2010; Harris, 1995; Harris, 2001; Magasi, 2008; Martin, n.d.).

As previously mentioned, the SCM is a key tenet of DS and it is in part because of this inclusionary stance and its multidisciplinary nature that DS serves as an umbrella for other subfields like dis/ability critical race studies (DisCrit), DS in education (DSE) and feminist DS. While DS focuses primarily on the ways in which socially constructed dis/ability labels impact peoples' lives, the subfields of DS such as DisCrit and feminist DS are intersectional perspectives of DS, which reflect the experiences of people who encounter oppression at the nexus of dis/ability, race and gender, respectively. The field of DSE, which was particularly relevant to this project, sprouted from DS as a means to address the ways in which labeling and diagnosing people with dis/abilities contributed to their isolation within school settings and subsequent social spaces, as well as perpetuating ideas regarding the segregation[21] of people with dis/abilities as beneficial (Connor *et al.*, 2008). DSE considers not only the ways in which society is constructed to alienate people with dis/abilities, but also the ways in which medical and educational professionals contribute to that alienation by making decisions regarding the educational trajectories of the individual without considering their wants, needs or desires. This ultimately compromises their autonomy (Connor *et al.*, 2008). DSE like DS is a field that is strongly rooted in social and political transformation. Its grounding in the SCM facilitates the questioning of institutions and special education with a final aim of increasing the integration of people with dis/abilities into mainstream (education) settings (Taylor, 2006).

For many reasons, the SCM was a valuable theoretical stance for this project. First of all, as previously mentioned, it has been shown that dis/ability labels impact entire families, not just individual children (Mehan, 1993). Thus, the SCM affords me a lens with which to understand and interpret the ways in which schools perceive students' abilities and how these are discussed and presented juxtaposed with the ways in which mothers perceive their children's ability levels. Second, it incorporates an additional level of criticality with which to discuss the ways labels, beyond race, class and gender, further contribute to the stigmatization of immigrant families and families of color. Third, the SCM highlights the blurriness that surrounds judgment-based dis/abilities like learning disabled which relates to the ongoing discussions regarding the overrepresentation of linguistically diverse children within special education. It challenges the assumption that children *possess* disabilities in exchange for a framework that understands that in many cases disabilities labels are thrust upon children. In other words, the SCM understands that children are categorized not in an effort to support them but in an effort to maintain the (exclusionary) status quo (McDermott, 1993). Fourth, DSE uses the SCM as a way to place a strong emphasis on privileging the voices of the labeled above the voices of those doing the labeling. Fifth, DSE and the SCM's emphasis on creating counter-narratives allows for the production and presentation of discourse which pushes back against ideologies that frame professionals as experts by acknowledging the ways in which these ideologies disempower families while at the same time expecting them to be equal partners. Lastly, one of the first pieces of research to hint at the need for an SCM stance within education was a report titled 'The Six-Hour Retarded Child' which 'showed that many children placed in special education, especially those from minority groups, were only "retarded" during school hours and functioned perfectly well at home and in their communities' (Taylor, 2006: xvii).

The EBLADs presented in this book are not only students who are 'dis/abled' for six-hours a day, but many are also forced monolinguals for that same period of time. This is all because of judgments that deem them not only as dis/abled, but also incapable of bilingualism 'without regard to [their] adaptive behavior, which may be exceptionally adaptive to the situation and community in which [s/he] lives' (President's Committee on Mental Retardation, 1969, as cited in Taylor, 2006).

Similarly to the previously discussed lenses, the SCM within a DS/DSE framing helped to ground the study in the ideals that not only acknowledge but also perceive differences as neutral attributes of individuals rather than inherent deficits. Additionally, this aspect of the theoretical framework also allows for a critical understanding of the way in which people are minoritized because of the ways they are evaluated and subsequently valued, and not on the basis of any fundamental features or causes.

From theory to reality

If we are to truly change the way we work with MoEBLADs and their families then it is important that we understand the ways in which they have been devalued, disregarded and disenfranchised. However, understanding is not enough, we must also actively deconstruct the White, monolingual, normative and patriarchal gaze with which they have been viewed and approached. Knowing that there are alternative ways to understand people's experiences is integral to growing as a society, to bringing into the center those who have been relegated to the margins. It is for this reason that I have spent so much time breaking down the theories that not only undergird this book but also shape my understandings.

All of the theories presented within this framework are grounded in criticality, social justice, advocacy and activism. Most importantly, they are all grounded in the understanding that individual experiences are complex and must be presented in multidimensional ways. To attempt in any way to fully parse matters of language from matters of dis/ability or motherhood from the lives of the participants in this study would be reductionist and disingenuous. The fact that previous research about this population has attempted to juxtapose life at home with life at school without tending to the intricate ways in which they bleed into each other highlights the ways in which previous research has failed such communities. Hints of other theories and theorists, like hints of cinnamon and chocolate in a cup of freshly brewed coffee, can be found throughout this book. Still, intersectionality, LHR and the SCM of disability are the notes that can be noticed in more palpable ways. It is by combining these theories that we can begin to see these women and their children as whole. It was with the aim to present these mothers as the complex beings they are that their stories were gathered outside of the school space, in houses of worship, in community centers, in their homes; on weekdays and weekends, in mornings and evenings; alone, with their families, with other mothers; through interviews and observations. However, as we move into the second part of the book, where we meet the mothers and their children, I hope that you enter this space understanding the complexity of it all: that these stories are but mere snapshots into the lives of complex women navigating complicated systems that were not designed with them or their children in mind.

Notes

(1) While Crenshaw is credited with naming the term and popularizing it in modern scholarship, many scholars acknowledge that the ideas from which she derives her theory hark as far back as the 1800s as evidenced by the critical stance that Sojourner Truth put forth in her speech 'Ain't I a Woman' and as recently as the 1960s and 1970s as evidenced by the work of bell hooks and Angela Davis (Bates, 2017; Bowleg, 2012; Yuval-Davis, 2006).

(2) This is not an attempt to engage in 'Oppression Olympics' but rather an attempt to show the added ways (and spaces in which) Spanish-speaking, monolingual Latinx women are disadvantaged (Yuval-Davis, 2012).

(3) The term 'dis/abled by proxy' is used here in order to describe a phenomenon by which the non-dis/abled members of a family with a member who is identified/labeled as dis/abled experience treatment that somehow equates the individual's dis/ability as a family dis/ability; this is particularly true for parents and siblings. See Barber, 2014; Mobley, 2015; Nicholls, 2008.

(4) #BlackLivesMatter often focuses on the victimization of Black men at the hands of law enforcement while #EqualPayForEqualWork primarily focuses on gender with White women often serving as the face of the movement. In the case of #BlackLivesMatter, Crenshaw has argued that focusing on men reinforces patriarchal standards of power within United States society thus ignoring the fact that women of color also die at the hands of police disproportionately, while #EqualPayForEqualWork ignores the fact that the pay gap is even greater for women of color (Swann, 2015). In response to the lack of intersectionality within #BlackLivesMatter, Black feminists created the hash tag #SayHerName as a way to make the experiences of women with regard to police brutality more visible (The African American Policy Forum, n.d.). For more see 'The Danger of a Single Story' by Adichie (2009).

(5) Intersectionality continues to dominate a large part of mainstream feminist discourse (Bloom, 2015; Rogers, 2015; Sathish, 2015). This is most evident in recent (social and traditional) media coverage surrounding the development and enactment of the Women's March on Washington. These discussions centered on issues of exclusion and alienation that arose when women of all walks of life demanded a seat at the table. Some chose to see this discourse as necessary, while others opted

not to participate in the march because doing so would amount to a betrayal of their feelings that the march was much more focused on the needs of able-bodied, White, cis-gendered women than on all women, and for many White women these conversations felt like the Oppression Olympics and as such counterproductive to progress. For examples of this see Anti-Defamation League (2017), Bates (2017), Chester (2017), Gebreyes (2017a, 2017b), Lachenal (2017), Ladau (2017) and Wilhelm (2017).

(6)   While I prefer to use the term 'home language' and do not personally ascribe to the label 'mother tongue' to describe the languages students use outside of school, I have included the term here for two reasons: First, it is an integral part of Skutnabb-Kangas' discourse around linguistic human rights and second, given that this study is grounded in the experiences of mothers, it feels appropriate to use the term 'mother tongue' as a means to underline the way language is embedded in the very personal connection that exists between a mother and a child.

(7)   'For the purpose of linguistic human rights, mother tongue(s) is/are the language(s) one has learned first and identifies with' (Skutnabb-Kangas, 1994: 361).

(8)   Based on the United Nations Genocide Convention (Articles IIb and IIe and its Final Draft Article III1), linguistic genocide refers to active (short- and long-term) practices that lead to the eradication of a language from an individual's or community's repertoire thus contributing not only to a loss of a language but also cultural identity (Skutnabb-Kangas, 2001, 2002).

(9)   The Hague Recommendations, formally known as 'The Hague Recommendations Regarding the Education Rights of National Minorities', are 'A set of High Commissioner on National Minorities Recommendations on the education rights of national minorities' that 'seek to provide guidance to [the Organization for Security and Co-operation in Europe] participating States on how best to ensure the education rights of national minorities within their borders. They cover the spirit of international instruments, measures and resources, decentralization and participation, public and private institutions, minority education at primary and secondary levels, minority education in vocational schools, minority education at the tertiary level and curriculum development' (Organization for Security and Co-operation in Europe, n.d.)

(10) For more on assimilation in the United States, see Alba (2005), Brubaker (2001) and Vigdor (2008).

(11) For more on nationalism in the United States, see Baum (2015), Gidda (2016), Meyer (2016) and The Economist Group (2016).

(12) In 2016, multiple instances of language-based harassment were reported. In one case, a Swahili speaker in Minnesota was attacked by a White woman who proclaimed 'In America, we speak English' before hitting the victim with a beer glass and causing serious injury to her face (Lynch, 2016). In another incident, a woman was harassed at a local retail store by a White customer who exclaimed 'Speak English, you're in America' (Chuck, 2016). Only the first accoster faced any legal consequence.

(13) The Mexican government has declared that it 'plans to have all of its students speaking English as well as Spanish within two decades' with an added expectation 'that every school could have an English teacher in 10 years' (Partlow, 2017). One of the ways the Mexican government intends to increase its English education labor force is by training and employing deported citizens as English teachers upon their return to Mexico (Baverstock, 2017).

(14) The percentages of Americans who feel this way are over 50% regardless of party affiliation. '[M]ore than eight-in-ten Republicans (83%) say language proficiency is a very important requisite for being truly American. [While f]ewer independents (67%) share that strong belief and even fewer Democrats (61%) agree' the sentiment is still strong (Stokes, 2017).

(15) While it may seem unorthodox to discuss a field of research and practice in relation to theory, for many the field of DS (and as such DSE) is synonymous with the social

construction model and vice versa. Additionally, because the study was grounded in the educational experiences of MoEBLADs, it is necessary to discuss not only the SCM but also the fields of DS and DSE, which guide its application.

(16) While the term 'people with dis/abilities' is used here to refer to individuals who identify and/or are identified as having an impairment, this term was not used within the design of the study because the 'people' with dis/abilities are children who are neither aware of their label nor have identified any sense of ownership or sense of identity associated with it.

(17) The difference between the social construction model, social interpretations and the minority (group) model is primarily semantics. In the social construction model 'disability is primarily understood as a result of oppressive social arrangements' (Connor *et al.*, 2008). However, Finkelstein (2004, 2007), who had originally introduced the idea of a social model, argued against calling it a model because he felt the term 'model' was too general and could be easily co-opted. He offered the term 'social interpretations' as a more precise way of understanding the ways in which society's views of disability impact the ability of people with impairments to move throughout the world (Finkelstein, 2001). The minority (group) model identified people with disabilities as a minoritized group similar to those who identify, or are identified, as African Americans, women and LGBTQ. The minority (group) model was developed by members of the Society for Disability Studies 'in the late 1970s and was influenced by the American Civil Rights Movement's claims to equal status for minority groups [...]. Proponents of this model asserted that minority group members experience stereotyping, marginalization, and discrimination' (Connor *et al.*, 2008).

(18) It is also important to note that within the social construction model there is a clear distinction between impairment and dis/ability. The term 'impairment' refers to the form, function or behavior embodied by the body (or body part), while the term 'disability' refers to the values and patterns of meaning attributed to those bodies (Baglieri *et al.*, 2011; Garland-Thomson, 2005; Taylor, 2006).

(19) Ideas around what it means to be normal are often referred to as normalcy. For more on normalcy and its historical and scientific development, see Davis (1995), Dudley-Marling and Gurn (2010) and Gallagher (2010).

(20) The term 'minoritizing' is used to implicate the active process by which people are given labels that place them within minoritized categories by external figures such as government entities or medical professionals. This is not exclusive to dis/ability labels as one can be minoritized on the grounds of race, ethnicity, language and class.

(21) *Segregation:* The act of separating students from the general population within a school on the basis of demographic factors such as spoken language and/or dis/ability label. As such students may be placed in inclusive classrooms, self-contained special education classrooms as opposed to participating in a general education classroom.

References

Aceves, T.C. (2014) Supporting Latino families in special education through community agency–school partnerships. *Multicultural Education* 21 (3/4), 45–50.

Adichie, C.N. (2009) The Danger of a Single Story. See http://www.ted.com/talks/chima manda_adichie_the_danger_of_a_single_story (accessed 24 February 2016).

Alba, R. (2005) Bright vs. blurred boundaries: Second-generation assimilation and exclusion in France, Germany, and the United States. *Ethnic and Racial Studies* 28 (1), 20–49. https://doi.org/10.1080/0141987042000280003

Anti-Defamation League (2017) What the Women's March teaches us about intersectionality. *Anti-Defamation League*, 24 January. See https://www.adl.org/blog/what-the-w omens-march-teaches-us-about-intersectionality (accessed 12 April 2017).

Asad, A.L. and Rosen, E. (2019) Hiding within racial hierarchies: How undocumented immigrants make residential decisions in an American city. *Journal of Ethnic and Migration Studies* 45 (11), 1857–1882. https://doi.org/10.1080/1369183X.2018.15 32787

Baglieri, S., Valle, J.W., Connor, D.J. and Gallagher, D.J. (2011) Disability studies in education: The need for a plurality of perspectives on disability. *Remedial and Special Education* 32 (4), 267–278. https://doi.org/10.1177/0741932510362200

Barber, C. (2014) Disability discrimination (2): Four UK laws to be aware of. *British Journal of Healthcare Assistants* 8 (7), 352–355.

Bates, K. (2017) Race and feminism: Women's March recalls the touchy history. *NPR.Org*, 21 January. See http://www.npr.org/sections/codeswitch/2017/01/21/510859909/race-and-feminism-womens-march-recalls-the-touchy-history (accessed 12 April 2017).

Baum, C. (2015) Nationalism in United States Foreign Policy in the Post 9/11 Era. *Dissertations and Theses.* https://doi.org/10.15760/etd.2528

Baverstock, A. (2017) Deportees back in Mexico offered free training to become English teachers. *FoxNews.Com*, 8 March. See http://www.foxnews.com/world/2017/03 /08/deportees-back-in-mexico-offered-free-training-to-become-english-teachers.html (accessed 12 April 2017).

Bloom, E. (2015) How economic issues turned into feminist issues. *The Atlantic*, 12 November. See https://www.theatlantic.com/business/archive/2015/11/how-economic -issues-turned-into-feminist-issues/415587/ (accessed 14 January 2021).

Bowleg, L. (2012) The problem with the phrase women and minorities: Intersectionality – an important theoretical framework for public health. *American Journal of Public Health* 102 (7), 1267–1273. https://doi.org/10.2105/AJPH.2012.300750

Brah, A. and Phoenix, A. (2013) Ain't I a Woman? Revisiting intersectionality. *Journal of International Women's Studies* 5 (3), 75–86.

Brown, S. (2003) *Movie Stars and Sensuous Scars.* Lincoln, NE: iUniverse. See https://bo oks-google-com.ezproxy.gc.cuny.edu/books/about/Movie_Stars_and_Sensuous_Sca rs.html?id=7DL9mfh8ygQC

Brubaker, R. (2001) The return of assimilation? Changing perspectives on immigration and its sequels in France, Germany, and the United States. *Ethnic and Racial Studies* 24 (4), 531–548. https://doi.org/10.1080/01419870120049770

Chester, C. (2017) Why the disability march is an important part of the Women's March on Washington. *The Mighty*, January. See https://themighty.com/2017/01/disability -march-on-washington/ (accessed 12 April 2017).

Chuck, E. (2016) 'Speak English, you're in America': Shocking rant caught on camera. *NBC News*, 22 December. See http://www.nbcnews.com/news/latino/speak-english -you-re-america-woman-tells-latina-shoppers-rant-n698776 (accessed 21 April 2017).

Cohen, S.R. (2013) Advocacy for the 'Abandonados': Harnessing cultural beliefs for Latino families and their children with intellectual disabilities. *Journal of Policy and Practice in Intellectual Disabilities* 10 (1), 71–78. https://doi.org/10.1111/jppi.12021

Connor, D.J., Gabel, S.L., Gallagher, D.J. and Morton, M. (2008) Disability studies and inclusive education: Implications for theory, research, and practice. *International Journal of Inclusive Education* 12 (5–6), 441–457. https://doi.org/10.1080/136031108 02377482

Crenshaw, K. (1991) Mapping the margins: Intersectionality, identity politics, and violence against women of color. *Stanford Law Review* 43 (6), 1241–1299. https://doi .org/10.2307/1229039

Darling, R.B. and Heckert, D.A. (2010) Orientations toward disability: Differences over the lifecourse. *International Journal of Disability, Development and Education* 57 (2), 131–143. https://doi.org/10.1080/10349121003750489

Davis, K. (2008) Intersectionality as buzzword: A sociology of science perspective on what makes a feminist theory successful. *Feminist Theory* 9 (1), 67–85. https://doi.org/10 .1177/1464700108086364

Davis, L.J. (1995) *Enforcing Normalcy: Disability, Deafness, and the Body*. London: Verso.

Dudley-Marling, C. and Gurn, A. (2010) *The Myth of the Normal Curve*. New York: Peter Lang.

Finkelstein, V. (2001) *The Social Model of Disability Repossessed*. Manchester: Manchester Coalition of Disabled People.

Finkelstein, V. (2004) *Modeling Disability: Yesterday's Model*. Leeds: University of Leeds.

Finkelstein, V. (2007) *The 'Social Model of Disability' and the Disability Movement*. Manchester: Greater Manchester Coalition of Disabled People. See http://pf7d7vi404s1d xh27mla5569.wpengine.netdna-cdn.com/files/library/finkelstein-The-Social-Model-o f-Disability-and-the-Disability-Movement.pdf (accessed 4 May 2017).

Fish, W.W. (2008) The IEP meeting: Perceptions of parents of students who receive special education services. *Preventing School Failure* 53 (1), 8.

Gallagher, D.J. (2010) Educational researchers and the making of normal people. In C. Dudley-Marling and A. Gurn (eds) *The Myth of the Normal Curve* (pp. 25–38). New York: Peter Lang.

Garcini, L.M., Murray, K.E., Zhou, A., Klonoff, E.A., Myers, M.G. and Elder, J.P. (2016) Mental health of undocumented immigrant adults in the United States: A systematic review of methodology and findings. *Journal of Immigrant & Refugee Studies* 14 (1), 1–25. https://doi.org/10.1080/15562948.2014.998849

Garland-Thomson, R. (2005) Feminist disability studies. *Signs* 30 (2), 1557–1587. https://doi.org/10.1086/423352

Gebreyes, R. (2017a) This woman just nailed the importance of intersectionality at the Women's March. *Huffington Post*, 22 January. See http://www.huffingtonpost.com/entry/intersectionality-womens-march-on-washington_us_5883e2bce4b096b4a2324 8bb (accessed 12 April 2017).

Gebreyes, R. (2017b) Women's March organizers address intersectionality as the movement grows. *Huffington Post*, 27 January. See http://www.huffingtonpost.com/entry /womens-march-organizers-address-intersectionality-as-the-movement-grows_us _5883f9d9e4b070d8cad314c0 (accessed 12 April 2017).

Gidda, M. (2016) How Donald Trump's nationalism won over white Americans. *Newsweek*, 15 November. See http://www.newsweek.com/donald-trump-nationalism-r acism-make-america-great-again-521083 (accessed 12 April 2017).

Gonzales, R.G. (2016) *Lives in Limbo: Undocumented and Coming of Age in America*. Berkeley, CA: University of California Press.

Groce, N. (1985) *Everyone Here Spoke Sign Language*. Cambridge, MA: Harvard University Press. https://books-google-com.ezproxy.gc.cuny.edu/books/about/Everyone _Here_Spoke_Sign_Language.html?id=AY_JCgAAQBAJ

Gu, M., Patkin, J. and Kirkpatrick, A. (2014) The dynamic identity construction in English as lingua franca intercultural communication: A positioning perspective. *System* 46, 131–142. https://doi.org/10.1016/j.system.2014.07.010

Hancock, A.-M. (2007) When multiplication doesn't equal quick addition: Examining intersectionality as a research paradigm. *Perspectives on Politics* 5 (1), 63–79.

Hankivsky, O. (2014) Intersectionality 101. *Cal* 64 (1), 238.

Harris, J. (2001) One principle and three fallacies of disability studies. *Journal of Medical Ethics* 27 (6), 383–387. https://doi.org/10.1136/jme.27.6.383

Harris, P. (1995) Who am I? Concepts of disability and their implications for people with learning difficulties. *Disability & Society* 10 (3), 341–352. https://doi.org/10.1080/0 9687599550023570

Harry, B. (2008) Collaboration with culturally and linguistically diverse families: Ideal versus reality. *Exceptional Children* 74 (3), 372–388.

Ijalba, E. (2015a) Understanding parental engagement in Hispanic mothers of children with autism spectrum disorder: Application of a process-model of cultural

competence. *Journal of Multilingual Education Research* 6 (6), 91–110. http://for
dham.bepress.com/jmer/vol6/iss1/6

Ijalba, E. (2015b) Effectiveness of a parent-implemented language and literacy intervention
in the home language. *Child Language Teaching and Therapy* 31 (2), 207–220. http:/
/dx.doi.org.ezproxy.gc.cuny.edu/10.1177/0265659014548519

Jenkins, J. (2013) *English as a Lingua Franca in the International University: The Politics
of Academic English Language Policy.* London: Routledge.

Jenkins, J. (2015) Repositioning English and multilingualism in English as a lingua franca:
Englishes in practice. *Englishes in Practice* 2 (3), 49–85.

Jenkins, J. and Leung, C. (2013) English as a lingua franca. In A. Kunnan (ed.) *The Com-
panion to Language Assessment* (pp. 1607–1616). Hoboken, NJ: John Wiley & Sons,
Inc. https://doi.org/10.1002/9781118411360.wbcla047

Lachenal, J. (2017) Do I have a place in your movement? On intersectionality at the Wom-
en's March on Washington. *The Mary Sue*, 24 January. See https://www.themarysue
.com/intersectional-feminism-womens-march/ (accessed 12 April 2017).

Ladau, E. (2017) Why are disability rights absent from the Women's March platform?
The Establishment, 16 January. See https://theestablishment.co/disability-rights-are-
conspicuously-absent-from-the-womens-march-platform-1d61cee62593#.6qgkqxl3w
(accessed 12 April 2017).

Lalvani, P. (2015) Disability, stigma and otherness: Perspectives of parents and teachers.
International Journal of Disability, Development and Education 62 (4), 379–393.

Lynch, J. (2016) Woman pleads guilty to hitting immigrant with beer mug. *CNN*, 18
October. See http://www.cnn.com/2016/10/18/us/applebees-immigrant-attack-minne
sota-trnd/index.html

Magasi, S. (2008) Infusing disability studies into the rehabilitation sciences. *Topics in
Stroke Rehabilitation* 15 (3), 283–287. https://doi.org/10.1310/tsr1503-283 (accessed
21 April 2017).

Martin, J.L. (n.d.) Legal implications of RTI and special education identification. *RTI
Action Network.* See http://www.rtinetwork.org/learn/ld/legal-implications-of-res
ponse-to-intervention-and-special-education-identification (accessed 25 May 2016).

McCall, L. (2005) The complexity of intersectionality. *Signs* 30 (3), 1771–1800. https://doi
.org/10.1086/426800

McDermott, R.P. (1993) The acquisition of a child by a learning disability. In C. Chaiklin
and J. Lave (eds) *Understanding Practice: Perspectives on Activity and Context* (pp.
269–305). New York: Cambridge University Press.

Mehan, H. (1993) Beneath the skin and between the ears: A case study in the politics of
representation. In C. Chaiklin and J. Lave (eds) *Understanding Practice: Perspectives
on Activity and Context* (pp. 241–268). New York: Cambridge University Press. https
://doi.org/10.1017/CBO9780511625510.010

Meyer, D. (2016) Trump's American nationalism. *The Seattle Times*, 18 December.
See http://www.seattletimes.com/opinion/trumps-american-nationalism/ (accessed 21
April 2017).

Mobley, C. (2015) Is my whole family disabled by proxy? – Raising children with disabilities. *FireFly Community*, 18 August. See http://community.fireflyfriends.com/
blog/article/is-my-whole-family-disabled-by-proxy-raising-children-with-disabilties
(accessed 12 April 2017).

Montelongo, A. (2015) Latino parents' perceptions of IEP meetings. *McNair Scholars
Journal* 16, 109–130.

Nash, J.C. (2008) Re-thinking intersectionality. *Feminist Review* 89, 1–15.

National Center for Education Statistics (2016) *English Language Learners.* Washington,
DC: US Department of Education. https://nces.ed.gov/fastfacts/display.asp?id=96

Nicholls, A. (2008) Disability discrimination by proxy: Employment and HR – UK.
Mondaq, 2 October. See http://www.mondaq.com/x/67056/employee+rights+labour
+relations/Disability+Discrimination+By+Proxy (accessed 12 April 2017).

O'Regan, J.P. (2014) English as a lingua franca: An immanent critique. *Applied Linguistics* 35 (5), 533–552. https://doi.org/10.1093/applin/amt045

Organization for Security and Co-operation in Europe (n.d.) *The Hague Recommendations Regarding the Education Rights of National Minorities | OSCE* [..Org]. Organization for Security and Co-Operation in Europe. See http://www.osce.org/hcnm/32180 (accessed 21 April 2017).

Partlow, J. (2017) Analysis | Mexico wants its kids speaking English as well as Spanish within 20 years. *Washington Post*, 15 March. See https://www.washingtonpost.com/news/worldviews/wp/2017/03/15/mexico-wants-its-kids-speaking-english-as-well-as-spanish-within-20-years/ (accessed 21 April 2017).

Ramirez, A.Y.F. (2003) Dismay and disappointment: Parental involvement of Latino immigrant parents. *The Urban Review* 35 (2), 93–110.

Ramirez, N. and Monk, G. (2017) Crossing borders: Narrative therapy with undocumented Mexican women on a journey beyond abuse and violence. *Journal of Systemic Therapies* 36 (2), 27–38. https://doi.org/10.1521/jsyt.2017.36.2.27

Reeves, D. (2015) Intersectional invisibility: A comparison among Caucasian, African-American, and Latino men and women. *HIM 1990–2015*. See http://stars.library.ucf.edu/honorstheses1990-2015/1737 (accessed 4 January 2019).

Rodriguez, R.J., Blatz, E.T. and Elbaum, B. (2013) Strategies to involve families of Latino students with disabilities: When parent initiative is not enough. *Intervention in School and Clinic* 49 (5), 263–270. https://doi.org/10.1177/1053451213513956

Rogers, T. (2015) This movement is uniting Latinos, blacks, and whites. *Fusion*, 11 November. See http://tv.fusion.net/story/231101/how-the-fight-for-15-is-uniting-latinos-blacks-and-whites-in-a-movement-the-nation-should-pay-attention-to/ (accessed 17 April 2017).

Sathish, M. (2015) Here's exactly how intersectional feminists are challenging the status quo. *Bustle*, 6 November. See https://www.bustle.com/articles/122144-heres-exactly-how-intersectional-feminists-are-challenging-the-status-quo (accessed 17 April 2017).

Scheer, J. and Groce, N. (1988) Impairment as a human constant: Cross-cultural and historical perspectives on variation. *Journal of Social Issues* 44 (1), 23–37. https://doi.org/10.1111/j.1540-4560.1988.tb02046.x

Shields, S.A. (2008) Gender: An intersectionality perspective. *Sex Roles* 59 (5–6), 301–311. https://doi.org/10.1007/s11199-008-9501-8

Simons, G.F. and Fennig, C.D. (eds) (2017) *Ethnologue: Languages of the World, Twentieth edition*. Dallas, TX: SIL International. https://www.ethnologue.com/statistics/size

Skutnabb-Kangas, T. (1994) Killing a mother tongue: How the Kurds are deprived of linguistic human rights. In T. Skutnabb-Kangas and R. Phillipson (eds) *Linguistic Human Rights: Overcoming Linguistic Discrimination* (pp. 347–370). Berlin: Mouton de Gruyter.

Skutnabb-Kangas, T. (1997) Human rights and language policy in education. In R. Wodak and D. Corson (eds) *Encyclopedia of Language and Education* (pp. 55–65). Dordrecht: Springer Netherlands. https://doi.org/10.1007/978-94-011-4538-1_6

Skutnabb-Kangas, T. (2001) Murder that is a threat to survival. *The Guardian*, 22 March. See https://www.theguardian.com/education/2001/mar/22/tefl3 (accessed 21 April 2017).

Skutnabb-Kangas, T. (2002) Linguistic human rights in education: Western hypocrisy in European and global language policy. In T. Lahdelma, J. Jankovics, J. Nyerges and P. Laihonen (eds) *Power and Culture, Plenary Sessions: 5th International Congress of Hungarian Studies* (pp. 115-156). Jyväskylä: University of Jyväskylä. http://www.tove-skutnabb-kangas.org/pdf/Linguistic_Human_Rights_in_Education_Western_Hypocrisy_in_European_and_Global_Language_Policy_Tove_Skutnabb_Kangas_Jyvaeskylae_2002.pdf

Skutnabb-Kangas, T. (2005) Language policy and linguistic human rights. In T. Ricento (ed.) *An Introduction to Language Policy: Theory and Method* (pp. 273–291). Malden, MA: Blackwell.

Smooth, W. (2011) Standing for Women? Which Women? The Substantive Representation of Women's Interests and the Research Imperative of Intersectionality. *Politics & Gender*, 7(3), 436–441. doi:10.1017/S1743923X11000225

Stokes, B. (2017) What It Takes to Truly Be 'One of Us'. *Pew Research Center's Global Attitudes Project*, 1 February. See http://www.pewglobal.org/2017/02/01/what-it-t akes-to-truly-be-one-of-us/ (accessed 21 April 2017).

Swann, J. (2015) Gloria Steinem joins the fight for 15: Fast-food wages are a feminist cause. *TakePart*, 8 June. See http://www.takepart.com/article/2015/06/08/fast-food-gloria-steinem (accessed 17 April 2017).

Taylor, S.J. (2006) Before it had a name: Exploring the historical roots of disability studies in education. In S. Danforth and S.L. Gabel (eds) *Vital Questions Facing Disability Studies in Education* (pp. xiii–xxiii). New York: Peter Lang Publishing.

The African American Policy Forum (n.d.) #*SayHerName*. AAPF. See http://www.aapf .org/sayhername/ (accessed 17 April 2017).

The Economist Group (2016) The new nationalism. *The Economist*, 19 November. See http://www.economist.com/news/leaders/21710249-his-call-put-america-first-donald -trump-latest-recruit-dangerous (accessed 21 April 2017).

Turney, K. and Kao, G. (2009) Barriers to school involvement: Are immigrant parents disadvantaged? *The Journal of Educational Research* 102 (4), 257–271. https://doi.org /10.3200/JOER.102.4.257-271

Vandergrift, J. and Greene, A. (1992) Rethinking parent involvement. *Education Leadership* 50 (1), 57–59. https://repository.asu.edu/attachments/70910/content/Rethinking .pdf

Vigdor, J.L. (2008) Measuring Immigrant Assimilation in the United States. Civic Report No. 53. Manhattan Institute for Policy Research. See https://eric.ed.gov/?id =ED501689

Wilhelm, H. (2017) 'Women's March' morphs into intersectional torture chamber. *Chicagotribune.Com*, 12 January. See http://www.chicagotribune.com/news/opinion/co mmentary/ct-womens-march-washington-white-black-perspec-0113-20170112-story .html (accessed 17 April 2017).

Wolfe, K. and Durán, L.K. (2013) Culturally and linguistically diverse parents' perceptions of the IEP process. *Multiple Voices for Ethnically Diverse Exceptional Learners* 13 (2), 4–18.

Yuval-Davis, N. (2006) Intersectionality and feminist politics. *European Journal of Women's Studies* 13 (3), 193–209. https://doi.org/10.1177/1350506806065752

Yuval-Davis, N. (2012) Dialogical epistemology: An intersectional resistance to the 'Oppression Olympics'. *Gender & Society* 26 (1), 46–54. https://doi.org/10.1177 /0891243211427701

Zadnik, E., Sabina, C. and Cuevas, C.A. (2016) Violence against Latinas: The effects of undocumented status on rates of victimization and help-seeking. *Journal of Interpersonal Violence* 31 (6), 1141–1153. https://doi.org/10.1177/0886260514564062

Zeigler, K. and Camarota, S.A. (2016) Nearly 65 Million U.S. Residents Spoke a Foreign Language at Home in 2015. Center for Immigration Studies. See http://cis.org/Nearl y-65-Million-US-Residents-Spoke-a-Foreign-Language-at-Home-in-2015 (accessed 21 April 2017).

3 Other People's Stories

The purpose of this research is not abstraction or generalization, but extended, active, layered, perhaps intersubjective engagement with others [...] Thus the processes, by forgoing prediction and explanation and judgment, produce a context of meaning and significance for a different aim: to recognize and remember and revalue the richness and complexity of human beings.

(Himley & Carini, 2000: 129)

This book is anchored on the stories of women. Like all things, the stories we tell, regardless of whether or not we were part of the original narrative, have their origin in one of two places: they are based on what we *saw* and they are based on what we *heard*. While I have already written about the theories and values that shaped the lenses with which I understood the stories I gathered, it is just as important to understand the values and processes that guided the work. As such, this chapter will focus on the two ideologies that heavily influenced what I saw and what I heard leading up to this book: the first is a valuing of stories as testimonios and the second is the process of gathering information through descriptive inquiry (DI).

Testimonios: Her Story is Everybody's Story

A central ideology undergirding this story-gathering work concerns not only the use of narratives as a data collection method, but also the valuing of narrative as a political and intentional act. *Testimonio*[1] refers to the intentional and political act of telling a singular experience – or a collection of interconnected/related experiences – in the hope of exposing an injustice that is both personal and systemic (Acevedo, 2001; Bernal *et al.*, 2012; Beverley, 1989; Huber, 2009a; Passos DeNicolo & Gonzalez, 2015; Reyes & Rodríguez, 2012). *Testimonios* have a long-standing history in Latin American politics and activism and it is in that spirit that they are included in this project. While *testimonios* are similar in nature to narratives, the fact that they are intentionally political as well as representative of a collective systemic issue makes them feel particularly relevant to the issues explored in this book. Additionally, given that the

focal community of this book is Latinx women of color, it is important
to use a lens that is connected not only to storytelling as a device, but also
to Latinidad, LatCrit, womanhood and Chicanx/Latinx feminist theory
(Acevedo, 2001; Bernal *et al.*, 2012; González *et al.*, 2003; Huber, 2009a,
2009b; Prieto & Villenas, 2012). Similarly to intersectionality, the importance of *testimonios* lies heavily in the epistemological understanding
that a woman's experience is influenced by the multiple identity markers she dons with particular attention to her gender, race and ethnicity.
Lastly, *testimonios* recognize and acknowledge the power difference that
exists between the speaker and the listener while also giving over a sense
of autonomy to the speaker by highlighting the fact that they choose
which narrative to share, when, how and to what end (Reyes & Rodríguez, 2012). While traditional narrative perspectives focus on the goals
of the listener/interviewer, *testimonios* focus equally, if not more so, on
the goals of the speaker (Beverley, 1989). It is also important to note the
importance of language in the word *testimonio*. The term '*testimonio*'
translates directly to testimony – yet, the direct translation does not fully
encompass the weight of the Spanish word which refers to the unpack-
ing and unloading of a story to a witness with an allusion to both a legal
confession and a religious one (Beverly, 1989). By maintaining its Spanish
presentation, the word *testimonio* also acknowledges that language is an
important part of the speaker's narrative and that some meaning can be
lost in the translation (Bernal *et al.*, 2012). This final point is of critical
importance and relevance to this project given that all of the interviews
were conducted in Spanish in order to privilege the voices of the speakers. This was also done in an effort to reveal the strength and value of
Spanish, of home language practices, which are so often devalued in
relation to the economic value of English. However, given my role as
an interlocutor, they must be translated into English in order to make
them widely available and accessible. Thus, *testimonio* also serves as an
analytical guide.

   Testimonios are a multipurpose instrument. They can serve as a
theory, a literary device, a methodology, a process, a product and a
pedagogical tool (Bernal *et al.*, 2012; Beverley, 1989; Huber, 2009b; Passos DeNicolo & Gonzalez, 2015; Reyes & Rodríguez, 2012). *Testimonios*
date back to the 1970s when Latin American activists began using them
as a literary mode by which to voice their oppressive experiences to the
outside world (Reyes & Rodriguez, 2012). In time, the *testimonio* was
developed into a theory for understanding the positionality of both the
speaker and the interlocutor/researcher who promoted and disseminated
the narrative that was shared (Huber, 2009a, 2009b). In the last 20 years,
it has also emerged as a methodology employed by LatCrit and Chicanx/
Latinx feminist scholars as a way to explore their own (and other speakers') oppressive experiences (Huber, 2009a, 2009b; Reyes & Rodriguez,
2012). Regardless of the platform upon which they are employed,

testimonios are universally used as a means to center the knowledge and document the experiences of oppressed groups, and to denounce injustices whether they take place on the farmland, in the political arena or in the classroom (Reyes & Rodríguez, 2012). *Testimonios* also aim to create a connection between the *Testimonialista/s* and the reader in order to effect change by making the reader bear witness, thus politicizing the narrative and leading the reader to understand that the personal is political and vice versa (Beverley, 1989).

While *testimonios* can arise from multiple mediums, be they oral histories, interviews, confessions, etc., there are many elements that define them. According to Huber (2009b), some of those elements include, but are not limited to, a verbal journey, an authentic narrative and a transformational storytelling. However, it seems as though one of the major factors that distinguishes a *testimonio* from a traditional Eurocentric narrative is the role of the gatherer/researcher. Unlike traditional narratives, the role of the researcher/listener/interlocutor is very important to the development of a *testimonio*. Rather than just sustain the 'common training of researchers to produce unbiased knowledge, *testimonio* challenges objectivity by situating the individual in communion with a collective experience marked by marginalization, oppression, or resistance' (Bernal *et al.*, 2012: 363). As such, it allows a researcher like me to connect with those stories and the *Testimonialista/s*[2] who share them on a sociocultural level in which I am able to acknowledge my own subjectivity as a Latinx woman. This connection between the researcher and the participant is based on a 'Chicana/Latina *femenista* sensibility and attempts to situate the researcher-participant in a reciprocal relationship where genuine connections are made between the researcher and the community members' (Bernal *et al.*, 2012: 366). Ultimately, '[t]estimonio, then, can be understood as a bridge that merges brown bodies in our communities with academia' (Bernal *et al.*, 2012: 364). This bridge harks back to Gloria Anzaldúa's work on the borderlands and mestiza consciousness through which Anzaldúa explored connections between the mind and the brown body across different sociocultural spaces (Anzaldúa, 1999; Reuman & Anzaldúa, 2000; Yarbro-Bejarano, 1994). This bridge is also significant because it extends Spivack's work on the subaltern by recognizing that women of color who have moved from traditional subversive and voiceless spaces into academic/formal spaces can still find themselves in the role of *Testimonialistas* whose *testimonios* have the power to uncover and vocalize experiences of oppression and resistance (Acevedo, 2001; Bernal *et al.*, 2012; Spivak, 1988).

The inclusion of *testimonios* as an ideological anchor for this project is reflective of multiple aims. The shape and design of the study allowed for the natural production of *testimonios* because it is grounded in the Latinx experience, immigrant histories and language. Additionally, the interactions between the participants and the researcher focused more on storytelling that was grounded in trust and relationship building than on questions and answers. As a result, the participants were able to have some control over the direction of the interactions and share only the stories and experiences that they wanted to expound.

One of the overarching goals of this book is to reframe the narrative around emergent bilinguals labeled as dis/abled (EBLADs) mothers through the use of their own voices, making their experiences worthy of consideration in the development of educational policies. Secondly, the focus on this particular population arose from the fact that White, middle-class values and experiences are often privileged above those who are other[ed]/minoritized/marginalized and so it is important to include a theoretical standpoint that originates from a cultural and historical place that is reflective of the experiences being shared by the participants. Third, the focus is on storytelling as a vehicle for community building, as a means to center the knowledge of the silenced which can provide healing through sharing, and as an entry point for change. This is compatible with Patricia Carini's work on DI which was employed in the study as a data collection method (Himley & Carini, 2000). The compatibility between *testimonios* and DI lies in how both practices demand that the subject be seen, heard and understood based on their positionality, not the observers or the interviewers. Both practices push us to accept the being and their stories as they are, without our own desire to contextualize or negotiate their experiences with our own. This is of particular importance for marginalized communities who so often have their talents and struggles qualified and quantified with those of the majority; their needs and gifts are never valuable on their own, they must always be put alongside, and in relation to, those of the majority. These stances and approaches also recognize that individuals are members of communities, especially linguistic communities. Thus, what happens to children impacts parents and vice versa (Gallo & Hornberger, 2017; Ricento & Wright, 2008). Lastly, one of the desired outcomes of this project is not only to raise awareness to the challenges of these individual participants, but also to gather individual voices to address a collective injustice that is being overlooked within an intersectional community. In the end, viewing the stories shared through a *testimonio* perspective allows for each mother's experience to be valued on its own, while also building a collective voice of dissent and hopefully a collective call to action.

To approach the stories that were being shared with me as *testimonios* allowed me to see power not only in the narratives but in the women sharing them. So often, work that is centered on communities like the one featured in this book focuses on the struggle, often evoking pity, shame and resentment. Approaching this work using *testimonios* allowed me not only to see more than the struggle, but also to show more than the struggle. Still, the ability to see complexity in things is not borne solely from *testimonios*, it also arises from my years of training in the use of DI processes.

Descriptive Inquiry: A Process for Gathering and Sharing

I have been engaged in the work of DI for my entire career as an educator. I was introduced to the descriptive processes in 2005, as a graduate student at Long Island University (LIU) – Brooklyn Campus.[3] The dean of the school of education at the time, Cecelia Traugh, had been engaged in this work for over 30 years and made it her mission to bring it to LIU, where it was part of the graduate course sequence. First, we learned to describe children's work, then we learned about gathering data through observations and using it to form narrative descriptions of children to help guide not only our instruction of individual students but also our overall practice. Throughout this learning, we were being trained on how to do this work without enacting the judgmental and deficit-centered language that seeped into our day-to-day discourse. It was a challenge. Describing work feels like it should be easy: a house, a dog, a tree. However, describing only what is there and not what you think is there or, more importantly, what you think it means and says about a child's psychological and academic development is excruciatingly hard. Many of us are hard-wired as educators to constantly gather data and quickly evaluate it for what is being done well and what problems need to be mitigated. While the work of DI is hard work, it is also worthy work. In a time when we are so consumed by test scores and rankings, it is nice to slow down – to look closely, to dive deeply. It was for this reason that DI appealed to me as a bilingual special education teacher. I saw the potential of this work to help expand my understanding of my students, to be able to see them where they were, to identify their strengths and build on them, and why I knew it was critical to this study.

You may be asking yourself how a process that is grounded in looking at children's work could be valuable to a study focused on mothers. The answer is simple: it is not about who we look at and it is about how. As such, instead of observing children in classrooms, I observed mothers in their homes; instead of focusing on how children take up space or interact with others, I focused on how mothers took up space in their homes, how they negotiated space with their children, how they interacted with them. From these observations, I developed questions for the mothers, questions that would elicit narratives representative of their lives, their experiences, their own individual (and collective) families and their mothering practices. Instead of developing recollections that would serve as entry points for connecting with children's work, I adapted recollections for mothers to be able to find points of connection with each other, with their particular kind of motherhood, etc. The goal of this study was to create full and complex depictions of these mothers and their children. At its core, DI is a guide for how to look at people, how to understand what they do and, most importantly, it is a guide for sharing. If ever a child were to be described as 'excited' or 'erratic', DI demands that we follow that qualification with a rich description of the behaviors that a child enacted in order for the describer to reach that conclusion – this is also the core of any and all data analysis. As with *testimonios*, DI is grounded in the idea that the maker is always intentional; there are no mistakes, there are no slips or accidental omissions. At the same time, all work is a work in progress – perhaps that child only filled half the page because there was a time restriction, perhaps they had something blocking their view; regardless, they drew what they drew and we can only analyze what the child included, we cannot speculate about what was left out or why. Similarly, what is shared in an interview is intentional – the participants say what they do because they want to; there are no omissions or mistakes, we cannot speculate as to why someone said or did something (not enough time? lack of information?), we can only work with what was said because that is what they wanted us to have access to. This understanding of the speaker and maker as intentional is grounded in empowerment. It is this focus on intentionality, on strength, on valuing the maker and on describing only what is there, that binds *testimonios* and DI in my work and in this book.

The specific components of DI that were used in this study were observations and recollections. A recollection is a component of a descriptive review (DR). DRs are a pedagogical and epistemological practice that was developed at the Prospect School in Bennington, Vermont, in the 1960s by Patricia Carini. As part of a DR, educators, and occasionally parents, gather to listen to detailed descriptions of a child/ student. These descriptions are based on five areas: physical presence and gestures, disposition and temperament, modes of thinking and learning, connections to others and strong interests and preferences (Himley & Carini, 2000). These descriptions come from deep observations that are enacted by the reviewer (in most cases a teacher).

A recollection is what Carini calls the gathering of a group of people to remember and share their individual experiences around a guiding question or theme. These are often carried out by educators prior to engaging in a DR of a child. The recollections are typically used to 'alert adults to the inner world of adolescents, of the new life beginning by grounding that experience in our own. The Descriptive Review of an Adolescent is intended to safeguard that interiority and to honor the young person's sense of self' (Himley, 2011: 23). The recollections also serve as a way to ground the participants in the practice of description and to prepare them to hear a very detailed description of a child, free of judgment and pathologizing. As such, the recollections usually center on a topic or theme connected to the child or the focusing question being presented.

In this study, the recollections did not focus on a childhood event but rather on a time when each Testimonialista helped her child with a school-based task because the focus of this study is on the experiences of the mother and not on the experiences of the child. Recollections were included in this study in order to give the participants an opportunity to hear their stories alongside each other. Additionally, recollections have an ability to create entry into a community as well as highlight a connection among participants (Himley, 2011).

The ways in which DI and *testimonios* were integrated into the study itself are explained in the following section.

The Gathering of Stories

The focus of this study was first and foremost to center the lived experiences and the narratives of the mothers; as such, their testimonios were central to this study. A variety of interview methods were used not only to elicit narratives, but also to help the discourse move beyond the joys of motherhood into the unfiltered reality. The configuration of processes enacted in this study relate back to the ideology and practices enacted by the DI process established by Patricia Carini at the Prospect School (Himley, 2011; Himley & Carini, 2000). While the processes were not enacted in their entirety, the philosophical stance behind them served as a guide for developing the study design.

The data originated from a combination of narrative interviews that called forth testimonios, observations, communal storytelling through recollections and the gathering of relevant artifacts. This complex approach to data collection was used in order to construct as complete an image of these matriarchs as possible so as to best counter the deficit-based perspectives that currently permeate their presence within the literature and society. Additionally, in order to offer a space to those mothers who have received the least amount of attention within the current scholarship, the data for this project was gathered primarily in Spanish.

The participation of the mothers in this study occurred in two phases.

The first phase took place from October to December 2016. This phase was marked by two interview stages. During the first stage, ethnographic interviews were conducted with all 10 Spanish-speaking Latinx mothers individually. These interviews consisted of general questions to collect demographic information and an inventory of the family, as well as open-ended questions in order to elicit narratives related to their children's bilingualism, dis/ability labels, the mother's parental identity and their relationship with the school. The second stage focused explicitly on the mother–child relationship. The Phase 1 interviews took place in one of three places: a local community center, a local church or the participant's home. At the end of this phase, three participants were identified for participation in Phase 2.

The remaining core group of three mothers, who will be referred to as the Testimonialistas, then participated in four additional narrative interviews grounded in their experiences, and on the collection of interviews conducted in Phase 1 (Figure 3.1).

In addition to new interviews, the second phase of the study also included two unstructured observations of each Testimonialista and her child in the home, as well as one observation in which the Testimonialista and her child were observed performing a focused task that required oral communication. There was also an individual interview with each child in which they were asked to talk about their mother. Phase 2 interviews were conducted in either a community church or the participant's home, again as determined by the participant. However, all observations were conducted in the participant's home, and while a secondary site option was not provided, mothers were told they could decline the observations. In addition to the interviews and observations, artifacts such as individual education plans (IEPs), report cards, homework and school–home communication were also collected as appropriate. There was also an opportunity to interview each Testimonialista before and after she took part in an IEP meeting at the child's school.

The final part of Phase 2 consisted of gathering the inner circle of mothers in order for the Testimonialistas to come together through their experiences by sharing a memory facilitated through a recollection. I also participated in sharing my own recollection. Afterward, we had dinner together and talked about our experiences and lives as mothers and the

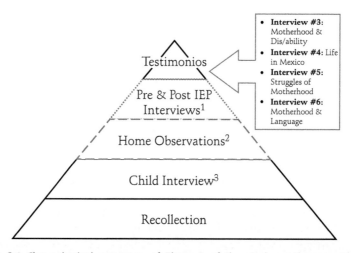

Figure 3.1 Chronological sequence of Phase 1 of the study – ethnographic case studies. [1]The IEP interviews were conducted throughout the second phase since each family's meeting took place at different points in the school year. [2]The home observations and child interviews took place between individual interviews #5 and #6. [3]The child interview took place immediately after home observation #2

ways in which our stories intersected and diverged. For this final session, the mothers were invited to my home.

Through these interviews, the mothers shared their perspectives on disability, bilingualism and motherhood. They also shared factors that impact their capacities as mothers and the types of parental engagement they take up, factors that I had not accounted for when I designed my study. Often, these factors went beyond the scope of what schools, teachers and education researchers, like me, recognize or consider because they often occur outside of school, factors such as domestic violence, social isolation, caring for aging parents, traumatic immigration journeys and transnational parenting. It is interesting to me that while these issues were not at the forefront of my mind when I started this journey, I now realize that they are inextricably connected. Just as I hope this book allows us as educators to see children as whole, my hope is that we can do the same for mothers, focusing not only on their needs but also on their resilience and resounding strength particularly as exhibited in their efforts to ensure their children's academic and social-emotional needs are met, at any cost (e.g. financial, physical and emotional).

Notes

(1) The use of *testimonio* italicized is meant to honor the original definition of 'a novel or novella-length narrative told in the first person by a narrator who is also the real-life protagonist or witness of the events he or she recounts' like Î, Rigoberta Menchú. An Indian woman in Guatemala (Beverley, 1991: 2). Thus, the italicized use references a genre while the standard use (i.e. testimonio) in this book refers to the testimonios gathered through this study.
(2) The producer of the testimonio.
(3) For the last 15 years, I have continued to engage with this work in a myriad of ways from monthly meetings with the Adolescent Study Group to training teachers on the descriptive processes. At the core of this has been traveling to Vermont for one to two weeks each summer to continue engaging with the descriptive processes with educators from around the country. The summer institutes were first offered by Carini through the Prospect Archive and Center for Education and Research, and more recently are run by the Institute for Descriptive Inquiry Inc.

References

Acevedo, L. del A. (ed.) (2001) *Telling to Live: Latina Feminist Testimonios*. Durham, NC: Duke University Press.

Anzaldúa, G. (1999) *Borderlands*. San Francisco, CA: Aunt Lute Books.

Bernal, D.D., Burciaga, R. and Carmona, J.F. (2012) Chicana/Latina testimonios: Mapping the methodological, pedagogical, and political. *Equity & Excellence in Education* 45 (3), 363–372. https://doi.org/10.1080/10665684.2012.698149

Beverley, J. (1989) The margin at the center: On testimonio (testimonial narrative). *MFS Modern Fiction Studies* 35 (1), 11–28. https://doi.org/10.1353/mfs.0.0923

Beverley, J. (1991) 'Through all things modern': Second thoughts on testimonio. *Boundary 2* 18 (2), 1–21. doi:10.2307/303277

Gallo, S. and Hornberger, N. (2017) Immigration policy as family language policy: Mexican immigrant children and families in search of biliteracy. *International Journal of Bilingualism* 23 (3), 757–770. https://doi.org/10.1177/1367006916684908

González, M.S., Plata, O., García, E., Torres, M. and Urrieta, L. Jr (2003) Testimonios de Inmigrantes: Students educating future teachers. *Journal of Latinos and Education* 2 (4), 233–243. https://doi.org/10.1207/S1532771XJLE0204_4

Himley, M. (ed.) (2011) *Prospect's Descriptive Processes: The Child, the Art of Teaching, and the Classroom and School.* North Bennington, VT: The Prospect Archives and Center for Education and Research. http://cdi.uvm.edu/resources/ProspectDescript iveProcessesRevEd.pdf

Himley, M. and Carini, P.F. (2000) *From Another Angle: Children's Strengths and School Standards: The Prospect Center's Descriptive Review of the Child.* New York: Teachers College Press.

Huber, L.P. (2009a) Beautifully Powerful: A LatCrit Reflection on Coming to an Epistemological Consciousness and the Power of Testimonio Symposium: LatCrit XIV: Outsiders Inside: Critical Outsiders Theory and Praxis in the Policymaking of the New American Regime, October 1–4, 2009: Outsider intellectuals: Identity, responsibility and method. *American University Journal of Gender, Social Policy & the Law* 18, 839–852.

Huber, L.P. (2009b) Disrupting apartheid of knowledge: Testimonio as methodology in Latina/o critical race research in education. *International Journal of Qualitative Studies in Education* 22 (6), 639–654. https://doi.org/10.1080/09518390903333863

Passos DeNicolo, C. and Gonzalez, M. (2015) Testimonio as a pedagogical tool for exploring embodied literacies and bilingualism. *Journal of Language & Literacy Education* 2 (1), 109–126.

Prieto, L. and Villenas, S.A. (2012) Pedagogies from Nepantla: Testimonio, Chicana/Latina feminisms and teacher education classrooms. *Equity & Excellence in Education* 45 (3), 411–429. https://doi.org/10.1080/10665684.2012.698197

Reuman, A.E. and Anzaldúa, G.E. (2000) Coming into play: An interview with Gloria Anzaldúa. *MELUS* 25 (2), 3–45. https://doi.org/10.2307/468217

Reyes, K.B. and Rodríguez, J.E.C. (2012) Testimonio: Origins, terms, and resources. *Equity & Excellence in Education* 45 (3), 525–538. https://doi.org/10.1080/10665684.2012.698571

Ricento, T.K. and Wright, W.E. (2008) Language policy and education in the United States. In N.H. Hornberger (ed.) *Encyclopedia of Language and Education* (pp. 285–300). New York: Springer US. https://doi.org/10.1007/978-0-387-30424-3_21

Spivak, G.C. (1988) Can the subaltern speak? In R. Morris (ed.) *Can the Subaltern Speak?: Reflections on the History of an Idea* (pp. 21–78). New York: Columbia University Press. https://books-google-com.ezproxy.gc.cuny.edu/books/about/Can_the_Subaltern_Speak.html?id=cXInuU4BUDYC

Yarbro-Bejarano, Y. (1994) Gloria Anzaldúa's Borderlands/La frontera: Cultural studies, 'difference', and the non-unitary subject. *Cultural Critique* 28, 5–28. https://doi.org/10.2307/1354508

4 Setting the Stage: An Introduction to the Mothers and the Significance of a Place and Time

Every strong and memorable story has a few core elements, among them the characters and the theme, but equally important is the setting. In this study, the setting was also critical. Soon, we will dive deeper into understanding who the mothers are – the collective as well as the main characters, the testimonialistas. But first we must discuss the place: Sunset Park, Brooklyn, and the time that brought us together.

New York City: 'The Multilingual Apple'[1]

According to Erik Vickstrom, a Census Bureau statistician, '[w]hile most of the U.S. population speaks only English at home or a handful of other languages like Spanish or Vietnamese, the American Community Survey reveals the wide-ranging language diversity of the United States' (US Census Bureau, 2015: para. 3). In other words, while it is accurate to say that the United States is overwhelmingly monolingual, that statement does not address the multitude of linguistic variability that is found in both small towns and metropolitan regions across the nation. Still, this linguistic variety is more notable in urban and demographically diverse centers like New York City. New York is a multilingual, multiracial and multiethnic city (NYC Population Facts, 2016). In New York City, to be White and monolingual is to be in the minority (Population Estimates, July 1, 2015 (V2015), n.d.). More than a third of its citizens are foreign born (Population Estimates, July 1, 2015 (V2015), n.d.). Nearly half of all city dwellers speak a language other than English at home; more often than not that language is Spanish (2010–2014 American Community Survey 5-Year Estimates, n.d.). Over 200 different languages are spoken in New York City, making it one of the most linguistically diverse cities in the United States (NYC Population Facts, 2016). This figure does not even take into account 'the languages spoken by many thousands of residents [that] fall into the "Other language" categories of the census, [and so] this remains a dissatisfying underestimate', with some estimating that there are nearly 800 languages spoken in the city (Menken, 2011: 121). This diversity is replicated, if not intensified, within New York City's schools. As such, New York City is the perfect stage for a study focused on the kinds of access that students with disabilities have to multilingual learning spaces. Like many parts of the country, New York City is also identified as a racially (and linguistically) segregated city, thus we find that bilingual programs tend to be concentrated in communities that are populated by minoritized people: Mandarin programs in the Lower East Side and Chinatown; Bengali programs in Elmhurst, Queens; Russian programs in Coney Island; and Spanish programs in Washington Heights. Given that most of the city's middle schools and high schools are decentralized and enrollment is based on applications, we see the highest rate of availability of bilingual programs concentrated within community-based elementary schools.

Place: Sunset Park, an Immigrant Community

Sunset Park can be described as a neighborhood in flux. Historically an immigrant community established by Scandinavian newcomers, it has remained an immigrant enclave though the country of origin of the immigrants has changed (Hum, 2014). Sunset Park is a working-class community with a high concentration of Latinx and Asian immigrants. Some 52% of the population is foreign born, over 19% originating from Mexico – which has the largest Latinx representation by country of origin (King et al., 2015). More than 77% of the residents speak languages other than English at home of which ~40% speak Spanish (Statistical Atlas, 2015). Although the neighborhood is currently fighting back a wave of gentrification brought about by new developments in Industry City, a great deal of the community continues to live below the poverty level (Hum, 2014; King et al., 2015). This is particularly true for young children as is evident in the data regarding schools (King et al., 2015).

Sunset Park is home to eight elementary schools, three middle schools and two high schools (Polesinelli, 2017). All of the schools serve students predominantly from low-income, foreign-born and racially, culturally and/or ethnically minoritized households, and as such many qualify as Title I[2] schools (United Federation of Teachers, 2017; Zimmer, 2017). All but two of the participating mothers' emergent bilingual labeled as dis/abled (EBLAD) children attended one of four schools – three elementary and one middle school – in the Sunset Park neighborhood. The two students who were not enrolled in a school within Sunset Park at the time of data collection had at some point in their educational careers attended schools within the community. In those cases, one child attended a public elementary school in Park Slope, while the other attended a charter school in Carroll Gardens.

My connection to this community is both personal and professional. After immigrating to the United States at the age of seven, my family lived in this neighborhood. I attended the local elementary and middle schools and was an active member of community activities. I was enrolled in bilingual programs here from second through eighth grade. Upon earning my master's degree in education, I returned to this community as a bilingual special education teacher. I taught at the same elementary school my sister had attended as a child; the school that was started by my elementary school principal, originally named the Dual Language School for International Studies, as a way to center bilingual education in the community. Perhaps it is for this reason that I found the most success recruiting participants from this community. I was already a familiar face within the community which allowed community leaders to advocate for me and my work.[3]

Time: The 2016 Election

Presidential elections have the power to change a country; leadership influences policies, rhetoric and, more importantly, the way people behave. The shifts in the nation following the 2016 election have been palpable, especially the way in which immigrants are viewed and treated. Since November 2016, there has been a rise in hate crimes targeting minoritized communities and both the erosion of protections and the establishment of discriminatory practices directed at minoritized people, particularly Latinx undocumented immigrants. Along with the 'Muslim' ban, the surge of detention centers and the use of family separation, communities like Sunset Park have also seen a rise in the number of immigration raids and, as a result, entire neighborhoods are left feeling terrorized. Additionally, as is noted in Gallo's (2015, 2017) work, children are subsequently retraumatized when they are tasked with navigating academic spaces with language policies that limit their linguistic practices, thus compounding their trauma from deportations and state-sanctioned terror.

I started recruiting participants for this study in October 2016. However, I did not enroll a single participant until a few days before the election with the bulk of my participants signing on in the days after. I remember waking up the morning after the election feeling both defeated by this country and embarrassed for it. I was due to attend a Mexican Consulate event that morning to continue recruiting. I contemplated cancelling. How could I face these people, after what had happened? How would my presence there be any different than ambulance chasing? Ultimately, I went to the event because I needed to do my job and, more importantly, my work gave me purpose – it was the thing that would keep me going and has continued to motivate me throughout the administration's run.

The fact that the majority of my participants enrolled in the study after the election is indicative of the power of community and the power of storytelling. It is possible that more people enrolled in the study because I was a potential resource and they knew that it would be important to have allies in the coming months and years. Or, perhaps they understood that their lives in the United States had meaning, that their stories had value, that they were a part of this country as much as those who were trying to push them out. Perhaps they understood that this was an opportunity for them to raise their voices and counter the mainstream narrative that spoke of them but not to them. Although it was not a criterion for this study, at least 9 of the 10 mothers in the study identified themselves as undocumented residents in the United States. The tenth, whose status was unclear, had experienced the deportation of the father of her children. Carini would say this is all speculative – none of this is explicitly in the data and that's true. However, the history and legacy of *testimonios* tell me that there was intentionality in their choice, that they were acting politically and with urgency. They saw an opportunity to be seen and heard and they took it. As such, their participation in this study was neither accidental nor coincidental, and Carini would agree with that.

The Mothers

The 10 women who took part in the study represent a range of experiences. They varied in age, marital status, number of children, education level and time lived in the United States. All but one of the participants identified as Mexican national and most (8 of the 10) were married. Still, they were bound together by the shared experience of mothering emergent bilingual children who had been identified as having a disability; by their use of Spanish as their home language; and by their status as immigrants in the United States. Table 4.1 provides their demographic information followed by a brief description.

Carlota, age 47, was a college-educated Mexican national who had been living in the United States for over 25 years. She was a married mother of three boys, one of whom was classified as having a disability, and a survivor of domestic violence.

Paty, 40, imagined that her move to the United States would be short term, having left two young children behind in Mexico where she had received a primary school education. However, after having two other children in the United States, she had not returned to Mexico in 11 years and, as a result, was raising four children, one of whom was identified as having a disability, in two separate countries.

María, 34, moved to the United States at the age of 24 from Mexico where she had earned a professional degree. María had two sons, both of whom were receiving special education services.

Table 4.1   Maternal background information

Name	Nationality	Age	Marital status	No. of Children	No. of children w/IEPs	Highest level of education	Time in the United States (in years)
Carlota	Mexican	47	Married	3	1	College	25+
Paty	**Mexican**	**40**	**Married**	**4; 2 in Mexico, 2 in United States**	**1**	**Primary school**	**11**
María	**Mexican**	**34**	**Married**	**2**	**2**	**Professional degree**	**10**
Elodia	Mexican	36	Married	3	2	Primary school	12
Rosa	Ecuadorian	33	Single	3	1	Sixth grade	15
Nancy	Mexican	47	Married	5; 1 deceased	2	High school	15+
Ana	**Mexican**	**36**	**Married**	**2**	**1**	**Primary school**	**12**
Carmela	Mexican	42	Married	5	2 (1 decertified)	High school	19
Rosario	Mexican	24	Single	2	2	High school	9
Sara	Mexican	38	Married	4	2	Fifth grade	19

Note: All names are pseudonyms of the participants choosing. Rows in bold denote a mother who is part of the Testimonialistas. IEPs, individual education plans.

Elodia, 36, emigrated to the United States from Mexico, where she had received a primary school education, at the age of 24. She had three children, two of whom had been identified as needing special education services.

Rosa, 33, studied until the sixth grade in a small town in Ecuador. She had been living in the United States for 15 years and was raising three children, one of whom had a disability, as a single parent following the deportation of her husband.

Nancy, 47, earned a high school degree from a Mexican school. She had lived in the United States for over 15 years and was at the helm of a mixed-status family of five children; some of her children had been born in Mexico and others in the United States. She had mothered six children, one died at a young age, another two had disability labels.

Ana, 36, had been living in the United States for 11 years. She had completed primary school in Mexico and was a stay-at-home mom to two children, one of whom was diagnosed with a disability at a young age.

Carmela, 42, shared many points of commonality with Nancy. They both earned high school degrees in Mexico, both were raising five children and both had two children who had been diagnosed as having a disability. Unlike Nancy however, Carmela had been successful at getting her oldest son decertified. Carmela was also experiencing her own version of family separation: raising children in the United

States and Mexico simultaneously, over the course of her 19 years in the United States.

Rosario, 24, was the youngest mother in the study and the only mother who had been educated in the United States. Having come to the United States at the age of 15, she completed high school in New York City. She had two daughters, both of whom were identified as students with disabilities.

Sara, 38, completed fifth grade in Mexico. She had been living in the United States for 19 years and was raising four children, two of whom were receiving special education services at school.

From this pool of 10 women, three were invited to serve as Testimonislistas: Paty, María and Ana.

The Testimonialistas grouping (which was like a focus group, but were treated differently, according to *testimonios*' and Carini's epistemologies) was developed in order to explore more deeply themes and ideas that had arisen in Phase 1 (Englander, 2012). Participant selection for Phase 2 was intentional and purposive (Polkinghorne, 2005). Mothers for Phase 2 were selected based on their enthusiasm for discussing their children's education and their willingness to share further. Attention was also given to their and their children's demographic data, which ensured that the participants were representative of the overall sample. The mother of a fifth grader and a second grader was included because it reflected the two most popular grades in the sample. Additionally, two of the mothers had only completed primary school, and this was representative of the sample.

Using three of the five descriptive review headings (physical presence and gestures; disposition and temperament; and connections to others) developed by Carini as guides, I present a more expansive description of each Testimonialistas that attempts to be free of judgment and grounded in my observations while still recognizing that their presentation is filtered through my eyes. These descriptions arise from observation notes and memory as with traditional descriptive reviews of children:

Ana – *Physical presence and gestures:* Ana is a small and mildly fullfigured woman. She has fair skin and medium length, light brown hair that she regularly wears up. She dresses in very boxy clothing that conceals her figure: oversized hoodies, slacks and work boots. Her clothing is often part of a dark neutral color palate with the exception of a red parka. She is very soft-spoken; I regularly had to ask her to speak up during one-on-one conversations to ensure the recorder would pick her up. *Disposition and temperament:* When she laughs, she exudes a very youthful and feminine giggle. When she is sad or upset, she tends to touch her face and cover her mouth as if she's telling a secret. When she cries, she wipes the tears before they reach her cheeks. Her overall body language is very insular/protective – she speaks quietly, makes herself small; she doesn't carry many belongings with her but when she does, she keeps them close to her. She does not to take up much space. She tries to present herself as a very happy person and her life as very serene. When she's around her children, she is very even-tempered. One cannot tell outright from her behavior if she feels stress or frustration. She never raises her voice. She often speaks using diminutive terms. *Connections to others:* While she does not volunteer much information, she is always open when asked a follow-up question. She answers questions honestly and frankly; when she doesn't want to talk about something, she often repeats the phrase 'no quiero recorder' [*I don't want to remember*] but still proceeds to share. She believes that if she doesn't talk about something, it isn't real. At the end of one particularly emotional conversation, she appeared to be angry with me for making her remember, even though I had only asked a benign follow-up question: how did you learn to text 'by chance'? She is a very private person who lives her life with a code of solitude: 'me reservo lo mío' [*I keep my things to myself*]. Lastly, she speaks very positively of her children, especially María Teresa. At home, she is very patient and attentive to her children's needs, often asking them if they need anything: 'una meriendita' [*a little snack*], 'una agüita' [*a little water*]. She also engages in projects with them; during one household observation, she was helping her children build paper mache Easter baskets using household items.

María – *Physical presence and gestures:* María is a short, medium-build woman. She has an olive skin tone and wavy, medium length, dark hair. She dresses in clothing that conforms to her shape: soft cotton tops and jeans or slacks. Her clothing is often part of a varied color palate; she wears a lot of blues, purples, reds and white. She walks very quickly and purposefully. Her tone of voice is even but when she gets excited she raises her voice, the ends of her sentences are higher pitched and she engages her hands. *Disposition and temperament:* When she laughs, she has a guttural, almost belly laugh that is infectious. When she is sad or upset, she tends to sink into her seat and cock her head to one side. When she cries, her voice changes and sounds deeper, heavier. Crying often seems to catch her by surprise as she is often scrambling for tissues in her bag as tears stream down her face. However, she is able to readily access her emotions and seems at ease with crying. Often, when she is done, she sighs, almost as if to communicate relief. She believes in 'llorar para desahogar' [*crying for relief*]; this perception of crying as purposeful is supported by Gračanin *et al.* (2014), who have asserted that crying is a self-soothing behavior which supports mood improvement and regulation. She answers questions openly and often speaks in stories or events. Due to the nature of her son Justin's disability, she has become a very precise planner, always making sure that her schedule is in keeping with what she told him to expect. *Connections to others:* María makes an effort to connect with other women. She was the only participant who brought someone with her to any of the interviews. While I expected this to result in more muted conversations, it did not. She brought her close friend Jessenia, 'ella es la que me apoya' [*she is the one who supports me*] and 'me comprende' [*understands me*], to one session. She also brought her mother to another session because even though she is binational, she 'ayuda' [*helps*] and 'apoya mucho' [*offers a lot of supports*]. It seems as though she is transparent with people she trusts. When her mother is in town, she enlists her help with household tasks so that she can focus more on the children and educational supports for Justin (her mother is a retired teacher). She speaks very positively of her children, but there is a sense of tiredness when she talks about them. However, at home, she is energetic, collected and very attentive to her children's social-emotional needs. As soon as they get home from school, she engages them in play and talks to them about their day.

Paty – *Physical presence and gestures:* Paty is a petite woman with a thin to medium-build. She has tan skin although her face has some red/pink undertones. When we met, she had shoulder length, dark brown hair, which she cut into a medium length bob during Phase 2 of the study. We often met after she had come home from work, so she was usually dressed in a shirt and pant uniform reminiscent of a hotel maid or a home health aide. When she had not been working, she wore casual yet tailored clothing – button shirts, cardigans and slacks. She would also wear deep red lipstick. Paty was one of the loudest participants. She often spoke authoritatively and fast. She has a very particular accent that reminds me of the way Cantinflas[4] used to talk; with intermittent high-pitched sounds that don't necessarily follow any pattern. Her body seems to always be in motion even when she's sitting down. *Disposition and temperament:* When she laughs, she has a very open mouth laugh and a twinkle in her eye. She laughs at herself easily. However, she also has a lot of self-doubt. After answering questions regarding Dan's education, she often ended the statement by saying 'no sé si hago bien o hago mal' [*I don't know if what I'm doing is right or wrong*] and shrugging her shoulders. She would also often seek approval by asking '¿qué piensa usted maestra?' [*what do you think teacher?*]. Paty also views herself as a fighter – she is constantly 'peleando por mis hijos' [*fighting for [her] children*]. For the most part, Paty comes across as a happy, jovial and loud person. However, when she is upset, her face gets very red and her voice softens. When she cries, she wipes the tears with her bare hands, in a brushing motion. *Connections to others:* In conversation, Paty often seeks physical contact. She touches a hand or gestures in the direction of the listener. Paty is an incredibly open person, she is very honest and frank. She can often answer multiple questions in just one narrative and can speak for minutes on end. She is an engaging storyteller. However, as mentioned above, she frequently seeks affirmation from the listener.

Lastly, she speaks very truthfully about her children, especially Dan. She acknowledges that she treats Dan differently than his sister Tanya, in part because he is a boy and in part because he pushes back more. While she engages with her children, she does so while also managing the household – she is often in the kitchen yelling over at Dan '¿terminaste de leer?' [*did you finish reading?*], '¿terminaste la tarea?' [*Did you finish the homework?*] and 'apaga el teléfono' [*turn off the phone*]. Paty is also very concerned with taking care of others; at every visit, she would offer me a bottle of water or a snack or she would invite me to stay for dinner.

Even though all three of the Testimonialistas were different in terms of personalities and demeanor, they came together to form a diverse and dynamic representation of a community with shared experiences. Lastly, while I was able to develop incredibly rich and meaningful relationships with at least three of the mothers featured in this book, all 10 of them can be described as fascinating, open and incredibly dedicated to others.

Notes

(1) A play on 'The Big Apple', the city's new nickname was given to it by García and Fishman (2011) in homage to the diverse languages of its inhabitants.
(2) According to the US Department of Education, Title I schools are schools that receive additional funding under Title I, Part A (Title I) of the Elementary and Secondary Education Act. Title I 'provides financial assistance to local educational agencies (LEAs) and schools with high numbers or high percentages of children from low-income families to help ensure that all children meet challenging state academic standards. Federal funds are currently allocated through four statutory formulas that are based primarily on census poverty estimates and the cost of education in each state' (US Department of Education, 2015: 1).
(3) My recruiting efforts originally spanned the entire city.
(4) 'Cantinflas, original name Mario Moreno (born August 12, 1911, Mexico City, Mexico—died April 20, 1993, Mexico City), one of the most popular entertainers in the history of Latin-American cinema. An internationally known clown, acrobat, musician, bullfighter, and satirist, he was identified with the comic figure of a poor Mexican slum dweller, a *pelado*, who wears trousers held up with a rope, a battered felt hat, a handkerchief tied around his neck, and a ragged coat' (The Editors of the Encyclopedia Britannica, n.d.: para. 1).

References

2010–2014 American Community Survey 5-Year Estimates (n.d.) US Census Bureau.
Englander, M. (2012) The interview: Data collection in descriptive phenomenological human scientific research. *Journal of Phenomenological Psychology* 43 (1), 13–35. https://doi.org/10.1163/156916212X632943

Gallo, S. and Link, H. (2015) 'Diles la verdad': Deportation policies, politicized funds of knowledge, and schooling in middle childhood. *Harvard Educational Review* 85 (3), 357–382. https://doi.org/10.17763/0017-8055.85.3.357

Gallo, S. and Hornberger, N. (2017) Immigration policy as family language policy: Mexican immigrant children and families in search of biliteracy. *International Journal of Bilingualism* 23 (3), 757–770. https://doi.org/10.1177/1367006916684908

García, O. and Fishman, J.A. (2011) *The Multilingual Apple, Languages in New York City* (2nd edn with a new foreword, 2002). New York: De Gruyter Mouton. http://www.degruyter.com/view/product/47449

Gračanin, A., Bylsma, L.M. and Vingerhoets, A.J.J.M. (2014) Is crying a self-soothing behavior? *Frontiers in Psychology* 5, 1–5. https://doi.org/10.3389/fpsyg.2014.00502

Hum, T. (2014) *Making a Global Immigrant Neighborhood: Brooklyn's Sunset Park.* Philadelphia, PA: Temple University Press.

King, L., Hinterland, K., Driver, C., Harris, T., Gwynn, R., Linos, N., Barbot, O. and Bassett, M. (2015) *Community Health Profiles 2015, Brooklyn Community District 7: Sunset Park* 31 (59), 1–16. See https://www1.nyc.gov/assets/doh/downloads/pdf/data/2015chp-bk7.pdf

Menken, K. (2011) From policy to practice in the Multilingual Apple: Bilingual education in New York City. *International Journal of Bilingual Education and Bilingualism* 14 (2), 121–131. https://doi.org/10.1080/13670050.2011.544117

NYC Population Facts (2016) City of New York. See http://www1.nyc.gov/site/planning/data-maps/nyc-population/population-facts.page (accessed 28 May 2016).

Polesinelli, M. (2017, May 5) Sunset Park Schools (personal communication).

Polkinghorne, D.E. (2005) Language and meaning: Data collection in qualitative research. *Journal of Counseling Psychology* 52 (2), 137–145. https://doi.org/10.1037/0022-0167.52.2.137

Population Estimates, July 1, 2015 (V2015) (n.d.) See http://www.census.gov/quickfacts/table/PST045215/3651000 (accessed 28 May 2016).

Statistical Atlas (2015) Languages in Sunset Park, New York, New York (Neighborhood): Statistical Atlas. Statistical Atlas. See http://statisticalatlas.com/neighborhood/New-York/New-York/Sunset-Park/Languages (accessed 4 May 2017).

The Editors of the Encyclopedia Britannica (n.d.) Cantinflas | Mexican actor. In *Encyclopedia Britannica.* See https://www.britannica.com/biography/Cantinflas (accessed 8 February 2018).

United Federation of Teachers (2017) New York City 2016–17 Title I Funding. See http://files.uft.org/nyc-titlei-funding-by-schools.pdf (accessed 5 May 2017).

US Census Bureau (2015) Census Bureau Reports at least 350 languages spoken in U.S. homes (No. CB15-185). US Census Bureau. See https://www.census.gov/newsroom/press-releases/2015/cb15-185.html (accessed 7 September 2020).

US Department of Education (2015, October 5) Title I, Part A Program (Program Home Page). See https://www2.ed.gov/programs/titleiparta/index.html?exp=0 (accessed 19 February 2017).

Zimmer, A. (2017) City schools could lose $500M in funding under Trump, teachers union fears. *DNAinfo New York*, 9 January. See https://www.dnainfo.com/new-york/20170109/sunset-park/nyc-schools-title-1-funding-vouchers (accessed 5 May 2017).

5 At Home with the Testimonialistas

Although the women presented in this book came together as a result of their children's identification as emergent bilinguals labeled as dis/abled (EBLADs), they are also connected by the ways in which they mothered. In general, all 10 women followed one principle: 'primero están mis hijos' [my children come first].

For these women, being a mother is the central role in their lives and so their children always come first. This is evident in the ways they interact with their children, the concerns that they shield their children from while allowing themselves to be consumed by them. Their relationships with their children also nourish and encourage them to keep moving forward. Mothering is an exhausting task; this chapter will showcase my testimonio of some of the activities recorded during the home observations with the Testimonialistas. The physical manifestation of mothering can be seen in the ways that mothers spend time with their children and in the ways they communicate with them.

As part of their participation in this study, the three Testimonialistas granted me access to their home. There, I was able to witness their interactions with their children, the ways in which they communicate and the roles other family members play. What follows is a brief description of each of the three mothers' homes, and their interactions with their children through my eyes.

Ana

Ana and María Teresa (MT) live above a storefront on the top floor of a fourth-floor walkup. To the left of their building's entrance is a Mexican bakery that specializes in ornate, multi-tiered cakes. To the right is a Salvadoran restaurant, which is known for its traditional and delicious pupusas as well as its rowdy patrons. The stairs to their apartment are very narrow and made narrower still by the bicycles and kids' toys that line it. This space seems to serve as secondary storage for the families that

live here. Ana's apartment is the only one on her floor. When you open
the front door, you are faced with the living room:

> The space is very pink – [lacey] pink curtains line the walls [and win-
> dows]; a pink Disney princess blanket lines the couch/futon. There is
> a small altar in between the windows. The room is sparsely furnished.
> There is a futon, a folding table and three folding chairs. There is also
> a hutch that contains different figurines – cake toppers, coffee cups, and
> disposable plates. There are two heart shaped helium balloons floating
> in the ceiling and a small happy face and a pink hair bow balloon. (Ana,
> Observation #1)

María Teresa and Ana live here with David, the younger child, and
Ana's husband. He was working during my visits so we never met. This
was a three-room apartment with a small kitchen off the living room and
a bathroom in the living room. Beyond the living room there appeared to
be two bedrooms: one for the family, and one that was previously rented
out to a roommate/tenant.

I visited Ana in late winter/early spring. During the first visit, she was
helping María Teresa with her math homework:

- Ana guides María Teresa through the math HW – suggest that she use
  her fingers to add: 'las manos en frente yo te enseñe como – suma'.

  A: Cinco mas cinco
  MT: diez
  A: Más cuatro?
  MT counts on fingers: 'Catorce'
  A: Suma tú sola, ya sabe – con los dedos.

- María Teresa counts on her fingers as mom points to each number
  sentence.

  (Ana, Observation #1)

Ana not only provided María Teresa with a strategy: 'con los dedos'
[with your fingers], but she also modeled with her own hands and manip-
ulated María Teresa's hands whenever necessary:

> María Teresa works silently at times and mom looks on, waiting for her
> to write something down or ask a question. – There is a lot of model-
> ing and prompting – she contorts María Teresa's fingers to match the
> number by which María Teresa will be adding on. (i.e. Pon tus siete
> [put up your seven] – sets up seven fingers using both of María Teresa's
> hands – Ahora cuenta de ocho [now count up from eight]). María Teresa

counts up from 8 designating a number to each finger until she reaches the end of her hand, which indicates she has reached an answer. (Ana, Observation #1)

This continued for almost an hour until nearly half of the worksheet was completed (Figure 5.1). Ana was incredibly encouraging as they worked, often proclaiming: 'Ya te faltan poquitos para la primera línea' [just a few more left in the first column].

However, the time was not solely focused on work. In between math problems the family would take snack breaks together:

- [María Teresa] walks over to get cups 'ma ¿t_ú quieres?' ['mama do you want?'] Mom shakes her head. [María Teresa] grabs only two cups from the hutch.
- They take another family break to have snack, chat and drink juice.

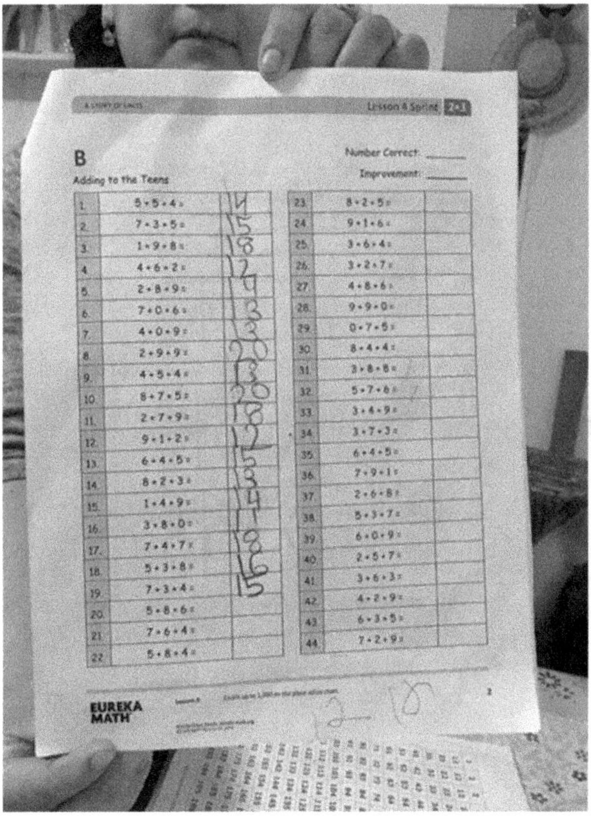

Figure 5.1 Ana holds up María Teresa's math homework worksheet

During my second visit, the family was working on paper mache Easter baskets:

* [María Teresa] is helping mom by bringing materials in from the kitchen to the small table – which has been set up next to the couch.
* [María Teresa] brings out plastic to-go cylindrical containers. (like the soup kind and the big sherbet ice cream kind).
* [María Teresa] asks her mom if she is going to make one as well.
* The kids then sit at the table waiting for mom.
* 'Ya casi está listo, espérenme'
* [María Teresa] and David chat [in Spanish] about the size of the bowls discussing which one is bigger.
   [...]
* They then discuss what kind of animal theme David's basket will have. He decides on a frog theme.
* Mom comes in from the kitchen and [María Teresa] shares with her David's decision regarding animal themes.

There were many moments like this where the siblings interacted in Spanish while mom tended to something. As a matter fact, the first English utterance that I recorded during one of my visits came from Ana. She said 'please' when asking María Teresa to do something.

Overall, this home was a very quiet, light and airy space. The children spoke softly and moved about as if they were figure skaters gliding across an icy floor. In many ways, it resembled Ana, whose personality could also be described as quiet, light and airy.

María

My first home observation with María and Justin did not actually begin at home but rather at school (Figure 5.2):

I met [María] at school; there we picked up Justin and then Jaden [the younger son]. [María] introduced me to each child individually. When she introduced me to Justin she told him: 'Esta es la maestra de la cual te estuve contando, ¿te acuerdas? Ella vendrá a casa con nosotros hoy'. [This is the teacher I told you about, remember? She's coming home with us today.] Justin then introduced himself [to me] using his whole name. A few minutes later we walked towards their home. While on the walk I fell back behind the group, Justin positioned himself next to me and signaled for me to hold his hand. I presented him with my open hand, he took it and interlaced his fingers between mine. We walked this way for a few minutes. He told me about what he planned to do at home: he was going to play games, he was going to draw and read.

Figure 5.2 Justin holds my hand as we walk to his house

A few minutes later he drops my hand. Moments later he returns and intertwines his fingers in mine. I explain to him that we can talk during the walk but that once I get to the house when I open my computer I wont be able to talk to him – he nods in understanding and proceeds to ask me what's in my backpack. After a few minutes of walking hand in hand I start to get cold. I ask him if he's cold and wants to put his hand in his pocket. He releases my hand and places his in his pocket. (María, Observation #1)

From the very beginning, Justin exhibits the very caring and loving nature that his mother talked about during our interviews. She also showed the ways in which she accommodates his need for consistency by reminding him of who I was and what I was doing: 'Esta es la maestra de la cual te estuve contando, ¿te acuerdas? Ella vendrá a casa con nosotros hoy' [This is the teacher I told you about, remember? She's coming home with us today]. This introduction not only helped him feel more at ease but also facilitated my entry into the space.

María and Justin live a few blocks away from the school in a small building with fewer than eight units. Unlike the other Testimonialistas, María does not live in the Spanish-speaking part of the neighborhood; she lives in the area that has been dubbed 'Brooklyn's Chinatown'. Once in the home, I got a glimpse into why María feels so overwhelmed; unlike Ana's space, which felt very serene, María's home felt very active. There was a lot of furniture and each room served as a multipurpose room: the living room was also a bedroom, the kitchen was also the dining room and the parents' bedroom was also the children's bedroom.

> There is no common area in the home, what would be a living room is being used as a common room and bedroom – there are two beds towards one side of the room (a large one and a twin) on the opposite wall there is a fish tank, a dresser/TV stand with a TV on top. There are pictures of children hung up above the beds. There are also two armoires. There is a bouquet of flowers on the 'TV stand'; there is a medium sized (about 10 inches tall) figurine next to the flowers. The furthest bedroom in the back – street facing – has a large bed and a set of bunk beds presumably where the kids sleep. (María, Observation #1)

María and Justin live here with Jaden, the younger brother, María's father, María's husband and, when she's in town, her mother. During my observations, María's mother was visiting from Mexico, so I had the opportunity to not only meet her but also talk to her. I did not meet any of the men in the family; I gathered that the reason for this had to do with work. Nonetheless, with just the women at home, there was plenty to do. In the span of two hours, the children played games, drew pictures, read books, ate supper and prepared for their tutoring sessions.

> Justin proclaims that they are done with the fire truck puzzle and that they can clean up. Mom asks them to put it away slowly – Jaden picks it up whole.
> While putting it away they talk about the importance of teamwork.
> When they are done putting the dino[saur] puzzle away they begin taking apart and putting away the fire truck puzzle
>
> **Ju:** Quiere otro juego [I want another game]
> **M:** ¿Qué quieres jugar [...] [What do you want to play]?
> **Ju:** pintar o leer [painting or reading].
> **M:** quieres pintar [you want to paint].
>
> (María, Observation #1)

María uses every opportunity available to teach her sons. In one instance, she discusses the importance of teamwork with them, in the next she is working on vocabulary.

> The kids gather their materials. Justin sets up on the TV stand (next to me). Jaden has decided to work alone in the bedroom.

M: ¿Qué es eso [What's this]?
Ju: Un caboose [a caboose]
M: ¿Un bus o un tren [a bus or a train]?
Ju: Caboose [caboose]
M: ¿Qué es eso, caboose [what's that caboose]?
Ju: No sé [I don't know]
M: Entonces cómo […] laughs [then how…]
Ju: Caboose es lo que viene al fin del tren. [Caboose is what comes at the end of the train.]

(María, Observation #1)

At first, María gets confused by Justin's use of the word 'caboose'. Part of this confusion may relate to the fact that the boys had been speaking exclusively in Spanish to their mother. However, rather than correcting him, she attempts to get Justin to explain what a caboose is. This is not true in Spanish; when Justin makes a mistake in Spanish, María is very quick to correct him:

Ju: Trajelo, trajelo
M: Tráelo
Ju: Tráelo

(María, Observation #1)

She does this repeatedly during their time together. During my first observation she also corrected his pronunciation of the word 'favor' and during the second she corrected his use of the words 'arcoiris' [rainbow] and 'pescado' [fish]. María was the one mother who engaged most actively in direct instruction of her children. She taught through play, she used vocabulary flashcards and YouTube videos as her teaching materials. However, this was not viewed as sufficient support for María. At the end of our first observation, María was getting Justin ready to meet with his math tutor. While she tried to give adequate attention to her other son, María was still very focused on making sure that Justin's needs were met, perhaps because she perceives him as being the most needy.

Paty

Like María, Paty also lives in a home that she shares with family members beyond the nuclear family. The apartment, located a half a block from the main commercial strip, is on the first floor of a small rental building (fewer than 12 units). Paty, her husband and their two children (Dan, the child in the study, and Tanya, an older daughter) share one bedroom in the three-bedroom apartment. Paty has two brothers who each occupy another bedroom.

Common area in the home. There are three bedrooms and two bathrooms – the kids and their parents inhabit one, there are uncles in the
other two. The family uses one bathroom exclusively for them and the
uncles the other. The common area is located offset from the entrance in
between the two bathrooms. It is sparsely furnished with a simple table
with six chairs, a toy storage basket, a bookcase, a refrigerator and two
additional chairs. There are also two bicycles one of which is electric that
dad uses for work and is charging. The kitchen is off to the side – on the
right of the entrance. (Paty, Observation #1)

One of Paty's greatest sources of pride was that the apartment had
two bathrooms, so her family did not need to share with her brothers
whom she identified as being considerably messy. Nonetheless, she – as
the 'woman of the house' – was responsible for all the cleaning. Although
the living room is a communal space, it is obvious that this is a space used
mostly for and by the children. Dan arrives home from school before his
mother. He waits for her in the living room with his sister Tanya, while
their father sleeps in the bedroom. There is not much talk between the
children and their father. This is starkly different from how they interact
with their mother and how she interacts with them:

From the moment [Paty] opens the door there is non-stop dialogue. The
first set of questions are about school then about homework:

Paty: Hello [Dan] how are you?
D: malo [bad]
P: ¿Y por qué? [and why]?
D: Porque tengo mucha tarea [because I have a lot of homework]

They debate in Spanish whether he will read or do his homework first
Dan walks over to backpack 'mira toda la tarea que tengo' [look at
everything I have to do]

P: ¿La puedes hacer solo? [can you do it alone]?
D: yeah
D: dos chapters de math [two math chapters]
D: dos questions de reading. Un difficult libro [two questions for
reading. A difficult book]
P: un libro dificultoso [a difficult book]
D: yeah
P: ¿en español? [in Spanish]?
D: 'English'

Mom repeats the word 'dificultoso'
Dan shows mom his homework written in his notebook but struggles
to read it – mom tries to repeat after him. (Paty, Observation #1)

From this exchange, one can see that even for the mothers who work outside of the home, the primary focus is the children. Although she is tired from a long day at work – she identifies herself as a housekeeper and her job is very physical – she does not find rest at home. Instead, she begins to ask her child/ren about homework, ensuring that they are set up with their work before she can begin to take on any of the household tasks that await her: laundry, cooking, cleaning. This exchange is also significant because it indicates the ways in which English and Spanish interact in the home. English is used primarily by Dan to discuss his homework, but Paty is the first person to speak in English when she says, 'Hello [Dan] how are you?'. Yet he replies in Spanish, 'malo' [bad]. Paty's household was the one household in which English and Spanish interacted the most, a great deal of this was reflective of the outside world, work and school, coming into the home:

> Mom receives a text message and asks [Dan] to read it and respond. He translates, mom replies. [Tanya] translates the message mom has requested for [Dan] to write. The message seems related to work – [can you work Saturday or Sunday?]
>
> It takes [Dan] a while to write the reply – mom suggest that the sister write it (~minute 5:30) [Dan] walks away, finishes the text – then returns to read it out loud to mom: 'I've got to do something'. [Tanya] takes phone – to correct [Dan]'s text. [Dan] talks to [Tanya] in English – then turns to mom to explain the issue [whether or not the word is necessary in the message or if it can just be replaced with an apostrophe or period – He speaks to mom in English]. [Tanya] reads the messages to mom in English for approval – sent – mom tells them to add 'sorry'.
>
> All three engage in a conversation about school supplies – the kids mention needing more pens – the dialogue is in Spanish with the exception of the word 'pens'. (Paty, Observation #1)

Collaborative communication was very common in this home. Dan and Tanya would help their mother communicate with her employer/s in English, while Paty and Tanya would help Dan communicate in Spanish. Additionally, all three would use their entire linguistic repertoire to help with homework. The best way to describe the language practices in this household is through translanguaging. Paty and the children made regular use of all of their linguistic resources in order to effectively communicate with each other and with the outside world:

> [Dan] and [Tanya] talk to each other about math in English. But as soon as mom joins in they shift to Spanish/English:

> **D:** Tu eres bueno en writing, pero yo soy bueno en math. Yo tengo muchos As Bs en math [you are good in writing but I am good at math. I have a lot of As Bs].

> (Paty, Observation #1)

This was also true when they talked about the readings. Dan would read a text in English, which Paty would also try to read and then would ask questions. However, at times her engagement frustrated Dan to the point that he exclaims 'Ya mami, ya no quiero más. Es too much' [enough mom, I don't want any more, it is too much].

Dan seems frustrated.

D: Ya mami, ya no más [enough mom, no more]. Mom keeps pushing on.
P: ¿Qué es esto? [what is this]?
D: Resources, un land [resources, *a* land]
P: ¿Qué es? [what is it]?
D: Un land [a land]
P: En Spanish [in Spanish]
D: Un land. [A land]
D: Ya mami, ya no quiero más. Es too much [enough mom, I don't want any more, it is too much]
P: Que ni que too much, órale [what, not too much, let's go]
P: ¿Qué es esto? [what is this]?
D: Mississippi
P: ¿Qué es Mississippi? [What is Mississippi]?
D: Mississippi es un countdown [Mississippi is a countdown].

(Paty, Observation #2)

Paty indicates the ways in which mothers are engaged with the children at home. So much so that at times they seem to push their children beyond comfort to ensure that they are advancing academically.

The other major noticing that I had while at Paty's house was the lack of involvement on the part of the father. While Ana and María's partners were not present when I observed in their homes, Paty's husband was often home, not just for the observations but also for the interviews. However, he was often sleeping or preparing to go to work:

[Dan] moves to the floor while [Tanya] works at the table with her mom. Dad is sleeping in the adjacent bedroom. (Paty, Observation #1)

Whether the lack of involvement is due to lack of interest or lack of opportunity is hard to tell. However, Paty and the other mothers did allude to the fact that for many of the men their primary role is as provider, while the mothers' is as nurturer, even if they worked.

Compared to any other participant, I spent the most time in Paty's home. This was mostly because Paty chose to be interviewed at her home rather than the local church. As a result, I got to see her interact with her children more than the other mothers. I also got to know both of her children more. The children also came to see me as a regular part of their household. I say this because whenever I visited I was offered meals and snacks. I was included in Tanya's birthday celebration, and I was introduced to the family pet (Figure 5.3).

I was pregnant at the time of these interviews and observations, which also drew the children's interest. Ultimately, my relationship to this family was greatly influenced by my access to their home. As a result, Paty's experience and family dynamic have in many ways become a part of my institutional memory. This is primarily due to the fact that my spending so much time in this home allowed me to witness a good deal of evidence that corroborates Paty's testimonios.

While the bulk of the data shared in this book is reflective of the narratives gathered during the study, the observations are an invaluable tool because they provide a context not only for the mothers' testimonies, but also for their desire to give a testimonio. Their homes are not places where they can find solace or relief. It is the site of their greatest and most

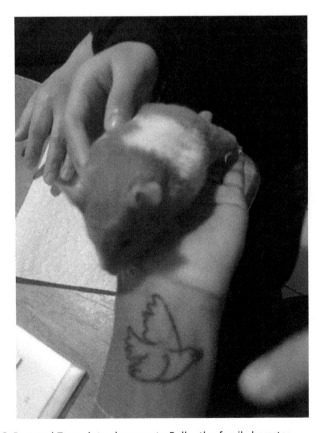

Figure 5.3 Dan and Tanya introduce me to Bella, the family hamster

taxing work. In many ways, the interview space (both the physical space and the metaphysical space) was a space that belonged to them more than any other space in which they interacted. In order to fully understand the effort that mothers make to support their children, it was important to get a glimpse into the place where most of their mothering takes place. Additionally, this context also serves as confirming evidence of the ways that mothers support their children's academic development.

Part 2

Testimonios: Mothers Speak

6 Mothering With, Through and Alongside Dis/ability Labels

A mother's understanding of a disability is heavily influenced by her experiences with her children and family. Yet, very few researchers – with the exception of Harry and Klingner (2014), Klingner and Harry (2006) and Harry *et al.* (2007) in collaboration with a few others – have discussed the lives of minoritized children beyond the school, much less centered the experiences of the mothers. This gap in research is significant and noteworthy. Yet, rather than focus on how these mothers are left out of the discourse, and in keeping with my desire to center the mothers' own experiences without qualification, you will find that these next few chapters limit the number of references to other studies. The gap in the literature stems specifically from this need to situate the experiences of these women in relation to others. What I, and a *testimonio* epistemology affirms, is that these women's stories and experiences are valid on their own. These are not counter-narratives. They are narratives that expand, that make space for more. So, let us start there: in order to expand the current notions regarding these students' realities, and in order to understand the impact that existing policies and practices have on families, we begin with the perception, values and ideologies that the mothers hold regarding dis/ability.

The mothers in this study were curious about the origin of their child's disability – was it hereditary? Was it an accident? Still, they viewed their children as normal and considered both the disability and the label to be temporary – able to be remedied by the service providers, and by God. Most studies ground Latinx mothers' beliefs around disability in religion (Balcazar *et al.*, 2012; Cohen, 2013; Salkas *et al.*, 2016; Skinner *et al.*, 1999; Zea *et al.*, 1994). However, the mothers in this study provide an alternative where disability perception is deeply rooted in disability as a social construct. They believed that the labels could help their children by offering resources, but they also recognized that they came with limitations. It was this tension that often reflected a disability studies stance; on the one hand, the disability was a part of their child just like any other feature and on the other, it was society – with its rigid, and often low, expectations – that limited their child, not the disability. However, even with holistic and affirming outlooks, the mothers discussed feelings of sadness and concern when their child was diagnosed with a disability. Mothers were also heavily concerned about the stigma that comes with a disability label and found ways to shield their children from it – primarily by keeping the diagnosis, and disability, a closely guarded secret.

Although the origin of their children's disability is seldom blamed on a curse, as in the past, the mothers wondered whether their child's disability was a test from God, due to a genetic condition or illness, an 'herencia' from some ancestor, or even an accident.

'Bendita herencia': Origins of Disability

Long gone are the mentions of disability being the result of a hex or curse (Larson, 1998, 1998; Mackelprang & Salsgiver, 2016). But most mothers wonder about its origin. For Nancy, her child's disability is viewed as 'una prueba' [a test] from God:

Ay, dios mío. ¿Qué hago? Pues yo siento que es una prueba que tendré que pasar, 'pero no la quiero pasar yo sola, quiero contigo, porque yo sola me vuelvo loca'.

[*Oh, my God. What do I do? Well, I feel like it is a test that I have to pass, 'but I don't want to go through it alone, I want it with you, because alone I will go crazy'.*]

Nancy believed that her child's disability was genetic, from her grandmother. She uses the word 'bendita' not as *blessed*, but as *damned*:

Cuando me dieron los resultados, yo le dije a mi esposo que me imaginaba que era una herencia de mi abuelita, porque yo recuerdo que mi abuelita era muy joven, y ella ya no veía y ya no oía. Yo le dije, 'Bendita herencia de mi abuelita', porque no me quedó de otra más que decirle eso.

[*When I got the results, I told my husband that I imagined that it was an inheritance from my grandmother, because I remember that my grandmother was very young, and she no longer saw and did not hear anymore. I said, 'Damned inheritance from my grandmother', because I had no other option but to say that to him.*]

Another mother, Ana, blames her own thyroid condition for her child's disabilities:

'La doctora me decía que es por los síntomas de la tiroides que yo le pasé'.

[*The doctor told me that it was because of the thyroid symptoms that I had passed on to her.*]

Carlota believed that her child's special education needs were the result of 'un accidente' [an accident] when the child was younger:

> [...] parece que esa fue la reacción, cuando él y yo tuvimos un accidente en la nieve. Caímos y él voló. Se me zafó de mis manos y él voló, y se golpeó la cabeza. De ahí fue la reacción, de que él dejó de hablar.

> [...] *it seems that was the reaction, when he and I had an accident in the snow. We fell and he flew. He slipped out of my hands and he flew, and hit his head. That's where the reaction came from, that he stopped talking.*

Despite the mothers' wonderings about the origin of their children's disability, it was surprising that they did not see disability as something their child had, in fact, most claimed that their children were 'normal'.

'Una niña normal': Disability as Social Construction

It was surprising that half of the group spoke of disability not as something inherently wrong with their child, but rather society's failure to recognize neurodiversity,[1] including Ana who, as cited above, was told by a doctor that her daughter's delays were due to genealogical factors. When asked whether or not they agreed with their child's disability label, these mothers responded by affirming that their child was like any other child. In the quotes that follow, the mothers assert that their child(ren) may be 'diferentes, pero no es discapacitado' [different but are not disabled] and the child 'no está enfermo' [is not sick]. Rather, these children just learn differently, they are simply children who are 'más lento' [slower], 'no pone atención' [don't pay attention] and 'no entendie' [don't understand]. Carlota does not believe that her child is disabled, but different:

> Yo no creo que nadie sea discapacitado. Tienen cosas diferentes, o–, diferentes, pero no es discapacitado. No creo que haiga un solo niño que sea discapacitado.

> *[I do not think anyone is disabled. They have different things, or–, different, but they are not disabled. I do not think there is a single child who is disabled.]*

Both Ana and Sara use the word 'normal' to describe their children:

Ana: Ella nació con unos poquitos problemitas [...] es una niña normal, es bien dulce, bien tierna, bien alegre, que todo el tiempo me anda diciendo, 'Mamá, mamá, te quiero', o así, con el papá, o con el niño. Pero ya en la clase, como que no pone atención, como–, no entiende lo que a ella le dicen.

[She was born with a few little problems [...] she is a normal girl, she is very sweet, very tender, very cheerful. All the time she is saying to me, 'Mom, mom, I love you', or so, with her dad, or with the boy [her brother]. But in class, it's like she does not pay attention, like..., she does not understand what she's being told.]

Sara: Un niño normal. Sí. [...] O sea, que–, pues como todos los niños. Le gusta jugar, comer, dormir, de todo.

[A normal child. Yes. [...] That is, what–, like all children. He likes to play, eat, sleep, everything.]

These mothers believe that their children are not deficient, they are merely different. María describes how she tells her younger son that his brother is not sick, he merely doesn't think like him:

Yo trato de explicarle a [su hermano menor] lo que es, que su hermano no está enfermo, sino que no piensa igual que él.

[I try to explain to [his younger brother] what he is, that his brother is not sick, but that he does not think the same as him.]

And Carmela views her son's disability as within the range of normalcy. He is merely slow, but not disabled:

Siento que hay niños que aprenden más rápido, otros más lento. En el caso de él, aprendió a hablar más lento. Pero eso no significa que tenga una discapacidad.

[I feel that there are children who learn faster, others slower. In his case, he learned to speak slower. But that does not mean that he has a disability].

It is interesting that these mothers understand disability as a social construction rather than an inherent deficit; at least half of the mothers expressed feelings that align with this perspective: 'un niño normal' [a normal child], 'no está enfermo' [is not sick]. This feels especially true when one notes the fact that 7 of the 10 participants used the word 'normal' to describe their child at some point in the study. These mothers feel not only that their children are like all other children, but also that the small ways in which they are 'diferente' [different] or 'lento' [slower] are used as ways to unfairly label and categorize them.

There is also an underlying sense that to be dis/abled is something grave. It is not simply a child who is 'lento' [slow], 'diferente' [different] or who 'no presta atención' [does not pay attention]. Although it is not named, to these mothers disability appears to be something much more profound than what their children exhibit.

Perhaps it is for this reason, combined with a dislike for the term 'disabled', that the mothers tried to explain away their child's disability as something other than a disability. The mothers did not believe their children's disability was serious or permanent. Many of them would use minimizing language to describe their child's struggles, or they would discuss the child's learning needs using transient language in an effort to indicate its temporary nature.

'Pequeñitos problemitas': The Minimizing of Disability

Upon closer inspection, one can see that the mothers also carry with them the negative feelings associated with being identified, or having a child that is identified, as *disabled*. They understood that disability *was* stigmatized (Lalvani, 2015; McHatton & Correa, 2005; Michie & Skinner, 2010). This is particularly evident in the ways that the mothers would attempt to minimize their children's needs. Some of this happened through minimizing language. Some used diminutive forms:

Ana talks about 'pequeñitos problemitas' [little problems] and says that the children 'tienen problemitas con el aprendizaje' [have little problems with learning]. María believes that her child's autism 'no es severo' [is not severe]. Many mothers highlight the ways in which the child has grown since the original evaluation/diagnosis. They have gotten 'mejor' [better] and know 'más' [more]:

Nancy: Lo que pasa [es] que él no lo necesita mucho, porque si yo me voy entre él y el niño grande, él habla mejor, el chiquito.

[*What happens is that he does not need it very much, because if I go between him and the older child, he speaks better, the small one.*]

Rosario: Cambió mucho, en que ella aprendió más. Aprendió más.

[She changed a lot, in that she learned more. [She] learned more.]

Carlota: [...] yo creo que ya, en este momento, ya él es demasiado–, es igual o mucho mejor que los otros niños. [...] Tengo tres hijos, pero es lo mejor que le ha pasado porque avanzó demasiado, yo creo que avanzó más que los niños regulares.

[[...] *I think that already, at this moment, he is already too much..., he is equal or much better than the other children. [...] I have three children, but it is the best thing that has happened to him because he advanced too much, I think he advanced more than the regular children.*]

Rosa: Él cuando era chiquito, no podía hablar bien. [...] pero ya–, o sea, bastante ha superado. Sí, bastante.

[*When he was little, he could not speak well. [...] but already..., that is, he has overcome quite a lot. Yes, quite a lot.*]

Not only have the children grown and even overcome their limitations, the mothers overwhelmingly feel that their children have learned and advanced 'más' [more] or 'bastante' [quite a lot] and even 'demasiado' [too much]. In fact, both Nancy and Carlota compare their emergent bilingual labeled as dis/abled (EBLAD) child to others and deem their child as 'mejor' [better]. Nancy believes that her EBLAD child is 'mejor' than her other child. Carlota thinks her child is now 'mejor' than her other two children.

Others would talk about their expectation or hope that the disability label (and/or the disability itself) would be temporary:

Nancy: Tengo que aceptar que el niño va a usar el aparato. Mi confianza es que sea por algún tiempo, porque también tengo la confianza que no hay mejor doctor que el de allí arriba, ¿verdad? Pero, todo eso lleva su proceso y si él no lo ha dado es porque a lo mejor no ha llegado el tiempo, ¿verdad?, todavía, pero algún tiempo. Y, pues lo he aceptado que el tiempo que él lo tenga que usar, lo ha de usar.

[I have to accept that the child will use the device. My faith is that it is for some time, because I also have the confidence that there is no better doctor than the one above, right? But, all that takes its process and if he [God] has not given it it is because maybe the time has not come, right?, not yet, but sometime. And, I have accepted that the time he has to use it, he has to use it.]

Carlota: Sí, yo sentía que me–, iba yo a tener el apoyo, para que el saliera de tener la–, de dejar pronto la–, los servicios. Y sabía yo que con la ayuda de ellas, y con mi ayuda, íbamos a sacarlo. Tengo un primo, que cuando era pequeño, lo único que sabía decir es, 'Sí, sí, sí, sí'. Ahora cuando él habla, son las palabras perfectas, simples. Simplificadas las palabras y perfectas. Entonces, yo decía, 'Oh, algún día mi niño también va a ser así'.

[Yes, I felt that I– I was going to have the support, so that he would get out of having–, to soon leave the–, the services. And I knew that with their help, and with my help, we were going to get him out. I have a cousin, who when he was little, the only thing he could say is, 'Yes, yes, yes, yes'. Now when he speaks, they are the perfect words, simple. Simplified words and perfect. So, I said, 'Oh, someday my child will also be like that'.]

Mothers have the 'confianza' [faith] that their children's disability is only 'por algún tiempo' [for some time] and 'algún día' [someday] everything will be taken care of. The mothers maintain their hope; they are not only hopeful, but also patient. They trust both God, 'el de allí arriba' [the one up there] and also the help of the therapists who work with their children and the help that they themselves give them: 'con mi ayuda' [with my help]. They are hopeful, patient and trust in God, in others and in themselves not only to overcome the disability, but also to terminate the services some day. In a way, for Carlota 'los servicios' [the services] and for Nancy 'el aparato' [the device] are the only indicators that their child has a disability. So when those are gone, so too is the *deficit*.

Another way that the mothers attempted to minimize the disability, or at least its impact on their child's life, was by limiting the number of people who knew that their child was identified as disabled. As a result, knowing about the disability was strictly on a need to know basis, often limited to school-based personnel, as we see in the next sub-section.

'Entre menos sepan, mejor': Disabilities as Closely Guarded Secrets

Mothers' ideologies around disability are complex. For the most part, they view their children like any other child – for them the concern arises when other people look upon their children as 'disabled'. Perhaps it is for this reason, and following in a long tradition, that many of them keep their child's disability diagnosis and label a secret (Anthony, 2013; Burghardt, 2015; Green, 2020; Wexler, 2005). In the following quote, Ana discusses why only a select group of individuals: 'las maestras' [the teachers], 'la doctora' [the doctor] and 'la trabajadora social' [the social worker] know about her daughter, María Teresa, and her dis/ability:

No, sólo con las maestras. Con la maestra o principalmente con la doctora o la trabajadora social, que a ella cualquier cosa le dejo saber. [...] porque–, no sé, pero yo siempre me reservo lo mío, y sólo cuando hay–. Por ejemplo, ahora en la escuela que estoy preocupada por [María Teresa] es donde yo le digo a la maestra, que tal vez es por ese defecto que tiene [María Teresa] en la cabecita, a lo mejor eso le estará afectando el aprendizaje.

[*No, only with the teachers. With the teacher or mainly with the doctor or the social worker, I let her know anything about it [...] because... I do not know, but I always keep my business mine, and only when there is–. For example, now in the school that I'm worried about [María Teresa] is where I tell the teacher, maybe it's because of that defect [María Teresa] has in her head, maybe that's affecting her learning.*]

For Ana, a person knowing that María Teresa has a disability is solely on a need to know basis. Unless there is a problem, there is no need to discuss the matter with anyone else. For her, 'entre menos sepan, mejor' [the fewer who know, the better]. This was noteworthy to me before Ana even decided to sign up for the study. Ana and I met during a community meeting where she, along with other moms from the schools' parent teacher association, were serving refreshments to those in attendance; my table with my poster and sign-up sheet was situated next to theirs. Ana's secrets regarding her daughter's disability label was such a private matter that I distinctly remember that as she walked over to my table to ask questions about the study and to affirm her interest in participating, her friend blurted out '¿[María Teresa] recibe servicios?' [receives services]. Ana slowly glanced up from the clipboard and quietly nodded in agreement. When asked about this exchange, Ana simply explained that she didn't want people to think of her daughter differently. She is so concerned with maintaining other people's perception of her daughter as 'una niña normal' [a normal girl] that she doesn't even talk about María Teresa's disability with her extended family:

> No, no. No one in the family. [...] Porque no. Sólo yo y el papá, y la mamá mía y la hermana mía. [...] No, para mí es una niña normal. Muy normal. Pero entre menos sepan, mejor.

> [No, no. No one in the family. [...] Because no. Only me and the dad, and my mom and my sister. [...] No, for me she is a normal girl. Very normal. But the fewer that know, the better.]

In a matter of sentences, Ana highlights the contradiction that so many mothers carry with them: the belief that their child is just like any other, that she is normal, and a huge sense of responsibility to keep any hint of difference private. Ana goes to such great lengths to guard this secret that she even keeps it a secret from María Teresa. It is also possible that since Ana suffers from epileptic seizures (and feared that she could lose custody of her children because of it) and is also someone who 'siempre me reservo lo mío' [always keep my business mine], keeping María Teresa's disability a secret may be a way for her to keep her own disability a secret and ultimately, protect her family. Still, keeping a disability a secret enforces the stigmatization that they themselves stand against. Additionally, despite the mothers' reluctance to accept the concept of disability, in the ways in which professionals described it, they saw the disability label as useful to their children and to them, as the next section describes.

Functions of the Disability Label

As presented in a previous section, most mothers talked about their children within the realm of neurodiversity; however, none of them had denied outright the designation or the diagnosis of their child as disabled. This was often due to the fact that the mothers felt as if they did not have agency in the evaluation process; evaluations were something they rarely chose to do so much as were told to do. Perhaps it is for this reason that after a designation was handed down, they chose to make strides toward reclaiming their agentive roles in their children's lives, often by reframing the disability labels as sources of support: a source of 'más' [more] resources for their children and information and relief for them.

The primary role that disability labels served in the lives of these families was in offering the children an individualized education focused heavily on services and small class sizes.

'Más': The disability label as a resource

Straying away from traditional notions of disability as secret or disability as stigma, many mothers said that the disabled label served a purpose; more often than not it provided the child with added support in school, with 'más' [more]. Mothers overwhelmingly acknowledged that the label meant that the teachers 'ayudan más' [help more] and 'ponen más atención' [pay more attention]. The repetition of the word 'más', when asked about the label, tells the story. There was not only more help, but there were also more teachers, 'dos maestras' [two teachers] and, in some cases, even 'tres' [three].

Elodia: [...] le ayudan un poco más con sus estudios.

[[...] *they help him a little more with his studies.*]

Rosario: Tiene dos maestras [...] según porque las ayudan más, y porque ella está como con esa discapacidad, entonces, ayudan más. Les ponen más atención a los niños. [...] Las otras clases, son clases regulares. Por lo que me explicaron a mí, son clases regulares, y entonces, en la clase que ella está, les ayudan un poco más. Por eso tienen dos maestros. Le han tocado tres maestros.

[*She has two teachers [...] supposedly because they help them more, and because she has that disability, then, they help more. They pay more attention to the children. [...] The other classes are regular classes. From what they explained to me, they are regular classes, and then, in the class that she is in, they help them a little more. That's why they have two teachers. She has had three teachers.*]

Paty: [Y]a está en una clase integrada, pero sigue habiendo los dos maestros. O sea, él me dice que los dos son maestros, y yo pregunté, 'El maestro, ¿cuál es?', que si la otra era una ayudante. Y me dijo que, 'No'. Los dos son ya maestros, maestros. Lo que pasa, que como ahorita ellos–, es un maestro de clase especial y un maestro normal. Entonces, tienen así. Dice que las opciones, de que ayudan más a los niños. Y a mí me gusta eso.

[[*H]e is already in an integrated class, but there are still two teachers. I mean, he tells me that they are both teachers, and I asked, 'The teacher, which is he?', if the other was an assistant. And he told me, 'No'. They are both teachers, teachers. What happens, right now they—it's a special education teacher and a normal teacher. Then, they have it like that. He says that the options, that they help the children more. And I like that.*]

Carlota: ... es muy bueno saber que tiene más apoyo porque tenía un bajo–, un nivel de que no podía hablar igual que todos los niños.

[*... it's very good to know that he has more support because he had a low - a level that he could not speak the same as all children.*]

As a result of being labeled as disabled, the qualifying children were enrolled in classes with lower student–teacher ratios and had access to specialized instruction designed specifically to meet their unique needs. Ultimately, the mothers thought that the individual education plan was a means to individualized learning and they appreciated it: 'es muy bueno' [it's very good], 'a mí me gusta eso' [I like that]. This was particularly true for mothers who came from countries where they themselves had not had access to a free and/or public education. In many ways, the special education system was viewed as a boutique education. It is perhaps for this reason that the mothers expressed great interest in keeping their children in self-contained classes, making sure to maximize the amount of services the child was receiving as well as securing a one-to-one para-professional for their child.

While many of these services may indicate a more restrictive environment for these mothers, it represented a more individualized and rigorous education, and certainly más, 'se siente más' [it feels like more], 'hace más' [he does more], he interacts with 'más niños' [more children] and even 'habla más' [speaks more]. Paty certainly feels that the disability label is providing her child with 'más' and this way the child 'avanza mucho' [progresses a lot], which she repeats twice.

[P]ues él–, lógico, todavía sigue con su retraso, ¿verdad?, porque no lo puede sacar. Pero sí, avanza mucho. Avanza mucho, y sirve que–, actúa con más niños, se siente él con más–, como que hace más–, convivir con más niños. Y pues siento que él se enseña así, a hablar más, y como ya no ser tan tímido.

[*[W]ell, he– logically, he still continues with his delay, right?, because he can't get it out. But yes, he advances a lot. He advances a lot, and it serves that–, he interacts with more children, he feels more–, it's as if he does more–, coexists with more children. And, well, I feel that he teaches himself like that, to talk more, and how to not be so shy anymore.*]

Paty encapsulates the mothers' sentiments when she states that her son's special education placement helps her child move forward. Being in small groups for services helps him make progress and overcome his shyness. In this way, more restrictive settings offer not only academic support but also support in social development.

The disability label was also beneficial to the mothers because it offered them an understanding of why their child had exhibited any delays, particularly in speech. As such, the disability label was a source of information.

'Yo no sabía': Disability diagnosis as information

The second function of the dis/ability label was as a source of information and relief for the mothers. Nine of the ten qualifying children in this study were initially referred for an evaluation by, or in conjunction with, their pediatrician or teacher. The most frequent indicator that something was 'wrong' was delayed speech.

Carmela: Él aprendió tarde para hablar.

[*He learned to talk late.*]

Rosa: Él cuando era chiquito, no podía hablar bien.

[*When he was little, he could not speak well.*]

Paty: [O] sea, simplemente era el defecto de que él no podía hablar.

[*Well, it was simply the defect that he could not speak.*]

Carlota: Para hablar, cuando él hablaba, que solo hacía: 'Ah, ah, ah'. Que yo no sabía [lo que decía] y yo decía: '¿Se va a quedar mudo?'

[*To talk, when he spoke, he only did: 'Ah, ah, ah'. That I did not know [what he was saying] and I said: 'Is he going to become mute?'*]

Nancy: a veces en las palabras, le sobraba o le faltaba. Yo, para mí que hablaba bien, pero ellos son los que decidieron. Pero no lo necesita mucho. Para mí la terapia del habla, no.

[*sometimes in words, there were extra [words] or missing [words]. I, for me he spoke well, but they are the ones who decided. But he does not need it much. For me, speech therapy, no.*]

These mothers felt that the problem was that their child was slow in speaking, but this was not considered a serious problem, although some were worried. It was when they were 'chiquito' [little] that they couldn't speak well, or it was 'simplemente' [simply] a defect, or for them 'no lo necesita mucho' [doesn't need it a lot]. And yet, the mothers were relieved to find people who knew more than they did and who were willing to answer their questions: 'Se va a quedar mudo?' [Is he going to become mute?]. Additionally, as Nancy indicates, the decision to label the child as having a disability and to enroll them in services was not one that the mothers made: 'ellos son los que decidieron' [they are the ones who decided], 'they' being the doctors, the teachers and the service providers. María spoke similarly about her situation:

Cuando yo empecé a notar más cosas distintas de él, yo hablé con el médico y fue que me mandó a un referido, para hacerle la prueba del autismo. Y ahí fue cuando lo diagnosticaron que tenía autismo, no es severo su autismo, pero sí tiene autismo.

[*When I started to notice more differences in him, I talked to the doctor and he sent me a referral, to test him for autism. And that's when he was diagnosed as having autism, his autism is not severe, but he does have autism.*]

Still, the label of disabled offered an explanation, an answer of sorts. However, Nancy and María's statements indicate that perhaps they do not have much choice and so they are making the best of the situation.

For these mothers, the disability labels offered the children many advantages, and the identification process offered them information. As a result, many of the mothers viewed the disability label as a source of relief. Before the diagnosis, the mothers were unclear about their child's needs, but after the diagnosis they had an understanding of their child's needs and the support the child needed to progress.

'No le entendía': The disability label as relief

In the end though, most mothers ultimately viewed the disability label as an informational tool – a tool that allowed them to understand why their child was not talking or behaving as 'expected'. This was particularly true for María:

En casa, igual le daban berrinches, y yo no sabía ni por qué. Yo pensé que porque él era un niño berrinchudo, y yo no sabía qué estaba pasando con mi niño. [...] Es bien difícil porque a veces–, cuando al principio me dijeron que el niño tenía autismo, yo no sabía qué era eso. Para mí fue como, '¿Qué es lo que le está pasando?'. No sabía cómo lidiar con él. [...] No, yo no sabía qué es lo que era el autismo. Y hasta después de que me lo diagnosticaron, yo supe qué era el autismo. Pero al principio fue muy alarmante y muy triste para mí, porque no tenía información de eso. [...] [E]staba un poco inquieta y preocupada, pero después como me fueron explicando las cosas, ya fui como tranquilizándome un poco más. Pero sí, no, me preocupaba, porque poco a poco, fue su aprendizaje, por lo mismo que él tenía autismo y yo no lo sabía. Entonces, ya fue poco tiempo que el empezó a hablar y decir sus primeras palabras. Y fue frustrante porque pues él no se podía comunicar conmigo ni yo con él. Y él lloraba cuando yo no le entendía las cosas. Y con las terapias, le digo, fue largo el tiempo que él estuvo para aprender, a decir palabras y comunicarse.

[*At home, he also had tantrums, and I did not know why. I thought that because he was a tantrumy child, and I did not know what was*

happening with my child. [...] It's very difficult because sometimes–
when I was initially told that the child had Autism, I did not know what
that was. For me it was like, 'What is happening to him?' I did not know
how to deal with him. [...] No, I did not know what autism was. And
even after he was diagnosed, I knew what autism was. But at the begin-
ning it was very alarming and very sad for me, because I did not have
information about that. [...] [I] was a little restless and worried, but after
they explained things to me, I was like settling down a little more. But
yes, no, I was worried, because little by little, it was his learning, because
he had autism and I did not know it. Then, it was not long before he
started talking and saying his first words. And it was frustrating because
he could not communicate with me or me with him. And he cried when I
did not understand things. And with the therapies, I tell you, it took him
a long time to learn, to say words and communicate.]

For María, learning that her child was autistic offered her not only an
explanation for her son's outburst but also a means by which to communicate with him and subsequently an understanding of how to support him. She repeatedly says, 'no sabía' [I didn't know], 'no entendía'
[I didn't understand], 'no tenia información' [I didn't have information].
So, although the label was 'alarmante' [alarming], 'triste' [sad] and
resulted in her being 'inquieta' [restless] and 'preocupada' [worried], the
label offered some measure of comfort and understanding.

This sentiment was shared by most of the mothers regardless of their
child's disability label. In many ways, the disability labels gave these
mothers access to information and to services, which ultimately gave
them access to their children. This is especially true for the mothers
whose children had delayed speech. For them, the diagnosis symbolizes
the line that marks the before and the after. In the before, the mothers
were unable to communicate with their children. Then, after receiving
a diagnosis and being enrolled in services, their child could talk – and,
equally as important, the mothers felt they could finally meet the needs
of their children.

Although the mothers openly discussed the ways in which the dis/
ability label benefited their child, this is not to say that those benefits did
not come at a cost; a cost that was most often paid by the mothers.

Disabled by Proxy?: Disability Labels' Impact on the Lives of Mothers of Emergent Bilinguals Labeled as Dis/abled (MoEBLADs)

While the mothers identified their child's additional support and
services by way of the disability label as a gain, they also expressed the
ways in which having a disability label had placed additional strain on
them and put into question their role as mothers and caregivers (Burke
& Hodapp, 2014; Dykens *et al.*, 2014; Findler *et al.*, 2016; Lee, 2013).

A child's disability label often placed an immeasurable strain on their emotional, psychological and physical health as well as their social interactions.

One of the most common feelings expressed by the mothers in this study was a sense of powerlessness. The mothers felt powerless to help, support, guide, educate or even advocate for their children.

'Impotente': The emotional toll

Several mothers also used the word 'impotente' [powerless] to describe how they felt in relation to their inability to support or do more for their child following a diagnosis. Although like others, they were 'triste' [sad] and 'preocupada' [worried], Carmela, Paty and María repeat the word 'impotente'. There was nothing that they could do to communicate with their child or 'ayudar' [help] nor could they 'apoyar' [support] their children; they didn't 'saber' [know] how.

Carmela: Bueno, siempre uno se siente un poco triste, pero como ya había pasado con la experiencia de mi otro hijo–, igual, cuando pasó la experiencia de mi primer hijo, sí, yo me sentía tan preocupada, tan como impotente de no poderle ayudar, de no saber por qué estaba tardando en hablar. [...], como ya había crecido, y vieron que realmente tenía el problema–, y entonces, yo quería que tal vez le dieran más terapias, pero ellos decidieron que solo necesitaba del habla. Entonces, a veces uno se siente impotente, porque quisiera conseguir más ayuda para los niños.

[*Well, you always feel a little sad, but since it happened with my other son – likewise, when this experience happened with my first child, yes, I felt so worried, so helpless I could not help him, I did not know why he was slow to speak, [...] as he had grown up, and they saw that he really had the problem– and then, I wanted them to give him more therapies, but they decided that he just needed speech. So, sometimes you feel helpless, because you would like to get more help for your children.*]

Paty: Yo me sentía impotente porque no podía ayudar a mi hijo, él no podía hablar. Él no más pedía leche, 'Mmhm, mmhm'. Le decía, 'Leche' y él me decía 'Le'. Algo así corto. Luego le decía, 'Vuélvelo a repetir', pero si él repetí dos veces, a la tercera ya no la repetía. Y na' mas empezaba señas, o llorar, y eso era como una impotencia para mí.

[*I felt helpless because I could not help my son, he could not talk. He only asked for milk, 'Mmhm, mmhm'. I would say, 'Milk' and he would say 'Mi'. Something like that, short. Then I would tell him, 'Repeat it again', but if he repeated it twice, the third time he would*] *not repeat it. And he just started signing, or crying, and that was like a helplessness for me.*]

María: Porque yo a veces me siento impotente, porque no estoy ahí como para apoyarlo.

[*Because I sometimes feel helpless, because I'm not there to support him.*]

Again, some of this may be reflective of the fact that none of the mothers identified a deficit in their child until an individual whom they viewed as an expert told them so. Even when they have something in mind for their child 'yo quería que tal vez le dieran más terapias' [I wanted them to give him more therapies], they get shut down: 'pero ellos decidieron que solo necesitaba del habla' [but they decided that he just needed speech]. This lack of power and control over the situation also made the mothers feel sad about the possibility that the disability label would erase their child's humanity.

'Me sentí mal': Disability labels as a source of sadness

Rosa was the only mother to state explicitly that she did not agree with her child's dis/ability label because she did not like the way it 'sounded'. She stated that:

O sea, como que suena algo–, ¿cómo sabría? No sé, no me gusta. Como–. [...] Como tristeza de–, o sea, porque de esa escuela lleva como un número de discapacitado, o algo así. Me sentía mal que–, la maestra de él–, él le va a llevar un número, que si va a una escuela, y él lleva un número. Entonces, eso, me sentí mal porque–, una tristeza.

[*I mean, like it sounds like something– how would I? I don't know, I don't like it. Like–. [...] Like a sadness of–, I mean, because from that school carries a disability number, or something like that. I felt bad that–, his teacher–, he is going to carry a number, that if he goes to a school, and he has a number. So, that, I felt bad because …, a sadness.*]

Rosa really struggles to articulate why she does not like her child being labeled as disabled. Ultimately, she worries that her child has become a number in school. Not just any number, a disabled number. That fills her with feelings of 'tristeza' [sadness]. This negative reaction to her child's diagnosis is emblematic of her desire that her child's teacher view him as complete, as a person and not a mere number. It is that invisibility that leads her to sadness and feeling 'mal' [bad]. This fear of invisibility could be residual from the mothers' own sense of invisibility during the evaluation process. This process often left them waiting in worry.

'No me daban respuesta': Worrying throughout the evaluation process

Being told that their child was not performing as expected was stressful for many mothers. In the end, none of these mothers identified a problem in their child until an external person made that conclusion. The evaluation process made the mothers feel 'preocupada' [worried] and often left them 'desesperada' [in despair]. These feelings continued even after a diagnosis was made.

Rosa was worried because of all the uncertainty:

Rosa: Me sentía preocupada. [...] Porque–, no sé qué va a pasar.

[*I felt worried.*] [...] [*Because–, I don't know what's going to happen.*]

Sara was desperate for answers and for information on how to help her child. When I asked how she felt during the evaluation process, she shared:

Sara: Un poco desesperada porque no me daban respuesta. [...] [Y me sentia] preocupada [...] Porque no sabía cómo ayudar a mi niño.

[*A little desperate because they would not give me an answer.*] [...] [*And I felt] worried*] [*Because I did not know how to help my child.*]

While the diagnosis did offer explanations as to why certain things were happening with their children, it also brought with it a great deal of uncertainty: something was wrong but 'no sabía cómo ayudar a mi niño' [I didn't know how to help my child] and, at the time, they did not know what to expect nor 'qué va a pasar' [what will happen]. Once again, we see that this is in part due to a shift in power dynamics. Because the mothers had not been the ones to identify a problem in their child, they no longer felt like experts on their children and those who they considered experts 'no me daban respuesta' [would not give [them] an answer].

Eventually, this increased sense of invisibility combined with feelings of powerlessness took a toll on the mothers' psychological well-being, often leading them to deny their own capacity as advocates for their children.

'¿Qué puedo hacer?': The psychological toll

The fact that the children were labeled as disabled by a school or medical professional results in some mothers not feeling 'conforme' [satisfied], yet feeling powerless because they believe that the label is 'necesaria' [necessary]. Even when they disagree with the label, the only question they feel that they can ask is, dismissively, '¿pero [...] qué puedo hacer?' [but [...] what can I do?]. When asked if they agreed with their child's disability label, Paty and Sara replied as follows:

Paty: Pues, no, no estoy conforme. Pero a veces, ¿qué puedo hacer? ¿Cómo podría ayudarlo yo?

[*Well, no, I'm not happy. But sometimes, what can I do? How could I help?*]

Sara: Pues, es necesaria.

[*Well, it's necessary.*]

In this case, neither Sara nor Paty acknowledges being in support of or in agreement with the disability label. Sara simply states that it is necessary. Paty, on the other hand, answers by saying that while she did not agree with the disability label, she did not feel that there was anything she could do – either to change it or to help her child.

For these mothers, these feelings of helplessness (Kwiatkowski & Sekulowicz, 2017) and powerlessness (Cole, 2007; Huang *et al.*, 2012) are a by-product of the disability evaluation process particularly because this event augments many of their social constraints. At one point or another, every single participant uses some version of the phrase 'ellos decidieron' [they decided]. These mothers, for the most part, have limited educational backgrounds and lack the linguistic resources necessary to access appropriate supports and information with which to push back against individuals who represent and are backed by powerful institutions. This results in compounded feelings of powerlessness that last beyond the evaluation and into the child's academic career.

While many of these disability labels have the most relevance at school, they often had consequences for the lives of the mothers beyond school. These mothers were limited in their ability to seek employment because they needed to always be available for their child even during school hours. In many ways, the mothers were beholden to the disability more than their children.

'Por eso no puedo...': Disability labels as confinement

This sense of powerlessness also extends to the choices that the mothers had over their own lives. As a result of having a child who was diagnosed with a disability, many mothers expressed feeling limited in their ability to access work, even when this resulted in additional financial strain on the families. This is the case of María:

[Y]o sé que si me pongo a trabajar, me puedan llamar en un rato y decirme 'Justin le pasó esto'. O me da miedo de que algún día se pueda salir del salón, ahora que no esté el Para con él. Y no encontrarlo. Como en kínder, que me lo perdieron. Entonces, por eso no puedo trabajar. Porque si yo me pongo a trabajar pueden llamar, y no voy a poder salirme del trabajo. Ese es el problema.

[[And] I know that if I go to work, they can call me in a little while and tell me 'this happened to Justin'. Or I'm afraid that someday he can leave the room, now that the Para is not with him. And they won't find him. As in kindergarten, they lost him. So, that's why I cannot work. Because if I go to work they can call, and I will not be able to leave work. That's the problem.]

María is hesitant to acquire employment out of fear that something might go wrong and she won't 'poder salirme del trabajo' [be able to leave work].

Paty discusses the complications that can arise from being the working mother of an EBLAD:

Yo, dos veces, tres veces en la semana, tenía que irme, salirme del trabajo, irme a recogerlo, porque él lloraba de una hora, hora y media, a dos horas. Y me hablaban porque decían, 'Tu hijo ya no sabemos cómo controlarlo, cómo callarlo'. '¿Pero qué le pasó?'. Yo salía tan nerviosa del trabajo, me iba para allá en taxi, en algo más fácil que yo llegara, y había días que lo encontraba llorando. Él, los ojos hinchados, rojos. Le decía a la muchacha, '¿Pero por qué, por qué, por qué?'. Y ella decía, 'Pues es que no sabemos, no sabemos, y no sabemos'.

[I, twice, three times a week, had to leave, leave work, go pick him up, because he cried from an hour, an hour and a half, to two hours. And they talked to me, 'because' they said, 'we no longer know how to control your son, how to keep him quiet'. 'But what happened to him?' I'd leave work so nervous, I'd go there by taxi, the easiest way for me to arrive, and there were days when I found him crying. Him, his eyes swollen, red. I said to the girl, 'But why, why, why?' And she said, 'Well, we do not know, we do not know, and we do not know'.]

For Paty, work was an additional source of stress because at any moment in time she could get a call from the school that would force her to leave work and rush to Dan's side. Often, the call came without any explanation from the school.

After learning of some of the ways in which these mothers have been tasked with constant availability in order to meet their child's needs, it is not surprising to learn that this overload also manifested itself in physical ways. Not only did the mothers talk about feeling tired, they often looked it.

'Me cansaba': The physical toll

This inability to work leads these women to be entirely dependent on their partners, which brings with it its own set of complications (for more on this, see Chapter 10). However, it is Ana who reveals how taxing this sacrifice can be on a mother's physical and mental health, and how difficult it was to have her young daughter, María Teresa, receive services:

Bueno, sí fue un poquito estresante para mí, porque desde que nació pues me costó crecerla yo sola. Aunque uno tiene familia, pero usted sabe que aquí uno se las tiene que ver solas. Entonces, de ahí creció, después cuando me dijeron que le iban a hacer evaluaciones, le hicieron las evaluaciones, y no las pasó. Que tenía que recibir las terapias. Fue un poquito muy complicado para mí. Yo creo que para ella también, porque también fue cansada. Y pues así fue pasando. [...] No, yo pensé que no más a los tres años. Como era bebé, nació prematuro y no se podía sentar.

[El que ella ha continuado a necesitar servicios es] un poquito difícil, pero ya ahora como que está pasando. Sólo [quedan] las preocupaciones de la escuelita. [...] [El proceso f]ue bueno, pero también estresante para mí. Para ella, un poco. [...] Estresante, porque desde que ella nació, necesitaba todo el tiempo estar conmigo, toda la atención. Y, hay veces que sí, a veces, como mamá, me cansaba. A veces ya llegaba a las ocho, a las nueve, yo lo que quería ya es dormir. Porque todo el día me la pasaba yo abrazando. Cuando el papá, él llegaba del trabajo, a veces, él la abrazaba y me quedaba yo dormida. De tanto cansancio. [... P]or una cierta parte es bueno quedarse con ellos. Pero, por otra parte, es un poco difícil, porque con el tiempo ellos se acostumbran a la mamá. [Y para mi es] un poquito difícil, porque cuando ella entró a la escuela, se la pasaba llorando, porque siempre me buscaba.

[*Well, it was a bit stressful for me, because since she was born it was hard for me to raise her on my own. Although you have a family, but you know that here you have to fend for yourself. Then, from there, she grew, then when they told me they were going to do evaluations, they did the evaluations, and she didn't pass them. That she had to receive the therapies. It was a bit too complicated for me. I think for her too, because she was also tired. And well that's how she was passing ... I thought it was only until she was three years. Since she was a baby, she was born premature and could not sit. [The fact that she has continued to need services is] a bit difficult, but now it seems she's passing. Only the concerns [left are] with school. [...] [The process] was good, but also stressful for me. For her, a little. [...] Stressful, because since she was born, she needed to be with me all the time, all the attention. And, sometimes I do, sometimes, as a mom, I got tired. Sometimes it would be eight o'clock, at nine o'clock, I just wanted to sleep. Because I spent all day embracing her. When the dad, he came home from work, sometimes, he hugged her and I would fall asleep. From so much fatigue. [...] In certain ways its good to stay with them. But, on the other hand, it's a bit difficult, because over time they get used to the mom. [And for me it's] a little bit difficult, because when she went to school, she would go crying because she was always looking for me.*]

When asked how it was to be a mother to Justin, María reveals the added burden that comes with a diagnosis and how she feels as opposed to her husband:

> [Teníamos una psicóloga] para nosotros. Para que nos ayudara para lidiar con Justin. Platicar como nos sentíamos. [...] Incluso teníamos como platicas de pareja. Porque también mi esposo casi no me apoyaba en eso. Él aún sigue renuente que el niño no tiene autismo. No acepta que el niño tiene autismo.

> Y [el diagnosis] fue más peor para mí, porque toda la carga y todo el estrés está en mí. Porque [mi esposo] se va a trabajar. Él ya llega tarde. Él casi no lidia con el niño. Soy yo la que tiene que estar lidiando con él.

> [[We had a psychologist] for us. To help us deal with Justin. Talk about how we felt. [...] We even had like couple talks. Because my husband also hardly supported me in that. He is still reluctant that the boy does not have autism. Do not accept that the child has autism.

> And [the diagnosis] was worse for me, because all the burden and all the stress is on me. Because [my husband] goes to work. He arrives [home] late. He does not really deal with the child. It's me who has to be dealing with him.]

Here, Ana and María reveal the overall effect of the disability label on an EBLAD family: for the child it means access to more support at school and at home, but for the mother it means shouldering 'toda la carga y todo el estrés' [all the burden and all the stress]. They are the only ones that their children seek, the only ones who can comfort them, the only ones who can 'lidiar con el niño' [deal with the child], and in some cases, as with María, the only ones who acknowledge that a disability is even present. At the end of the day, after tending to their children 'sola' [alone], they are left too 'cansada' [exhausted] to do anything other than 'dormir' [sleep].

Conclusion

In this chapter, the mothers revealed the complexity that arises from labeling a child with a disability. While these mothers can view the process that follows the evaluation and diagnosis process as beneficial, they also acknowledge the ways in which these same experiences can impact their capacity to mother their children and to be autonomous women. It is also worthy of note that some of what the mothers discussed in this chapter could be understood as conflations between how a child's disability manifests versus the diagnosis itself. However, the mothers did not speak of their children's disability as explicitly burdensome but rather the tasks that came with the diagnosis – the subsequent need for services, the parent workshops, etc. For them, this labor was not tied to the disability but to the diagnosis because in their minds what changed wasn't their child or the way they behaved but rather the framing of their child's behavior. This framing also influenced the way they viewed their own and their children's linguistic practices. As such, the issues presented here are further complicated by the role of language within these families as these mothers guide their children through life in and out of school. The next chapter focuses on the linguistic aspect of their life.

Note

(1) 'Neurodiversity is the idea that neurological differences like autism and ADHD are the result of normal, natural variation in the human genome. This represents new and fundamentally different way of looking at conditions that were traditionally pathologized; it's a viewpoint that is not universally accepted though it is increasingly supported by science. That science suggests conditions like autism have a stable prevalence in human society as far back as we can measure. We are realizing that autism, ADHD, and other conditions emerge through a combination of genetic predisposition and environmental interaction; they are not the result of disease or injury' (Robinson, 2013: para. 1).

References

Anthony, C.S. (2013) *Ida McKinley: The Turn-of-the-Century First Lady through War, Assassination, and Secret Disability.* Kent, OH: The Kent State University Press. https://muse.jhu.edu/book/33206

Balcazar, F.E., Suarez-Balcazar, Y., Adames, S.B., Keys, C.B., García-Ramírez, M. and Paloma, V. (2012) A case study of liberation among Latino immigrant families who have children with disabilities. *American Journal of Community Psychology* 49 (1–2), 283–293. https://doi.org/10.1007/s10464-011-9447-9

Burghardt, M. (2015) 'He was a secret': Family narratives and the institutionalization of people with intellectual disabilities. *Disability & Society* 30 (7), 1071–1086. https://doi.org/10.1080/09687599.2015.1076718

Burke, M.M. and Hodapp, R.M. (2014) Relating stress of mothers of children with developmental disabilities to family–school partnerships. *Intellectual and Developmental Disabilities* 52 (1), 13–23. https://doi.org/10.1352/1934-9556-52.1.13

Cohen, S.R. (2013) Advocacy for the 'Abandonados': Harnessing cultural beliefs for Latino families and their children with intellectual disabilities. *Journal of Policy and Practice in Intellectual Disabilities* 10 (1), 71–78. https://doi.org/10.1111/jppi.12021

Cole, B. (2007) Mothers, gender and inclusion in the context of home-school relations. *Support for Learning* 22 (4), 165–173. https://doi.org/10.1111/j.1467-9604.2007.00467.x

Dykens, E.M., Fisher, M.H., Taylor, J.L., Lambert, W. and Miodrag, N. (2014) Reducing distress in mothers of children with autism and other disabilities: A randomized trial. *Pediatrics* 134 (2), e454–e463. https://doi.org/10.1542/peds.2013-3164

Findler, L., Klein Jacoby, A. and Gabis, L. (2016) Subjective happiness among mothers of children with disabilities: The role of stress, attachment, guilt and social support. *Research in Developmental Disabilities* 55, 44–54. https://doi.org/10.1016/j.ridd.2016.03.006

Green, D.A. (2020) Shhh!!!! Can you keep a secret? A cultural bias against disclosing a mental disability & its impact on seeking reasonable accommodations for the bar exam. *Texas Hispanic Journal of Law and Policy* 26, 1.

Harry, B. and Klingner, J. (2014) *Why Are So Many Minority Students in Special Educa-tion?* (2nd edn). New York: Teachers College Press.

Harry, B., Klingner, J.K., Cramer, E. and Sturges, K. (2007) *Case Studies of Minority Stu-dent Placement in Special Education.* New York: Teachers College Press. See http://www.tcrecord.org.ezproxy.gc.cuny.edu/library/Abstract.asp?ContentId=14542

Huang, Y.-P., Kellett, U. and John, W.S. (2012) Being concerned: Caregiving for Tai-wanese mothers of a child with cerebral palsy. *Journal of Clinical Nursing* 21 (1–2), 189–197. https://doi.org/10.1111/j.1365-2702.2011.03741.x

Klingner, J.K. and Harry, B. (2006) The special education referral and decision-making process for English language learners: Child study team meetings and placement con-ferences. *Teachers College Record* 108 (11), 2247–2281.

Kwiatkowski, P. and Sekulowicz, M. (2017) Examining the relationship of individual resources and burnout in mothers of children with disabilities. *International Journal of Special Education* 32 (4), 823–841.

Lalvani, P. (2015) Disability, stigma and otherness: Perspectives of parents and teachers. *International Journal of Disability, Development and Education* 62 (4), 379–393.

Larson, E. (1998) Reframing the meaning of disability to families: The embrace of para-dox. *Social Science & Medicine* 47 (7), 865–875. https://doi.org/10.1016/S0277-9536(98)00113-0

Lee, J. (2013) Maternal stress, well-being, and impaired sleep in mothers of children with developmental disabilities: A literature review. *Research in Developmental Disabili-ties* 34 (11), 4255–4273. https://doi.org/10.1016/j.ridd.2013.09.008

Mackelprang, R.W. and Salsgiver, R. (2016) *Disability: A Diversity Model Approach in Human Service Practice.* New York: Oxford University Press. https://books.google.com/books/about/Disability.html?id=wgjnDAAAQBAJ

McHatton, P.A. and Correa, V. (2005) Stigma and discrimination perspectives from Mexican and Puerto Rican mothers of children with special needs. *Topics in Early Childhood Special Education* 25 (3), 131–142. https://doi.org/10.1177/02711214050250030101

Michie, M. and Skinner, D. (2010) Narrating disability, narrating religious practice: Rec-onciliation and fragile X syndrome. *Intellectual and Developmental Disabilities* 48 (2), 99–111. https://doi.org/10.1352/1934-9556-48.2.99

Robinson, J.E. (2013) What is neurodiversity? *Psychology Today*, 7 October. See http://www.psychologytoday.com/blog/my-life-aspergers/201310/what-is-neurodiversity (accessed 16 February 2018).

Salkas, K., Magaña, S., Marques, I. and Mirza, M. (2016) Spirituality in Latino families of children with autism spectrum disorder. *Journal of Family Social Work* 19 (1), 38–55. https://doi.org/10.1080/10522158.2015.1114060

Skinner, D., Rodriguez, P. and Bailey, D.B., Jr (1999) Qualitative analysis of Latino par-ents' religious interpretations of their child's disability. *Journal of Early Intervention* 22 (4), 271–285.

Wexler, A. (2005) Identity politics of disability: The other and the secret self. *Journal of Social Theory in Art Education* 25 (1), 210–224.

Zea, M.C., Quezada, T. and Belgrave, F.Z. (1994) Latino cultural values: Their role in adjustment to disability. *Journal of Social Behavior & Personality* 9 (5), 185–200.

7 Broken Promise: The Security of Bilingualism for the Future and the Ambiguity of Bilingualism in the Present

For the mothers in this study, bilingualism serves multiple functions. In the long run, bilingualism is not only a tool that helps them reinforce their children's Latinx heritage (Brooke-Garza, 2015; Sari *et al.*, 2018; Schwartz & Palviainen, 2016), but it is also a way to grant their children access to better jobs (Alonso & Villa, 2020; Subtirelu, 2017). In the more immediate and tenuous future, bilingualism allows their children to develop concrete relationships with their siblings living abroad (Hua & Wei, 2016; Lahaie *et al.*, 2009; Vázquez *et al.*, 2018) and it also prepares them for life in their ancestral home in case of the undocumented mothers' deportation (Gallo & Hornberger, 2017; Mangual Figueroa, 2013).

The Multilayered Meanings and Purposes of Bilingualism

For the mothers, where a person was born determined which language belonged to them; other languages were just add-ons. For example, the mothers were born in Mexico so Spanish is their language while English belongs to their children, at least to those who were born in the United States.

'Mi idioma': Country of birth = linguistic identity

Multiple mothers framed Spanish as 'mi idioma' [my language] and English as 'el idioma de ellos' [their language]. This was true for María and Carmela.

María: [El español] es su lengua materna, le digo. Y el inglés, porque el inglés aquí es su idioma de ellos.

[*[Spanish] is their mother tongue, I tell them. And English, because English here is their language.*]

Carmela: Si yo puedo enseñarle mi idioma, y conservar mi idioma, creo que va a ser un beneficio para él. [...] Entonces, yo siempre trato de que ellos conserven mi idioma.

[If I can teach him my language, and preserve my language, I think it's going to be a benefit for him. [...] So, I always try, for them to conserve my language.]

Although they all express an interest in bilingualism, it is also clear that for the mothers, their children's English is more important than their Spanish. For María, Spanish is 'lengua materna' [their mother tongue] but not in the sense that it is their 'native language' but rather that it is their mother's tongue.

Similarly, the mothers see English as the language of the country in which their children were born, and the language of the society in which they live. Sara, Carlota and Carmela express this thus:

Sara: es su idioma, de él, o sea, él nació—[aquí].

[it's his language, his, that is, he was born—[here].]

Carlota: [...] era más importante el inglés. ¿Cómo le voy a decir a un doctor: 'Tengo dolor de cabeza'?

[[...] English was more important. How can I tell a doctor: 'I have a headache'?]

Carmela: Son ciudadanos americanos, tienen que saber el inglés.

[They are American citizens, they have to know English.]

For them, the fact that their child 'nació' [was born] here and that 'son ciudadanos Americanos' [they are American citizens] means that English acquisition is and must be the primary focus. And yet, the mothers feel that Spanish is also important for their children for different reasons. One of the primary and oft-cited reasons relates to the perception that being bilingual affords one increased access to a more secure financial future through better career opportunities.

'Oportunidad': Bilingualism for financial security

Regardless of the child's disability label, all of the mothers who participated in this study expressed a clear interest in developing their child's bilingualism. Across the group, the primary value placed on bilingualism often referred to a future need. The women were clear that their child's Spanish is important to them, as Carmela says, 'Spanish/English bilingualism is an important "beneficio" [benefit], "una oportunidad" [an opportunity]'. It is the word 'oportunidad' that they repeat most. The mothers see their children's bilingualism as an important opportunity to get a job in the future or for a future profession, as Carmela and Rosario express:

Carmela: Pienso que es importante para mí, es importante conservar nuestro idioma. Y, también pienso que es importante aquí, en este país, hablar más de un idioma. [...] Por ejemplo, para conseguir un trabajo. Creo yo, que una persona que habla más de un idioma, tiene un poco más de oportunidad. Y si habla dos, o tres idiomas, pues mejor. [...] En mi área hay esa oportunidad, y yo trato de aprovecharla. [...] Entonces, yo aprovecho las oportunidades que hay acá para que ellos aprendan el idioma.

[*I think it's important for me, it's important to preserve our language. And, I also think that it is important here, in this country, to speak more than one language. [...] For example, to get a job. I think that a person who speaks more than one language has a little more opportunity. And if he speaks two, or three languages, even better. [...] In my area there is that opportunity, and I try to take advantage of it. [...] So, I take advantage of the opportunities that are here for them to learn the language.*]

Rosario: Sí. Sí es importante [que ella sea bilingual]. [...] Porque en un futuro le va a servir mucho. [...] En el futuro, por ejemplo, ya se está mirando que hay más oportunidades, en los trabajos casi se necesitan los dos idiomas o más idiomas, entonces para ella es mucho mejor. [...] En alguna carrera que ella quiera tomar, siempre es mejor que hable los dos idiomas.

[*Yes. Yes, it is important [that she is bilingual] [...] Because in the future it will be very useful. [...] In the future, for example, you can already see that there are more opportunities, in jobs you almost need two languages or more languages, so for her it is much better. [...] In any career that she wants to take on, it is always better to speak both languages.*]

This discourse around bilingualism for more opportunity is laced throughout the mainstream discourse on bilingual education (Bak *et al.*, 2014; Bialystok & Werker, 2017; Katznelson & Bernstein, 2017), so it is not surprising to see it arise among the mothers of emergent bilinguals labeled as dis/abled (EBLADs). But bilingualism is not only important for economic and future opportunities, it is also important because of the transnational lives these families live (Duff, 2015; Hirsch & Lee, 2018; Hua & Wei, 2016; King, 2016). Like most immigrant families, the families in this study maintained relationships with family members who remained in the mother's country of origin. Unlike most previous research, the mothers in this study indicated that these family members were not only of older generations but increasingly consisted of brothers and sisters who were never brought to the United States, as well as a select few who had voluntarily returned to Mexico. As such, bilingualism was a necessary tool in the interpersonal success of the child.

'Mi hermano, ¿le contestó?': Communicating with binational siblings

The connections that the mothers have to their country of origin appear as motivators for Spanish development. For some mothers, that connection is cultural or ancestral, but for Paty, it was one of living in the present. Paty was raising two children in Mexico at the same time that she was raising two children in the United States. Paty's younger children have never met her two older children and they have only had a relationship through text. She explains:

> Sí. Sí. [Tanya], como ella puede escribir el español, le textea a él, a uno de ellos. O a los dos les puede textear. Luego dice, 'Mamá, te mandó mensaje'. '¿Quién?', 'Mi hermano, ¿le contesto?', 'Okay, contéstale'. Y le dice, 'Hola, soy [Tanya]. Mamá está ocupada'. Y ya, ahí le va escribiendo. [Dan], a veces le tiene que decir a [Tanya] porque él no puede textearle en español... Entonces, a veces le textea en inglés, pero [el hermano en México] le dice, 'No te entiendo, no te entiendo'. 'Soy [Dan], soy [Dan]'. Y le dice el otro, 'Pero es que no te entiendo'.

> [*Yes. Yes. [Tanya], since she can write Spanish, she texts to him, to one of them. Or she can text them both. Then she says, 'Mom, he sent you a message'. 'Who?', 'My brother, do I answer?', 'Okay, answer him'. And she says, 'Hi, its [Tanya]. Mom is busy'. And like that she starts writing them. [Dan], sometimes he has to tell [Tanya] because he cannot text in Spanish ... Then, sometimes he texts in English, but he [the brother in Mexico] says, 'I do not understand you, I do not understand you'. 'Its [Dan], Its [Dan]'. And the other says, 'But it's that I do not understand you'.*]

In this family, Spanish is a necessary tool for communication particularly for the set of siblings who have never physically met. Because Dan is enrolled in an English-only class, unlike his sister Tanya who 'puede escribir español' [can write in Spanish] because she is in a bilingual program, his ability to communicate with his siblings is greatly hindered by his inability to read and 'textearle en español' [text them in Spanish]. Rather than getting to know each other, these text conversations result in moments of frustration where one brother is silenced by his inability to write in Spanish while the other is left saying 'no te entiendo, no te entiendo' [I do not understand you, I do not understand you].

Nancy lived a similar reality and noted that she has to serve as linguistic intermediary for her binational children:

Su hermana está en México, y entonces él me dice, 'Mami, le voy a mandar un mensaje a mi hermana'. Le digo, 'Sí, papi, pero mándaselo en español'. 'No', dice, 'Yo se lo mando en inglés porque ella me ha dicho'. Le digo, 'Pero yo quiero que tú aprendas a escribir en español'. 'Ah, bueno, pero me ayudas', me dice. Y le digo, 'Sí, sí, yo te ayudo'. Y ya le voy deletreando. Eso es no más–, es en los mensajes con su hermana o su tía.

[*His sister is in Mexico, and then he says, 'Mom, I'm going to send a message to my sister'. I say, 'Yes, honey, but send it in Spanish'. 'No', he says, 'I send it to her in English because she told me'. I tell him, 'But I want you to learn to write in Spanish'. 'Ah, well, then you help me', he tells me. And I say, 'Yes, yes, I will help you'. And I will spell it for him. That's it–, it's in the messages with his sister or his aunt.*]

In these families, bilingualism is important for intergenerational communication, so that children can talk to their grandparents or 'tía[s]' [aunts]; but these families also show that bilingualism is a necessary part of intragenerational communication, so that children can talk to their 'hermano[s]' [brothers] and 'hermana[s]' [sisters]. While it was unexpected to learn of mothers who were raising children in two nations, this reality was true for at least two other mothers in this study. Yet, this still did not create a pressing need for these mothers to have their children in bilingual education programs where they would also be taught in Spanish. Much more important was the very real fear of deportation, as the following section shows.

Being bilingual not only helped these children develop and maintain relationships with their siblings, but it also prepared them for the possibility of life in their mother's country of origin. Through their development as bilingual and biliterate people, EBLADs were given the tools they needed to ensure that they would have a smoother transition in a Spanish-dominant country and school system.

'Me puedan deportar': Bilingualism in case of deportation

Although it was not a criterion for this study, at least 9 of the 10 mothers identified as undocumented residents in the United States. The tenth, whose status was unclear, had experienced the deportation of the father of her children. The enrollment for this study occurred in the aftermath of the 2016 presidential election, and the interviews took place soon after. Given the anti-immigrant sentiment and rhetoric that was produced by the Trump campaign, it was no surprise that the fear of deportation was heavy on the minds of these mothers. Two mothers

alluded to an uncertain future in the United States for their children and
themselves. They have no assurances about where they are going to be in
the future, 'mañana no lo sé' [tomorrow I don't know]. As Nancy states,
they are aware that their children might one day live in a country where
only 'puro español' [pure Spanish] is spoken:

> Porque yo, ¿cómo le puedo decir? Porque yo estoy aquí ahora, ¿verdad?
> Mañana, no lo sé. Y si un día, yo pudiera ir con ellos a mi país, para
> que ellos entiendan, porque allí no está nada escrito en inglés. Ahí, puro
> español.

> [*Because I, how can I tell you? Because I'm here now, right? Tomorrow,
> I do not know. And if one day, I could go with them to my country, so
> that they understand, because there is nothing written in English. There,
> pure Spanish.*]

However, it is not language that these mothers fear, but an uncertain future, not knowing, 'yo no sé', whether they will indeed be with
their EBLAD children in the future. As María explains in the following
excerpt, one can understand how concerning this uncertainty can be:

> Siento preocupación porque él va creciendo, y yo no sé qué pueda pasar
> el día de mañana con él, y saber que no pueda estar con él, como que
> pienso mucho en eso. Pero tengo que ir viviendo al día a día con él. No
> quiero traumarme en el futuro, de que qué va a pasar con él si yo no
> estoy con él. Es difícil, pero solo Dios sabe por qué me mandó ese niño
> especial.... Porque no sé qué pueda pasar el día de mañana. Si me puedan
> deportar, si me pueda pasar algo y no poder estar con él.

> [*I am worried because he is growing, and I do not know what could hap-
> pen tomorrow with him, and knowing that I may not be with him, I think
> a lot about that. But I have to live day to day with him. I do not want to
> be traumatized by the future, [thinking about] what will happen to him if
> I am not with him. It's difficult, but God only knows why he sent me that
> special child.... Because I do not know what could happen tomorrow. If
> they can deport me, if something happens to me and I can't be with him.*]

Paty makes the 'foreignness' very explicit for her son. She tells him,
'Tú no eres de acá' [you are not from here] and that if she were deported
he would have to go with her. She does this so that he understands that
even though 'eres nacido acá' [you were born here], he can also be affected
by deportation and so he needs to 'aprender el español' [learn Spanish].

> [risas] Y por eso le digo a él, 'Tú debes de por eso aprender el español.
> Porque tú no eres de acá, de acá. Sí, eres nacido acá. Pero tus padres son
> mexicanos. Y si hubiera en el momento, no sé–', le digo a veces, 'si nos
> deportaran, lógico. Eres mi hijo. Te tengo que llevar. Y si ya no regreso,

no te puedo dejar acá solo. [...] Tú tienes que aprender el español porque del país que yo vengo, no se habla el inglés. Las escuelas no te dan el inglés. Entonces, habla Spanish'. Es como lo entendió.

[[laughs] And that's why I say to him, 'You must, therefore learn Spanish. Because you're not from here, from here'. Yes, you're born here. But your parents are Mexicans. And if there was a moment, I do not know–, I say sometimes, 'if they deported us, logical, you are my son. I have to take you. And if I don't come back, I can't leave you here alone. [...] You have to learn Spanish because in the country I come from they don't speak English. The schools don't teach you English. So, speak Spanish'. That's how he understood it.]

Paty clarifies that she loves her children, and she would never leave them here with family. For her, family isn't going to 'tratar [los] igual, como, como madre' [treat [them] the same as, as a mother]. So she tells them that they should learn English because it will be needed and it is their language, but they must learn Spanish in case she is deported and they have to go with her. She argues with me that she has no one to leave them here with:

¿Maestra con quién los dejaría acá? Tengo familia. ¿Usted cree que mi familia los va a tratar igual, como uno, como madre? No todas tenemos ese amor. [...] A ver, por eso les digo, 'aprovechen, aprovechen aprendan el inglés como el español, aprendan el inglés porque les va a hacer falta, porque es su idioma de ustedes, y el español por si algún día me deportan y se tengan que ir conmigo, que no le pido eso a Dios, pero por si las dudas, hay que prevenir de todos hijos', 'Tienes razón mamá'. [...] Por eso a veces yo siento que sí, es bueno que ellos aprendan los dos idiomas, que le digo a veces, 'Y no se les olvide que no son americanos, que también son mexicanos'.

[Teacher, who would I leave them with here? I have family but do you think that my family will treat them the same as, as a mother? We do not all have that love. [...] Let's see, that's why I tell them, 'take advantage, take advantage of learning English like Spanish, learn English because you're going to need it, because it's your language, and Spanish, in case one day I'm deported and you have to go with me. I do not ask God for that, but just in case, you have to prepare for everything children'. You're right mom. [...] That's why sometimes I feel like it's good for them to learn the two languages, which I say sometimes, 'And do not forget that you are not Americans, that you are also Mexicans'.]

While the mothers primarily discussed English for future jobs and opportunities, Spanish is framed as a means to survive. These mothers recognize that if they were to be deported, their children would go with them (Becerra, 2016; Olivos & Sobko, 2017). Without speaking Spanish, they would have a difficult time adjusting to their life in Mexico or elsewhere. Even though these mothers believe that both languages have value – the commodification of each language is dependent on a very tenuous future. Although the mothers feel strongly that their children should be bilingual, they accept the fact that their children are placed in monolingual classrooms. The next section addresses the reasons as to why this might be so.

From Spanish-Speaking Homes to Complicated Classrooms

There are many different settings in which emergent bilinguals labeled as dis/abled[1] can be educated (Figure 7.1). The restrictiveness of the placement often correlates to the perceived severity of the child's dis/ability label vis-à-vis the perceived limits of their academic function (Figure 7.2).

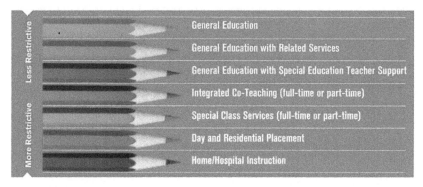

General Education

General Education with Related Services

General Education with Special Education Teacher Support

Integrated Co-Teaching (full-time or part-time)

Special Class Services (full-time or part-time)

Day and Residential Placement

Home/Hospital Instruction

Less Restrictive / More Restrictive

Figure 7.1 NYCDOE special education settings. *Least restrictive environment:* A clause within the Individuals with Disabilities Education Act (IDEA) that states: 'To the maximum extent appropriate, children with disabilities, including children in public or private institutions or other care facilities, are educated with children who are not disabled, and special classes, separate schooling, or other removal of children with disabilities from the regular educational environment occurs only when the nature or severity of the disability of a child is such that education in regular classes with the use of supplementary aids and services cannot be achieved satisfactorily' (Individuals with Disabilities Education Improvement Act of 2004 (PL 108-446), 2004). In essence, the least restrictive environment refers to the learning environment that is most similar to that which is inhabited by typically developing children as opposed to an environment that would result in the isolation and segregation of a student labeled as dis/abled from their typically developing peers (often called the most restrictive environment). *Most restrictive environment:* A setting within a school or community that would result in an increased level of segregation between a student labeled as dis/abled and their typically developing peers. While this term is colloquially used with regularity as the inverse of 'least restrictive environment', it does not appear formally in the IDEA (Source: Family Guide to Special Education Services for School-Age Children – A Shared Path to Success, 2014: 14)

Disability Classifications

Below is a list of classifiable disabilities:

- Autism
- Deafness
- Deaf-Blindness
- Emotional Disturbance
- Hearing Impairment
- Learning Disability
- Intellectual Disability
- Multiple Disabilities
- Orthopedic Impairment
- Other Health Impairment
- Speech or Language Impairment
- Traumatic Brain Injury
- Visual Impairment

Figure 7.2 NYCDOE dis/ability classifications (Source: Family Guide to Special Education Services for School-Age Children – A Shared Path to Success, 2014: 20)

These dis/abilities are further reduced to low-incidence and high-incidence disability categories. High-incidence dis/abilities are the most prevalent in children in US schools. These include, but are not limited to, the New York City Department of Education (NYCDOE) classifications of emotional disturbance, learning disability and speech or language impairment (Gage *et al.*, 2012). Low-incidence dis/abilities are rare and 'require significant supports' (Kurth *et al.*, 2014). These include, but are not limited to, the NYCDOE classifications of autism, intellectual disability and hearing impairment. More often than not, students with low-incidence dis/abilities are placed in more restrictive environments (Kurth *et al.*, 2014).

Currently, many bilingual students labeled as dis/abled are often placed in English-only special education programs under the misconception that learning bilingually is counterproductive to their academic growth (Cheatham & Barnett, 2016; Kangas, 2014, 2017). However, when students who speak Spanish at home are placed in English-only environments, not only is their learning impacted, but also the way that the family, particularly monolingual Spanish-speaking mothers, interacts with the school and is able to participate in the child's education. Alternatively, students at risk of being diagnosed with a dis/ability can be inappropriately placed in bilingual mainstream programs that do not fully meet their academic needs. This is often done because the learning issues are perceived as primarily language based and as a way to reduce the disproportionate representation of culturally and linguistically diverse (CLD) students in special education (Cartledge *et al.*, 2016; Fernandez & Inserra, 2013; Lerma & Stewart, 2016). Where bilingual special education programs do exist, they are considered a 'special class service' and thus a more restrictive environment (Family Guide to Special Education Services for School-Age Children – A Shared Path to Success, 2014). While the intentions of placing EBLADs in mainstream bilingual settings are altruistic, they can lead to serious issues in the home. In many cases, mothers are frustrated with their child's academic performance and are unable to adequately meet their child's academic needs because of a mismatch between the expectations placed on the child and their capacity. This can also lead to an English-only placement because the mother may place the blame on the bilingual learning environment. This often results in children being voluntarily placed in English-only settings, ultimately creating a linguistic disconnect between the home and the school. There are currently not enough settings in which all of an EBLAD's needs can be met.

The False Dichotomy: Remedy the Disability or Develop Bilingualism/Biliteracy

Although all of the mothers in this study expressed an interest in bilingualism, and in bilingual education for their children, only two of the children (Justin and María Teresa) were enrolled in a bilingual program at the time of the study. When asked to address this contradiction, the mothers would often reveal a dichotomous perspective in which a bilingual education could not be provided alongside or in conjunction with special education services. The following section addresses how difficulties in language, as evaluated in school, play an important part in how the mothers view their children's disabilities as well as influence their decisions to keep their children out of bilingual programs and, in some cases, remove them from bilingual programs.

'Dificultades en decirlo bien': Language as a disability marker

Ana reveals how because of her disability, María Teresa 'tiene dificultades' [has difficulties] learning English. For Ana, 'lo principal, de aquí, es el inglés' and so it is important that María Teresa at least learn English well:

Lo principal, de aquí, pues es el inglés. Y como ella tiene dificultades para aprenderlo, entonces, solo la voy a dejar en lo de inglés.

[The main thing, from here, well it's English. And since she has difficulties to learn it, then, I'm just going to leave her in English.]

In this brief statement, Ana reveals her rational for wanting to move María Teresa from the bilingual class she is now in to a monolingual English class.

Nancy, whose son is in a monolingual English class, feels that only after her son does well 'por lo menos el IEP' [on at least the IEP[2]], would she consider signing him up for a bilingual program:

La verdad lo he pensado [inscribirlo en un programa bilingüe], pero para mí siento que tiene muchísimos programas [...]. Pero ojalá, Dios quiera, lo supere por lo menos el IEP, entonces, ya hablaría yo [con la escuela].

[I really thought about [enrolling him in a bilingual program], but for me I feel that he has so many programs [...]. But I hopefully, God willing, he will exceed at least the IEP, then, I would speak [with the school].]

The mothers did not seem to recognize the inherent contradiction in this dichotomy. Whereas all of the mothers identified their child as Spanish speaking, they still seemed to believe that their child could not be formally educated in a bilingual setting as a result of their 'descapacidad' [disability] or 'problemas' [problems]. A reason for this may be that 'problemas de lenguaje' [speech issues] were the mothers' primary indication of a problem.

María acknowledges her son's difficulties with language, with words, with pronunciation, and ascribes these issues to his autism:

Porque por su discapacidad, de él que tiene autismo, tiene también problemas de lenguaje. No puede hablar ni pronunciar bien las palabras. Y le digo, a veces yo tengo que corregirlo en español. En inglés, tal vez lo corregirán en la escuela. Pero en cuestión de español yo trato de corre–. A veces no puede pronunciar una palabra. Yo trato, trato, trato de que vuelva a repetirlo, repetirlo, repetirlo hasta que pueda decirlo bien.

[Yes, yes. Because of his disability, he has autism, he also has language problems. He can not speak or pronounce words well. And I tell you, sometimes I have to correct him in Spanish. In English, maybe they correct it at school. But in a matter of Spanish I try to corre– Sometimes he can not pronounce a word. I try, I try, I try to get him to repeat it again, repeat it, repeat it until he can say it right.]

María states that her son has a difficult time expressing himself: 'no puede hablar ni pronunciar bien las palabras' [He can not speak or pronounce words well]. She focuses mostly on what Justin can't do and her need to 'corregirlo en español' [correct him in Spanish]. However, during all of the observations that took place at their home, she and Justin communicated solely in Spanish and did not present any issues. In addition, in her first interview, María stated that Justin felt most comfortable using Spanish when engaging in oral communication.

Why is it then that mothers accept monolingual placements in schools? The answer lies in what mothers reveal about what school professionals told them.

'Ellas me dijeron...': Monolingual ideologies among school professionals

In the following excerpt, Paty reveals why the mothers may feel that it is impossible for their EBLADs to be educated bilingually. It turns out that it is the educators in school who disseminate this idea 'que se confunden los niños' [that children get confused]. And yet, Paty herself feels that even though 'uno les habla español' [one speaks Spanish] at home, indicates, it seems that these mothers are savvier about bilingualism than the school professionals:

> Cuando estaba creo que en tercer grado, pregunté [sobre inscribirlo en una clase bilingüe] y ellas me dijeron que no podían porque a él lo iban a confundir. Dice que se confunden los niños. Porque realmente, a veces sí, el inglés que es el idioma de ellos les cuesta. Ahora, con otro idioma.

> [When he was there, I think that in the third grade, I asked [about placing him in a bilingual class] and they told me they could not because it was going to confuse him. They say that the children get confused. Because really, sometimes yes, the English, which is their language, is hard for them. Now, you add another language.]

And when I asked whether she agreed with the school professionals' decision, Paty says:

> Pues, yo siento que no, yo diría que no porque pues, como padres, pues uno les habla español. Y eso ya sería por parte de la escuela, el inglés. Porque, bueno, al menos yo eso sentí en la niña, que no fue problema. Porque ella, o quizás dependió de la mente de ella. Como ella es diferente a él.

> [Well, I feel like I do not, I would say no because, as parents, well one speaks Spanish to them. And that would already be on the part of the

school, English. Because, well, at least I felt that in the girl, it was not a problem. Because she, or maybe it depended on her mind. Since she is different from him.]

Paty states that she does not agree with the school's message that bilingualism would be confusing and she cites her child's actual linguistic practices as evidence. However, at the end, she compares her 'typically developing' daughter who is in a bilingual program, with her 'disabled' child, and so rationalizes her son's monolingual placement: 'como ella es diferente a él' [since she is different from him].

The fact that Paty was told by her child's school that bilingualism was too confusing was not unique to her. Multiple mothers shared similar stories. This was Elodia's experience:

Sí [ellos han ofrecido la opción de clase bilingüe], pero para él es muy difícil. [...] Porque es difícil que aprenda los dos idiomas, tanto para escribirlo, al leerlo ... para ellos es más fácil que aprenda sólo un idioma.

[Yes [they have offered the option of bilingual class], but for him it is very difficult. [...] Because it is difficult to learn both languages, both to write it, to read it ... for them it is easier to learn only one language.]

Carlota shares Elodia's view that a child with disabilities has difficulties learning two languages:

¿[T]e imaginas?, está aprendiendo a hablar. Y si tú le metes dos idiomas es más difícil, ¿no? Es mejor que hable solamente un idioma. Y ya hasta que empezara a estructurarse en su forma de hablar, ya meterle el otro idioma. Pero pobre niño, los niños que tienen esa discapacidad y hablan dos idiomas, yo creo que es mucho peor, ¿no?

[Can you imagine? He's learning to speak. And if you give him two languages it's more difficult, right? It is better to speak only one language. And until he begins to structure his way of speaking, then you can add the other language. But poor child, children who have that disability and speak two languages, I think it's much worse, right?]

Carlota, who previously said that her son spoke 'better' than his typically developing peers, now tries to convince herself that being bilingual would be 'difícil' [difficult].

Unfortunately, teachers and schools are a major factor in the distribution of misinformation regarding bilingualism and disability. Teachers have also told Ana that it is better for her daughter to learn only in English. Teachers tell her it is 'para el bien de ella' [for her own good], repeating the assertion that it is very complicated to learn two languages at the same time:

Yo creo que solo lo dejaría en inglés. Bueno, para el bien de ella. Para que lo aprenda, pero para el bien de ella. Pero pues por un lado, no. No sabría–, ¿cómo le diré?, no sabría calificarla yo, si lo está hablando bien. [...] Los maestros dicen que es mejor para ella. Para que solo en un–, solo en inglés se enfoque. Y no se le haga tan complicado aprender al mismo tiempo los dos idiomas.

[I think I would only leave it in English. Well, for her own good. To learn it, but for her own good. But on the one hand, no. I would not know ..., how can I tell him? I would not know how to rate him, if he is speaking well. [...] The teachers say it's better for her. So that only in one–, she focuses only in Engl. And it will not be so complicated to learn both languages at the same time.]

Ana is able to follow this recommendation in good conscience because she believes that the teachers are the experts and as such 'tratan de orientar a uno como papás lo más que pueden' [try to guide one as parents as much as they can]. When I asked Ana about how María Teresa's transition from a bilingual setting to a monolingual setting will impact her ability to support her daughter academically, she once again cites the teachers' recommendation:

Bueno, la recomendación fue de los maestros, que es mejor que estuviera en una clase–, en una clase de inglés, solo de inglés. Los niños que tienen problemitas con el aprendizaje de español a Inglés, es mejor dejarlos en una sola clase. Bueno, por un lado estaría bien, porque pues aprendería mejor el inglés. Pero por otro lado, en casa, pues yo no sabría–, ¿cómo le diré?, si ella no está aprendiendo bien. O en el español, pues lo hablaríamos el español en la casa, pues lo podría calificar. Pero el inglés, pues no. O por la–, ejemplo, ella me hablaría más inglés, pero yo no le entendería.

[Well, the recommendation was from the teachers, that it's better that she be in a class–, in an English class, just English. Children who have problems with learning from Spanish to English, it is better to leave them in a single class. Well, on one hand it would be good, because then she would learn English better. But on the other hand, at home, because I would not know ..., how can I tell you?, if she is not learning well. Or in Spanish, well because we would speak Spanish at home, so I could assess it. But English, well no. Or for the–, example, she would speak to me more English, but I would not understand her.]

Mothers like Ana feel totally incapable of assessing their children's progress in English, whereas they can do so in Spanish. Thus, they feel that they have to trust the teachers with recommendations about English. However, this trust comes at a cost. In this same excerpt, Ana explains the ways in which mothers are impacted when their children are moved to monolingual settings: 'en casa, pues yo no sabría [...] si ella no está aprendiendo bien' [at home, I would not know [...] if she is not learning well] and 'ella me hablaría más inglés, pero yo no le entendería' [she would speak more English, but I would not understand]. When children are placed in monolingual English settings, mothers rightfully worry that they will lose their ability to assess their child's learning and even their ability to communicate with their child. Still, Ana will support the school's decision to move her daughter to a monolingual English class the following school year because it is in the best interest of her child.

Ana and many of the other mothers are often so concerned with their children's welfare and advancement that they are willing to do everything they can in order to ensure that they make progress, even when that means promoting a linguistic policy that excludes them from their child's academic development. This shows the mothers' interest in their children's well-being and school success. For many, the only way to subvert this exclusion is by becoming language teachers in their own homes.

Notes

(1) The use of the term emergent bilinguals labeled as dis/abled (EBLAD) rather than English language learners with dis/abilities or English language learners with special education needs aims to dismantle the double deficit model that is produced by combining the term English language learner, which fails to acknowledge the linguistic resources that a student brings, with the terms 'with disabilities' or 'special education needs', which negate the social and structural power dynamics that are at play, making dis/ability a result of individual failure rather than systemic inequality. By using the term EBLAD, an attempt is made at acknowledging a student's full linguistic potential as well as emphasizing the imposing nature of labeling and categorizing children.

(2) IEP stands for individual education plan. According to the U.S. Department of Education, 'Each public school child who receives special education and related services must have an Individualized Education Program (IEP). Each IEP must be designed for one student and must be a truly *individualized* document. The IEP creates an opportunity for teachers, parents, school administrators, related services personnel, and students (when appropriate) to work together to improve educational results for children with disabilities. The IEP is the cornerstone of a quality education for each child with a disability' (Kupper, 2000: 1).

References

Alonso, L. and Villa, L. (2020) Latinxs' bilingualism at work in the US: Profit for whom? *Language, Culture and Society* 2 (1), 37–65. https://doi.org/10.1075/lcs.19013.alo

Bak, T.H., Nissan, J.J., Allerhand, M.M. and Deary, I.J. (2014) Does bilingualism influence cognitive aging? *Annals of Neurology* 75 (6), 959–963. https://doi.org/10.1002/ana.24158

Becerra, D. (2016) Anti-immigration policies and fear of deportation: A human rights issue. *Journal of Human Rights and Social Work* 1 (3), 109–119. https://doi.org/10.1007/s41134-016-0018-8

Bialystok, E. and Werker, J.F. (2017) The systematic effects of bilingualism on children's development. *Developmental Science* 20 (1), e12535. https://doi.org/10.1111/desc.12535

Brooke-Garza, E. (2015) Two-way bilingual education and Latino students. *Educational Leadership and Administration: Teaching and Program Development* 26, 75–85.

Cartledge, G., Kea, C.D., Watson, M. and Oif, A. (2016) Special education disproportion-
ality: A review of response to intervention and culturally relevant pedagogy. *Multiple
Voices for Ethnically Diverse Exceptional Learners* 16 (1), 29–49. https://doi.org/10.5
555/2158-396X.16.1.29

Cheatham, G.A. and Barnett, J.E.H. (2016) Overcoming common misunderstandings
about students with disabilities who are English language learners. *Intervention in
School and Clinic* 53 (1), 58–63. https://doi.org/10.1177/1053451216644819

Duff, P.A. (2015) Transnationalism, multilingualism, and identity. *Annual Review of
Applied Linguistics* 35, 57–80. https://doi.org/10.1017/S026719051400018X

Family Guide to Special Education Services for School-Age Children – A Shared Path
to Success (2014) New York City Department of Education. See https://docplayer.
net/1539776-A-shared-path-to-success.html

Fernandez, N. and Inserra, A. (2013) Disproportionate classification of ESL students in
U.S. special education. *The Electronic Journal for English as a Second Language* 17
(2), 1–11. http://www.tesl-ej.org/wordpress/issues/volume17/ej66/ej66a1/

Gage, N.A., Lierheimer, K.S. and Goran, L.G. (2012) Characteristics of students with
high-incidence disabilities broadly defined. *Journal of Disability Policy Studies* 23 (3),
168–178. https://doi.org/10.1177/1044207311425385

Gallo, S. and Hornberger, N. (2017) Immigration policy as family language policy: Mexican immigrant children and families in search of biliteracy. *International Journal of
Bilingualism* 23 (3), 757–770. https://doi.org/10.1177/1367006916684908

Hirsch, T. and Lee, J.S. (2018) Understanding the complexities of transnational family
language policy. *Journal of Multilingual and Multicultural Development* 39 (10),
882–894. https://doi.org/10.1080/01434632.2018.1454454

Hua, Z. and Wei, L. (2016) Transnational experience, aspiration and family language
policy. *Journal of Multilingual and Multicultural Development* 37 (7), 655–666. https
://doi.org/10.1080/01434632.2015.1127928

Individuals with Disabilities Education Improvement Act of 2004 (PL 108-446) (2004) See
https://www.congress.gov/bill/108th-congress/house-bill/1350 (accessed 17 February
2016).

Kangas, S.E.N. (2014) When special education trumps ESL: An investigation of service
delivery for ELLs with disabilities. *Critical Inquiry in Language Studies* 11 (4), 273–
306. https://doi.org/10.1080/15427587.2014.968070

Kangas, S.E.N. (2017) 'That's where the rubber meets the road': The intersection of special
education and dual language education. *Teachers College Record* 119 (7), 1–36.

Katznelson, N. and Bernstein, K.A. (2017) Rebranding bilingualism: The shifting discourses of language education policy in California's 2016 election. *Linguistics and
Education* 40, 11–26. https://doi.org/10.1016/j.linged.2017.05.002

King, K.A. (2016) Language policy, multilingual encounters, and transnational families.
Journal of Multilingual and Multicultural Development 37 (7), 726–733. https://doi
.org/10.1080/01434632.2015.1127927

Kupper, L. (ed.) (2000) *A Guide to the Individualized Education Program*. U.S. Department of Education. See https://eric.ed.gov/?id=ED444279 (accessed 14 January 2021).

Kurth, J.A., Morningstar, M.E. and Kozleski, E.B. (2014) The persistence of highly
restrictive special education placements for students with low-incidence disabilities.
Research and Practice for Persons with Severe Disabilities 39 (3), 227–239. https://doi
.org/10.1177/1540796914555580

Lahaie, C., Hayes, J.A., Piper, T.M. and Heymann, J. (2009) Work and family divided
across borders: The impact of parental migration on Mexican children in transnational families. *Community, Work & Family* 12 (3), 299–312. https://doi.org/10.1080
/13668800902966315

Lerma, L. and Stewart, M. (2016) Preparing preservice teachers to address the dispropor-
tionality of ELLs in exceptional education programs. *TAPESTRY* 4 (2). http://stars.li
brary.ucf.edu/tapestry/vol4/iss2/2

Mangual Figueroa, A. (2013) Citizenship status and language education policy in an emerging Latino community in the United States. *Language Policy* 12 (4), 333–354. https://doi.org/10.1007/s10993-013-9275-x

Olivos, E.M. and Sobko, S. (2017) Cuentos para dormir: Bedtime stories by deported parents. *Bilingual Review/Revista Bilingüe* 33 (5), Article 5. https://bilingualreview.utsa.edu/index.php/br/article/view/296

Sari, B.T., Chasiotis, A., Vijver, F.J.R. van de and Bender, M. (2018) Parental culture maintenance, bilingualism, identity, and well-being in Javanese, Batak, and Chinese adolescents in Indonesia. *Journal of Multilingual and Multicultural Development* 39 (10), 853–867. https://doi.org/10.1080/01434632.2018.1449847

Schwartz, M. and Palviainen, Å. (2016) Twenty-first-century preschool bilingual education: Facing advantages and challenges in cross-cultural contexts. *International Journal of Bilingual Education and Bilingualism* 19 (6), 603–613. https://doi.org/10.1080/13670050.2016.1184616

Subtirelu, N.C. (2017) Raciolinguistic ideology and Spanish-English bilingualism on the US labor market: An analysis of online job advertisements. *Language in Society* 46 (4), 477–505. https://doi.org/10.1017/S0047404517000379

Vázquez, A.M., Guzmán, N.P.T. and Mora-Pablo, I. (2018) 'I was lucky to be a bilingual kid, and that makes me who I am': The role of transnationalism in identity issues. *International Journal of Bilingual Education and Bilingualism* 0 (0), 1–15. https://doi.org/10.1080/13670050.2018.1510893

8 Teacher? Student? Both: Mothers as Language Brokers

Bilingualism within these families is understood in complex ways: on the one hand, it is a tool that helps their children prepare for the future; but, on the other hand, it is a barrier to their children's disability remediation. One of the ways in which the mothers deal with this contradiction is by letting the schools focus on remedying the disability, while making language learning the focus of the home.

The Linguistic Practices and Perceptions of Mothers of Emergent Bilinguals Labeled as Dis/abled (MoEBLADs)

For mothers, the disconnect between the home language (for Latinx families that language is often Spanish) and the school language (English) is one of the primary ways in which they feel limited in their capacity to support their children academically (Ryan *et al.*, 2010; Surrain, 2018). Ijalba (2015b) notes that mothers have linguistic needs that are also tied to their cultural needs. Whereas cultural needs get their fair share of attention, linguistic needs are often relegated to the recommendations' sections. A parent who does not feel capable of helping their child complete their homework is not going to feel confident addressing an English-speaking staff in order to advocate for the academic and social development needs of their child (Figueroa, 2011). Although many suggest the use of translators as a way to create entry for mothers, Aceves (2014) points out that translation services are not systematically offered. When they are offered, they are often unreliable and subject to bias, which further hinders parental participation (Aceves, 2014). Additionally, the use of interpreters and translators alone has not been shown to increase parental engagement during individual education plan (IEP) meetings or other pertinent meetings (Aceves, 2014; Cohen, 2013; Ijalba, 2015; Wolfe & Durán, 2013).

Most literature around Latinx parental engagement is inconsistent in its presentation of language as a stand-alone issue (Gaetano, 2007; Goodall, 2018; Jeynes, 2018; Ryan *et al.*, 2010). Whereas some leave out language completely, others include language in reference to cultural beliefs (i.e. bien educado [well educated], añoñar [spoil]), but most studies overwhelmingly frame language not as a cultural difference that both parties must traverse, but rather as a hurdle that schools must overcome in order to ensure parental engagement (Rodriguez *et al.*, 2013; Wolfe & Durán, 2013). Others associate language in relation to the school climate and social issues like policing (Landa *et al.*, 2020; McWayne *et al.*, 2016; Mundt *et al.*, 2015; Paredes Scribner & Fernández, 2017). The linguistic ideology behind this perspective values English above all other languages and faults the mothers for their inability to speak English rather than schools for their inability to communicate in the mothers' home language(s). As such, a parent's lack of English is a deficit that must be remedied by the schools by providing translators and translated materials (Rodriguez *et al.*, 2013). Others present a parent's inability to communicate in English as a burden upon the schools that they are required/mandated to mitigate (Montelongo, 2015). The most explicit framing of mothers who are speakers of languages other than English as deficient came from Wolfe and Durán (2013: 9) who stated that '"language barrier" refers to situations in which limited English proficiency hinders effective communication'. By presenting a language barrier as a parent problem/failing rather than a systemic one (i.e. '"language barrier" refers to situations in which [speakers do not share a common language which] hinders effective communication' (Wolfe & Durán, 2013: 9) inherently places mothers in a negative light, which puts them at fault for hindering effective communication. For many, the most immediate way to resolve this tension is to provide mothers with interpreters.

While interpreters are presented as the most effective and efficient way to open communication between the school and the home, this suggestion does not take into account that mothers may not feel comfortable discussing their child through an interpreter if the person is not a trusted person (Cohen, 2013; Ijalba, 2015; Wolfe & Durán, 2013). Additionally, school-based interpreters tend to be bilingual staff or teachers who are not typically trained as interpreters and may not be as informed about the needs of the particular child, so rather than translate word for word they may offer a summary (Reiman *et al.*, 2010). Alternatively, someone who translates word for word may not convey the gravity or intensity of the situation – and may not advocate for the parent as needed (Reiman *et al.*, 2010). Many mothers do not have access to an interpreter and those who do report feelings of dissatisfaction, particularly because they feel they experience unequal treatment with preference given to the professionals rather than the mothers (Reiman *et al.*, 2010; Wolfe & Durán, 2013). Lastly, the majority of references to translators, interpreters and translated materials are overwhelmingly one-sided, focusing on what the school could give the mothers, rather than what the school could gather from the mothers (Montelongo, 2015; Rodriguez *et al.*, 2013; Wolfe & Durán, 2013). This focus on school-to-parent communication emphasizes the need to make information accessible for the sake of the school meeting compliance, rather than creating a collaborative space in which both parties can discuss the student's needs, the family's goals and how both the school and the family can support each other.

A great deal of the literature devoted to MoEBLADs is not written for them or with them, but rather about them. As a result, these mothers are often the victims of the same deficit-based lens with which their children are viewed. Although researchers aim to change the minds of teachers and other stakeholders so that they view mothers as a resource, the continued use of deficit-based language (i.e. lack of..., in need..., requiring..., etc.) continues to subversively uphold the same values they are attempting to counter. For example, in Montelongo's (2015) article focused on Latino parents perceptions of IEP meetings, the term 'accommodate' was used to address the ways schools could support the families; this terminology was used by an administrator quoted in Rodriguez *et al.*'s (2013) article around strategies for increasing engagement among Latino parents of students with disabilities. The literature does a good job of presenting ways that schools can ensure that information reaches the families. However, by not suggesting that schools ask mothers about their own needs and the needs of their children, the literature paints mothers as empty vessels needing to be filled without taking account of the many resources they have to offer.

Language Learning at Home

While the mothers side with the teachers with regard to language learning at school, they don't completely give up the hope that their children will be bilingual. Instead, they find ways to support their children's home language development outside of school. They take on the role of language teachers themselves, they enroll their children in Spanish language catechism and they make efforts to learn English themselves, as a way both to expand their own linguistic repertoires and to model multilingual language learning.

'Yo le enseño': Home language education at home

One way that mother's support their children's bilingual development outside of school is by engaging them in direct Spanish instruction in the home, as Carlota previously indicated and asserts here once again: 'en casa, yo le enseño a leer, a escribir [en español]' [at home, I teach him to read, to write [in Spanish]]. Both Paty and Ana repeat that they are teaching their children Spanish at home. Paty says: 'Está aprendiendo el español, parte por aquí de la casa, y por la hermana. Pero él por parte de la escuela, no'. [He's learning Spanish, in part here at home, and through his sister. But on the part of the school, no]. And Ana repeats that even though the home might not be able to teach her child to read and write

Spanish, it definitely helps her learn Spanish: 'Pues el español tal vez no lo pueda escribir o tanto, pero sí lo podrá aprender lo que pueda en la casa'. [Well, Spanish, she may not be able to write it or so, but she can learn what she can at home].

Besides the home, mothers, interested in their children's development of Spanish, and especially their literacy development, see the Catholic Church and catechism instruction as a viable place where their children are learning to read and write Spanish. This is the subject of the next section.

'El catecismo en español': Teaching Spanish through God

Like other immigrants who value home language maintenance (Carreira & Rodriguez, 2011; Kim, 2011; Zhang & Slaughter-Defoe, 2009), these mother made strides to ensure their children would develop as bilingual individuals. As such, even though these mothers' desires to educate their children bilingually were subverted at school, many of the mothers ensured their children would learn to be biliterate not by enrolling them in language heritage programs as is common among Asian and Eastern European communities (Avineri, 2012; Li & Wen, 2015) but rather by enrolling them in Spanish catechism in the local Catholic Church. Rosa's statement is indicative of their thinking:

> Como aquí viene los domingos también el catecismo en español, entonces, ahí también. Ya va aprendiendo más. Y con la hermana, pues. [...] sí [, yo elegí que le dieran catecismo en español]. [...] Para ayudarle en las tareas. Porque yo en inglés, no sé absolutamente nada, entonces, yo no podría ayudarlo.
>
> [As since he comes here Sunday also the catechism in Spanish, then, there too. He is already learning more. And with the sister, well [...] yes [, I chose that be given a catechism in Spanish] [...] To help him in on the homework. Because I in English, I know absolutely nothing, then, I could not help him].

The mothers want to make sure that their children develop their Spanish. Thus, they teach them at home and find other opportunities for them to learn. Catechism classes provide them with such opportunities. But mothers are also engaged in trying to learn English so that they can help their children.

'Uno tiene que aprender el idioma': Mothers' efforts to learn English

While Rosa states that 'en inglés, no sé absolutamente nada' [in English, I know absolutely nothing], this debilitating monolingualism was not due to lack of desire or effort on the part of the mothers. The mothers were aware, even 'antes de venir' [before coming], that 'en este país el ingles' [in this country English] is critical. Ana says:

Porque pues el español lo hablo pero yo estoy aquí en este país el inglés, entiendo algunas palabras pero no diremos --. [...] por mi parte me hace falta mucho el inglés para enseñarles a mis niños y para entenderlos, si está bien en la tarea. Es muy importante saberlo, el idioma. [...] Estoy aprendiendo apenas, a hablarlo un poco.

[*Because I speak Spanish but I am here in this country English, I understand some words but we will not say – [...] for my part I need a lot of English to teach my children and to understand them, if they're doing well in their homework. It is very important to know, the language. [...] I'm just learning, to talk a little.*]

Paty is learning basic English through cassettes that her boss gave her:

[Antes de venir a los Estados Unidos] yo decía, 'uno tiene que aprender el idioma', pero me decía mi esposo, 'pero también ahí hay muchas personas que hablan español. [...] [Ya aquí, mi jefa me dijo] 'Te voy a comprar unos cassettes en inglés para que aprendas'. Le digo 'bueno'. Y sí, los compró, y aprendí, o sea, pero lo básico, lo que yo sentí que puedo para mi trabajo.

[*Before coming to the United States] I said, 'you have to learn the language', but my husband used to tell me, 'but there are also many people who speak Spanish. [...] [Once here, my boss said] 'I'm going to buy you some cassettes in English so you can learn'. I say 'good'. And yes, she bought them, and I learned, well, but the basics, what I felt I could for my job.*]

For María, the lack of English is embarrassing, and she was terrified that people would not understand her:

Yo sentía miedo de no poder que la gente me entendiera o comunicarme con las personas. Ese era mi miedo cuando llegué a este país, y lo sigue siendo porque pues no [risas], no hablo el inglés.

[*I was afraid of not being able to understand or communicate with people. That was my fear when I arrived in this country, and it still is because I do not [laughs], I do not speak English.*]

The mothers' efforts to learn English have often been met with serious challenges. The first challenge has been finding the means with which to pay for English classes, as María states:

Hay escuelas, pero uno tiene que pagar la escuela y mi esposo no creo que me daría dinero para pagar la escuela, [... Pero], si yo estuviera en una escuela, no hay como interrupciones, seria todo el año, eso me ayudaría mucho para poderlo aprender [ingles].

[There are schools, but one has to pay for school and my husband I don't think he would give me money to pay for school, [... But], if I were in a school, there are no interruptions, it would be all year, that would help me a lot so that I could learn [English].]

Even with limited financial resources, the mothers have sought out free or low-cost opportunities to learn English by listening to 'cassettes en ingles' [English tapes] and by attending English as a second language (ESL) classes in their children's 'escuelita' [school] and at the local 'iglesia' [church]. Ana goes to 'la escuelita'. She says:

Estoy tratando de aprender el inglés, pero ahí, más o menos. [...] Voy a la escuelita, ahí lo que la maestra enseña es lo básico, para una conversación, preguntas o una plática. Una plática corta.

[I'm trying to learn English, but there, more or less. [...] I go to the school, there what the teacher teaches is the basics, for a conversation, questions or a chat. A brief chat.]

Paty goes to the church:

Sí. Bueno, he tratado de aprender. Hace un año, aquí en la iglesia de [REDACTED], dieron un curso de inglés, bueno el año. Pero como mi esposo no trabajaba en la noche, yo lo agarré. Y pues sí, ahí sentí que yo podía hacer a veces–, como ellos dicen, los verbos. El maestro fue un chino. Muy buen maestro. [...] Eran martes y jueves. Esos dos días. Pero eran tres horas. A mí sí me gustaba mucho.

[Yes. Well, I've tried to learn. A year ago, here at the church of [REDACTED], they gave an English course, well a year. But since my husband did not work at night, I took it. And yes, there I felt that I could do sometimes – as they say, the verbs. The teacher was Chinese. Very good teacher. [...] It was Tuesday and Thursday. Those two days. But it was three hours. I did like it a lot.]

And María seeks out free courses, even though English is 'extenso' and she can't really learn it well:

Cuando hay cursos gratis es cuando yo aprovecho, pero, le digo –no es, como que el tiempo es muy corto y no puedo aprender, es mucho, el inglés es extenso y no puedo aprenderlo bien.

[When there are free courses, it's when I take advantage, but, I say – it's not like, the time is too short and I can not learn, it's a lot, English is extensive and I can not learn it well.]

The most common issue was that the free courses were offered at inconvenient times. For Ana, classes were offered at a time when she couldn't leave her son alone:

El año pasado hubo clases [de ingles] también, pero yo no podía ir porque el niño no había con quien dejarlo.

[Last year there were [English] classes too, but I could not go because I had no one to leave the little boy with.]

Paty narrates how she was learning a lot in classes, but the more advanced class was intensive and offered at a time when her husband worked:

Yo sentía que sí podía aprender ahí. Bueno, estaba aprendiendo muchas cosas. Pero este año, después me dijeron que acabó y que si quería seguir y yo le dije que sí. Entonces, cuando empezó la clase, me hablaron, pero mi esposo ya trabajaba. Y son tres horas. Entrábamos a las seis y salíamos a las nueve.

[I felt that I could learn there. Well, I was learning many things. But this year, they told me that it was over and that if I wanted to continue and I said yes. Then, when the class started, they talked to me, but my husband was already working. And it's three hours. We would get in at six and leave at nine.]

Classes were offered either during the day when some mothers worked or had to tend to young children or in the evenings when they needed to care for their families. Even if a mother 'sabía que [ella] podría aprender' [knew that [she] could learn] in these programs, finding 'con quien dejarlo' was enough to keep them from going, as Paty says:

Porque no puedo dejar los niños tres horas. No nos admiten con niños en la escuela. [...] porque dicen que distraen. A veces como nosotras, como mamás no nos podemos concentrar. Porque ustedes están mirando al hijo que no toque, que no haga esto.

[Because I cannot leave the children for three hours. They do not admit us with children in school. [...] because they say they distract. Sometimes like us, like moms we cannot concentrate. Because you are watching your child to not touch, to not do this.]

Paty's class was composed of 25 women and 4 or 5 men. She was told by a male teacher not to bring children to the class because when the children come, the parents are distracted and unable to concentrate.

Still, even when time was not an issue, good-quality English instruction was hard to come by. As a stay-at-home mom to school-age children, María had the ability to attend English classes during the day. However, the courses that were available only 'enseñ[an] lo básico' [teach the basics]:

Sí, he ido a clases en la escuela de mi niño, pero sólo son por dos meses y eso no, o sea, tal vez te enseñen lo básico como los números, el abecedario y eso. Pero así como para entablar una conversación, no. [...] Porque sólo el curso duran dos meses, entonces es muy poco tiempo para poder aprender muchas cosas.

[*Yes, I have been to classes in my child's school, but they are only for two months and that is not, that is, maybe they teach you the basics like numbers, the alphabet and that. But well enough to start a conversation, no. [...] Because the course only lasts two months, then it is very little time to learn many things.*]

Similarly, when I met Carlota she was in her second year of enrollment at a weekly ESL class in the local community center. However, classes were irregular and often cancelled due to low participation levels. Frequently, she was the only one to show up to class and the volunteer teachers – as she described, two blonde, monolingual English, stay-at-home moms – would simply cancel the class rather than 'waste' the lesson. Unfortunately, many people, including their children, continue to believe that these mothers are monolingual by choice, 'creerán que yo no quiero aprender el idioma' [they may think that I don't want to learn the language], rather than by circumstance. María expresses how she really would like to learn English to help her children. Her inability to speak English is a source of great frustration for her:

Me siento mal porque creerán que yo no quiero aprender el idioma, pero a mí me gustaría aprender el idioma. Porque así también puedo ayudar a mis hijos, con las tareas. Sobre todo, con la lectura y con escritura.

[*I feel bad because they will believe that I do not want to learn the language, but I would like to learn the language. Because I can also help my children with homework. Above all, with reading and writing.*]

Paty's son, Dan, blamed her for not speaking English and for not being able to help him with his homework. This made her very uncomfortable:

[Dan me decía] 'Tú tienes la culpa, porque yo no sé por qué tú no hablas el inglés. Tienes muchos años porque tú no eres una baby. Tienes muchos años mami y tú no sabes hablar el inglés'. [...] Porque dice que yo no pudiera hablar el inglés. El que yo no lo pueda ayudar en la tarea, porque como viene en inglés [...] Él me reprochaba. Y después yo me sentía más incómoda, más–, muy fuera de aquí.

[[Dan was saying to me] 'You are to blame, because I do not know why you do not speak English, you are many years old because you are not a baby, you are very old mom and you can not speak English'. [...] Because he says that I could not speak English. That I can not help him on the homework, because it comes in English [...] He shamed me. And then I felt more uncomfortable, more–, very out of place.]

It is possible that the mothers' own limitations in English contribute to their desire for their children to acquire English before Spanish – or better than Spanish. It is a way for them to spare their children the frustrations and social paralysis: 'me siento tan incómoda, tan inútil' [I feel so uncomfortable, so useless] that they have experienced as a result of not being able to fully communicate in English.

The children intrinsically perceive and understand that Spanish monolingualism presents a limitation in the mothers' lives. They try to remedy this by offering their mothers English lessons at home. This experience of children as English teachers is discussed in the next section.

'Es así en inglés ¿okay?': Reciprocal learning

While these mothers struggle to find appropriate learning environments outside of their homes, they are resourceful and find ways to make language learning at home reciprocal. Here, Nancy reveals that teaching goes both ways in her family. She teaches her son things when they are in the kitchen or in the store, and sometimes 'en vez de yo enseñarle, ellos me enseñan' [instead of I teaching them, they teach me].

Bueno, todo depende, ¿verdad? de qué cosas. Si es en la cocina, ya le digo, le pido algo, pero si él no sabe, voy y le enseño. Si es en la tienda, muchas veces, en vez de yo enseñarle, ellos me enseñan, porque hay cosas que están en inglés y yo no las entiendo. Y, '¿Qué es esto?', o, 'Estoy buscando esto'. Y como es que–, 'No lo encuentro'. Si no lo conozco, en vez de yo ayudarles, me ayuda él.

[Well, everything depends, right? On what things. If it's in the kitchen, I tell him, I ask him for something, but if he does not know, I go and show him. If it is in the store, many times, instead of teaching them, they teach me, because there are things that are in English and I do not understand them. And, 'What is this?', Or, 'I'm looking for this'. And how is that–, 'I cannot find it'. If I do not know it, instead of helping them, he helps me.]

Limited English proficiency was a cause of great distress for these mothers because it compounded many of their pre-existing marginalizations as was evidenced by their pursuit of ESL classes for themselves. Thus, the fact that their children speak English, even if they are 'disabled', is of great help to them. In those instances, the children are not disabled; the mothers are disabled. The role of teacher and student is reversed. The fact that the mothers can identify ways in which they learn from their children supports the mothers' perceptions of disability as socially constructed. Nancy identifies that her child is capable not only of learning but also of learning in Spanish: 'en la cocina... voy y le enseño' [in the kitchen ... I go and I show him]. Likewise, he is also capable of teaching her, 'me ayuda él' [he helps me]; flexing his bilingual muscle.

Paty reveals how her son has become her English teacher:

A veces diciéndole que: 'Mira, esto se llama así'. Yo no sé, a veces le digo: '¿Cómo es en inglés?', le digo: 'Anótamelo', a veces ahí en esa pizarra. Luego me dice: 'Mira, mamá, en español tú dices que se llama así, y es así en inglés, ¿okay?', y es una forma. No sé, que a veces siento que sea para los dos, tanto él como yo, que yo sepa cómo se dice esa cosa en inglés y él cómo se diga en español.

[*Sometimes telling him: 'Look, this is called that'. I do not know, sometimes I say: 'How is it in English?', I say: 'Write it down', sometimes there on that blackboard. Then he says: 'Look, mom, in Spanish you say it's called this, and it's like this in English, okay?', And it's a way. I do not know, that sometimes I feel it is for both of us, both he and I, that I know how to say that thing in English and he [knows] how it is said in Spanish.*]

Here, Paty shows that the children also understand that this is a reciprocal relationship. The mothers teach the children when they 'dice que se llama así' [say it's called this] in Spanish, and the children teach the mothers when they say that 'es así en ingles' [it's like this in English].

Conclusion

In Chapter 7, we learned that the mothers value bilingualism, but are much more concerned with ensuring their children's academic success in the now, centering English, than securing their future, particularly when the future, especially their ability to live in the United States, is ambiguous. Part of this is influenced by their perception of disability as something that can be remedied or remediated, but it is also heavily influenced by the information they receive from teachers and other educational professionals. In this chapter, we begin to understand how the mothers' inability to grasp English leaves them in a position where they have to trust what the teachers are saying even if the teachers are misinformed. This misinformation is often so convincing that the mothers themselves often miss the fact that their children are already bilingual based on the linguistic practices they exhibit at home and at school. This is a perfect example of the ways in which these mothers continue to make choices that are in the best interest of their children, even when they are not in their own best interest. Still, in this chapter, we see the ways in which they are subverting the school while also trying to secure bilingualism not only for their children but also for themselves.

In many ways this teaching of Spanish at home creates an opportunity for the mothers to be highly engaged in their children's academic development. As such, the one area where many of them feel in charge is *in* Spanish. Spanish is the one part of their child's life where they, not the school, are the authority: 'español es la lengua maternal' [Spanish is the mother tongue], 'el inglés es el lenguaje de este país' [English is the language of this country], 'yo le enseño español' [I will teach him Spanish], 'yo le puedo enseñar' [I can teach him], 'yo le ayudo' [I can help]. When students are placed in bilingual programs, the mothers feel empowered because they feel they can support their children, assess what they know and what they are being taught in school. However, when schools remove children from bilingual settings and place them in monolingual settings, they take away some of the mother's power and authority. Yet, these mothers find their roles as mothers to be so central to their identity and to their child's advancement that they recoup some of this power by engaging in other parts of their children's lives.

References

Aceves, T.C. (2014) Supporting Latino families in special education through community agency–school partnerships. *Multicultural Education* 21 (3/4), 45–50.

Avineri, N.R. (2012) *Heritage Language Socialization Practices in Secular Yiddish Educational Contexts: The Creation of a Metalinguistic Community*. Los Angeles, CA: University of California, Los Angeles. https://escholarship.org/uc/item/9f50n171

Carreira, M.M. and Rodriguez, R.M. (2011) Filling the void: Community Spanish language programs in Los Angeles serving to preserve the language. *Heritage Language Journal* 8 (2), 1–16.

Cohen, S.R. (2013) Advocacy for the 'Abandonados': Harnessing cultural beliefs for Latino families and their children with intellectual disabilities. *Journal of Policy and Practice in Intellectual Disabilities* 10 (1), 71–78. https://doi.org/10.1111/jppi.12021

Figueroa, A.M. (2011) Citizenship and education in the homework completion routine. *Anthropology & Education Quarterly* 42 (3), 263–280. https://doi.org/10.1111/j.1548 -1492.2011.01131.x

Gaetano, Y.D. (2007) The role of culture in engaging Latino parents' involvement in school. *Urban Education* 42 (2), 145–162. https://doi.org/10.1177/0042085906296536

Goodall, J. (2018) Leading for parental engagement: Working towards partnership. *School Leadership & Management* 38 (2), 143–146. https://doi.org/10.1080/13632434.2018 .1459022

Ijalba, E. (2015) Understanding parental engagement in Hispanic mothers of children with autism spectrum disorder: Application of a process-model of cultural competence. *Journal of Multilingual Education Research* 6 (1), 6. http://fordham.bepress.com/jme r/vol6/iss1/6

Jeynes, W.H. (2018) A practical model for school leaders to encourage parental involvement and parental engagement. *School Leadership & Management* 38 (2), 147–163. https://doi.org/10.1080/13632434.2018.1434767

Kim, J. (2011) Korean immigrant mothers' perspectives: The meanings of a Korean heritage language school for their children's American early schooling experiences.

Early Childhood Education Journal 39 (2), 133–141. https://doi.org/10.1007/s10643 -011-0453-1

Landa, L., Rangel, V.S. and Coulson, H. (2020) Parent engagement at a primarily Latinx high school campus. *Journal of Latinos and Education* 0 (0), 1–17. https://doi.org/10 .1080/15348431.2020.1794875

Li, G. and Wen, K. (2015) East Asian heritage language education for a plurilingual reality in the United States: Practices, potholes, and possibilities. *International Multilingual Research Journal* 9 (4), 274–290. https://doi.org/10.1080/19313152.2015.1086623

McWayne, C.M., Melzi, G., Limlingan, M.C. and Schick, A. (2016) Ecocultural patterns of family engagement among low-income Latino families of preschool children. *Developmental Psychology* 52 (7), 1088–1102. https://doi.org/10.1037/a0040343

Montelongo, A. (2015) Latino parents' perceptions of IEP meetings. *McNair Scholars Journal* 16, 109–130.

Mundt, K., Gregory, A., Melzi, G. and McWayne, C.M. (2015) The influence of ethnic match on Latino school-based family engagement. *Hispanic Journal of Behavioral Sciences* 37 (2), 170–185. https://doi.org/10.1177/0739986315570287

Paredes Scribner, S.M. and Fernández, E. (2017) Organizational politics of parental engagement: The intersections of school reform, anti-immigration policies, and Latinx parent organizing. *Educational Policy* 31 (6), 895–920. https://doi.org/10.1177 /0895904817719527

Reiman, J.W., Beck, L., Coppola, T. and Engiles, A. (2010) *Parents' Experiences with the IEP Process: Considerations for Improving Practice.* Eugene, OR: Center for Appropriate Dispute Resolution in Special Education (CADRE). http://eric.ed.gov/ ?id=ED512611

Rodriguez, R.J., Blatz, E T. and Elbaum, B. (2013) Strategies to involve families of Latino students with disabilities: When parent initiative is not enough. *Intervention in School and Clinic*, 49 (5), 263–270. https://doi.org/10.1177/1053451213513956

Ryan, C.S., Casas, J.F., Kelly-Vance, L., Ryalls, B.O. and Nero, C. (2010) Parent involvement and views of school success: The role of parents' Latino and White American cultural orientations. *Psychology in the Schools* 47 (4), 391–405. https://doi.org/10 .1002/pits.20477

Surrain, S. (2018) 'Spanish at home, English at school': How perceptions of bilingualism shape family language policies among Spanish-speaking parents of preschoolers. *International Journal of Bilingual Education and Bilingualism* 0 (0), 1–15. https://doi .org/10.1080/13670050.2018.1546666

Wolfe, K. and Durán, L.K. (2013) Culturally and linguistically diverse parents' perceptions of the IEP process. *Multiple Voices for Ethnically Diverse Exceptional Learners* 13 (2), 4–18.

Zhang, D. and Slaughter-Defoe, D.T. (2009) Language attitudes and heritage language maintenance among Chinese immigrant families in the USA. *Language, Culture and Curriculum* 22 (2), 77–93. https://doi.org/10.1080/07908310902935940

9 Bending Roles: Resisting Exclusion, Creating Paths for Engagement

While there are many ways in which the capacity of a mother of an emergent bilingual labeled as dis/abled (MoEBLAD) to engage in her child's academic development is stunted by the child's disability labels and monolingual placement, these mothers still make great efforts to support their children's learning. However, these efforts are not often recognized because they do not fit into the dominant culture's definition of academic involvement. The testimonios of the mothers in this study serve as a counter-narrative to what the literature portrays as lack of parental involvement. This chapter focuses on how the mothers in the study viewed and enacted their mothering role. In general, they followed one principle: 'primero están mis hijos' [my children come first].

Involvement of the Mothers with Their Children's Academic Development

Most of the academic literature frames MoEBLADs as disengaged, for a variety of reasons. However, that is not at all reflective of their actual mothering practices. On the contrary, like other immigrant parents, these mothers are extremely engaged, although not in traditional ways or in ways that are reflective of the schools' definition of parental academic engagement (Ishimaru *et al.*, 2016). There are two major ways that mothers exhibited engagement: (1) teaching their children and supporting them in their learning; and (2) outsourcing support for their children, whether engaging their other children, paying for a tutor or using technology.

'Trato, en lo que puedo...': Mothers as teachers

The mothers constantly reveal their support. In their discourse, the words 'apoyar' [to support], 'ayudar' [to help] and 'enseñar' [to teach] are common. María and Rosario reveal the type of support they give their children: they explain things and help them with everything especially with homework. Rosario also takes her daughter to the library.

Sí, cuando–, trato, en lo que puedo, ayudar en la tarea. Bueno, cuando no trabajaba, la llevaba yo a la librería.

[*Yes, when–, I try, in what I can, to help with the homework. Well, when I did not work, I would take her to the [library].*]

Paty rewards her son's efforts 'cuando él está bien, en las calificaciones' [when he's doing well, in his grades] by taking him to 'la tienda de libros' [the bookstore] on the weekends.

Sí. Yo le–, a él, ahora decir, cuando él está bien, en sus calificaciones, 'Mamá, tengo ganas de este libro'. 'Okay, este fin de semana nos vamos a la tienda de los libros, y escojan sus libros. [...] Sí, a veces yo les digo a ellos, 'Tienen derecho a dos libros. Un libro que yo piense que sea conveniente, y un libro que ustedes–, sea para ustedes'. Porque a veces él, no más le gustan puros dibujitos.

[*Yes. I told him, lets say, when he's doing well, in his grades, 'Mom, I'm looking forward to this book'. 'Okay, this weekend we're going to the book store, and you can pick your books. [...] Yes, sometimes I say to them, 'You have the right to two books. A book that I think is convenient, and a book that you–, that's for you'. Because sometimes he only likes [books with] just little drawings.*]

A monumental task in which the mothers are engaged is revealed by María who recounts that she had to teach her child how to bathe. And she is proud of her success – now 'él solo se baña' [he bathes by himself].

Yo siempre estoy apoyándolo en todo. Trato de que él lea más, ponga más interés en sus lecturas, le hago preguntas sobre las lecturas, para que él también vaya como [...] En cuestión de las escuelas, trato de apoyarlo lo más que yo puedo. Explicándole las cosas, la tarea y eso. En cuestión de la casa, si me costó trabajo a enseñarle cómo bañarse. Porque yo antes lo bañaba. Ahora ya él solo se baña.

[*I'm always supporting him in everything. I try to make him read more, put more interest in his readings, I ask him questions about the readings, so that he too goes like [...] In the matter of schools, I try to support him as much as I can. Explaining things, the homework and that. In regards to the house, yeah it was hard work teaching him how to bathe. Because I used to bathe him before. Now he bathes by himself.*]

The mothers indicated the non-traditional ways in which they support their children's academic development: they buy them books, take them to the library and teach them basic life skills like bathing and grocery shopping. However, they understood that the support their child needed often extended beyond what they could offer. In the next section, one can see the ways in which mothers ameliorated these situations by engaging their other children.

'Mi hija me ayuda': Mothering by proxy

While the mothers want to help, they also acknowledge that because the majority of their children's schoolwork is in English they 'no puedo ayudarlo' [cannot help [them]. In the following quote, Rosa highlights another way in which mothers support their children's academic development: turning to their other children. These children's support of their parents often correlates to their age; younger children help with home translations particularly of homework and correspondence. Rosa's 10 year old helps translate the homework:

[La tarea] se me hace bien difícil. A veces, no puedo ayudarle. Yo algo entiendo, pero a veces, no puedo ayudarlo. Y él dice, 'Mami ayúdame'. 'Pero, no entiendo. ¿Cómo hago?'. Entonces, yo a veces a mi hija, la de 10 años, le pido ayuda que–. [ella traduzca]

[[The homework] is very difficult for me. Sometimes, I cannot help him. I understand something, but sometimes, I cannot help him. And he says, 'Mommy help me'. 'But I do not understand. What can I do?' So, sometimes I ask my daughter, the 10-year-old, for help – she [translates]]

Sara's daughter helps her child do homework:

No [ayudo] mucho. [...] Porque no lo entiendo [porque son todas en inglés.] [...] Sí, mi hija es quien más lo ayuda [en las tareas]. Sí, porque yo–, aunque quisiera, no mucho le entiendo. Muy poquito.

[I do not [help] much [...] Because I do not understand [because they are all in English.] [...] Yes, my daughter is the one who helps [with homework] the most. Yes, because I– even if I wanted to, I do not understand much. Very little.]

and Carmela's son helps when absolutely necessary, when Carmela 'really can not':

Y cuando no puedo en algo, les pedimos ayuda a sus hermanos. Solamente cuando realmente no puedo, o salgo tarde del trabajo, bueno, dejo que alguien más lo ayude, pero por lo regular, trato de estar yo ahí con él.

[And when I can not do something, we ask their brothers for help. Only when I really can not, or I'm late from work, well, I let someone else help, but usually, I try to be there with him.]

Older children are sometimes tasked with attending individual education plan (IEP) meetings and offering translations in that setting, in addition to the home. Sara, for example, brings her other daughter with her:

> Mi hija va conmigo [...] No. No. [No hay un intérprete oficial de la escuela.] Sí [es mi derecho], pero a veces como que no hay nadie disponible, por cualquier cosa. [...] Pero parece que no es lo mismo, ¿verdad?, como si fueran nosotros mismos.

> [*My daughter goes with me [...] No. No. [There is not an official interpreter from the school.] Yes [it is my right], but sometimes like no one is available, for anything. [...] But it seems that it is not the same, right? as if it were ourselves.*]

Here, Sara explains how she relies on her daughter to go with her to official school meetings because she'd rather be prepared since 'a veces como no hay nadie disponible' [sometimes no one is available] to translate at the school.

Mothers are pushed out of their children's lives not only at home 'por que no lo entiendo' [because I do not understand [the English homework]] but also at school because they (and the schools their children attend) lack the resources necessary to facilitate their participation. Sara recognizes that having her daughter there as a translator 'no es lo mismo [...] como si fueran nosotros mismos' [not the same [...] as if it were [her]] doing the listening and talking. Nonetheless, this is just another way that mothers make use of all of their resources in order to stay active and engaged in their EBLADs education. Still, mothers did not place the entire onus on their other children, they also sought out external support by way of afterschool programs and hiring tutors, as presented in the next section.

'Yo busco a una persona': Seeking external support

In addition to turning to their other children, many of the mothers relied on outside help in order to ensure their child was academically successful. Ana enrolls her daughter in an afterschool program, PAZ:

> Bueno, a mí me preocupa [que ella este de bajo nivel] y me pongo a pensar, pues yo también ya no la puedo ayudar mucho, porque yo no tengo suficiente estudio, y pues más el inglés pues se necesita aquí, y pues yo no lo sé; yo la ayudo en la que yo puedo. Por eso la dejé en la tarde de PAZ[1] para que ahí por lo menos le ayuden algo en la tarea, el inglés. Y ya si no lo termina, el español yo le enseño en casa.

> [*Well, I'm worried [that she's of low level] and I start to think, because I can not help her too much, because I do not have sufficient education, and because more English is needed here, and well I don't know it; I help her where I can. That's why I left her in the PAZ in the afternoon so that*]

*at least they would help her wsome on the homework, the English. And
if she does not finish it, I teach her the Spanish at home.*]

And many of the mothers, desperate to provide their children with extra
help, even pay for tutors, as María and Paty express:

María: En Matemáticas, yo he buscado una persona para que le de
tutorías, aparte fuera de la escuela, porque tampoco no me gusta
dejarlo en [inglés] Afterschool. Entonces, yo busqué a una persona
que le de tutorías una hora, y veo que mi niño, así, con las tutorías,
mi niño va avanzando. ... Yo pago por eso.

[*In Mathematics, I have looked for a person to tutor him, apart from
school, because I also do not like to leave him in Afterschool. So, I
looked for a person to tutor him for an hour, and I see that my child,
well, with the tutorials, my child is moving forward. ... I pay for
that.*]

Paty: Okay. A [Dan] como yo no le entiendo el inglés, yo busco a una
persona que viene a ayudarlo. Viene una muchacha, le ayuda con la
tarea, le explica con las cosas que él no puede y le pone trabajos,
'Debes de hacerlo así, así y así'. [...] La conocí por mi vecina de allá
arriba, que también la ayuda a su niña con las tareas [...], Entonces,
ella me dijo, 'Yo tengo una muchacha', porque yo le platiqué. Le digo,
'Es que hay cosas que a veces no puedo', me dice, 'Oh, yo conozco
a una muchacha. Y está bien, porque ella sigue estudiando, es el idioma de ellos', le digo, 'Ahora sí me la pasa o me la presta', 'Sí', y así
es como yo conocí a esa muchacha. [...] No [es gratis], yo pago $15
la hora.

[*Okay. For [Dan] since I do not understand English, I look for a
person who comes to help him. A girl comes along, helps him with
homework, explains things to him that he cannot do and gives him
practice, 'You must do it like that, like that'. [...] I met her by my
neighbor up there, who also helped her daughter with her homework,
[...], she told me, 'I have a girl', because I talked to her. I told her,
'There are things that sometimes I cannot do', She says, 'Oh, I know
a girl, and it's fine, because she is still studying, it's their language', I
say, 'Now you have to share her or lend her to me', 'Yes', 'and that's
how I met that girl. [...] No [it's not free], I pay $15 an hour.*]

These supports do not go unnoticed. Paty's son, Dan, for example,
recognizes the support his mother gives him when she employs a tutor or
another person to help him with his homework. He also realizes that she
does this because it is 'something really important for me', even if 'she
has to waste our money':

[*Sometimes, trying to help me, she calls people to help me. [...] Like my cousin, and a lady that goes– a girl that goes to– a teenager that goes to college. [They help] by just telling me [in] easy words I can understand. [My mom calls them] Because sometimes she thinks, or sometimes she knows, that I actually have something [to do] and she calls them to help me. [...] Yes, [when she can't help me, she finds somebody else to help me] because last time we stayed up all night until finishing my math questions. [...] [When my mom calls other people to help me it makes me feel] a little—it says she's nice because she's doing something, even though she has to waste our money, and that's something really important for me.*]

Not only are these mothers using very limited financial resources to ensure that their children are getting the support that they need, but they are also sacrificing time with their children because each minute that a child spends with a tutor or in afterschool is a minute that the child is robbed of connecting with their mother and vice versa.

While seeking external support for their children was common, the mothers also found ways to maintain their role as their children's academic supporter. Mothers did this by bridging the linguistic divide through the use of technological platforms such as Google Translate.

'El traductor del teléfono': Using technology

Many mothers were able to maintain a presence in their child's academic endeavors, while still meeting their needs: using technology to help them bridge the language gap that was created by school. None of these families had internet at home, but they all had phones, which they used to translate the child's homework, do the homework with their child and then translate it back to English for their child to submit. This was a time-consuming task, and yet, they engaged in it regularly.

Carmela, Ana and Carlota discuss the importance of Google Translate. As the mothers sit down to help their children with homework, they use their phones to find out the pronunciation and meanings of words. For Carmela, the cell phone helps her find out how words in the homework are pronounced, something she previously had to do with dictionaries:

Sí [yo siento que participo], porque–, ¿cómo dicen ellos?, la discapacidad que tiene, yo trato de hacer la tarea con él, de sentarme con él a escuchar para ver cómo está leyendo, y aunque yo no sé inglés, yo lo escucho para ver si él está leyendo. A veces buscamos en el diccionario cómo se pronuncia una palabra. Ahora que todo se puede buscar en el teléfono, en el Internet. De esa manera, yo lo ayudo.

[*Yes [I feel that I participate], because–, how do they say?, the disability that he has, I try to do the homework with him, to sit down with him*

*to listen to see how he is reading, and although I do not know English, I
listen to him to see if he is reading. Sometimes we look in the dictionary
for a word to be pronounced. Now that everything can be searched on
the phone, on the Internet. That way, I help him.*]

Ana uses her cell phone to find out the meaning of words in the
homework, and she regularly uses it to find words both in English and
in Spanish:

Porque ahorita con el español y el inglés, hay cositas que se me hacen
un poco difíciles enseñárselas. O estarlo escribiendo en el teléfono buscando, qué significa para yo orientarla.

[*Because right now with Spanish and English, there are things that make
it a bit difficult for me to teach them. Or I'm writing on the phone looking, what does it mean, for me to guide her.*]

Ana's experience is especially troubling because María Teresa was
enrolled in a bilingual inclusion class, yet most of her homework assignments were in English.

This was also true for María whose son Justin was enrolled in a
transitional bilingual education class. During one of the early interviews,
María noted that even though Justin is supposed to be in a bilingual class,
all of the homework was assigned in English:

Todas las tareas son en inglés, matemáticas, lectura, escritura, todo es
en inglés.

[*All assignments are in English, math, reading, writing, everything is in
English.*]

Even when a child is enrolled in a bilingual program, the mothers are
confronted with English-only work. María also made a point of sharing
that she's not the only one; other moms have to do this too:

Y no solo soy la única, somos todas las mamás. Jessenia [her friend], le
pasa lo mismo también. Y peor que ahora son dos niños, estar mucho
tiempo sentados traduciendo tarea de uno o tarea del otro.

[*And I'm not the only one, it's all us moms. Jessenia [her friend], the
same thing happens to her too. And worse that now there are two children, sitting for a long time translating one's homework or the other
one's homework.*]

The mothers use the internet on their phone not only for homework but also for living with their children. The gap between the
English language practices of their children and the Spanish of the

mothers sometimes makes communication difficult. For example, Carlota explains how when her child wants to say or explain something to her that is in English, he uses three resources: pointing and gesturing, his siblings and Google.

> Sí, y si no, el me señala. Me señala, o busca en Google para ver qué es la respuesta, o pide ayuda con sus hermanos.

> [*Yes, and if not, he points things out to me. He points at me, or searches on Google to see what the answer is, or asks for help with his brothers.*]

Google has become a most important resource for these mothers to communicate with their children.

Working with their children in these ways, both for homework and for living, takes a large investment in terms of time. But despite the investment in time, mothers are willing to make the sacrifice, as María explains:

> [C]uando trataba de hacer tareas con él, primero medio me tardaba como dos, tres horas con él haciendo tareas, y él se desesperaba, porque era mucho tiempo yo lo que yo lo tenía sentado ahí haciendo tareas. Porque yo tenía primero que traducir toda la tarea, para poder explicarle lo que iba a hacer. [Usaba] el traductor del teléfono.

> [*[W] hen I tried to do homework with him… first it took me as long as two, three hours with him doing homework, and he would get anxious, because it was a long time for me to have him sitting there doing homework. Because I had to translate the whole task first, in order to explain what he was going to do. [Using] the phone's translator.*]

The mothers are savvy about technology programs that are available on their phones and that their children could use to read and learn. For example, María tells us about one such program:

> Ahorita hay un programa que se llama Raz-Kids, ese lo lee primero en el teléfono y ya despés él lo tiene que leer. Y algunas palabras que él todavía no comprende. Y luego, 'Mami, ¿cómo dice aquí?'. Tengo que regresarme a ver cómo es la palabra correcta para poder pronunciarla, porque no es lo mismo que yo se la diga como yo la entiendo, a que cómo es la palabra, porque lo confundo más.

> [*Right now there is a program called Raz-Kids, I read it first on the phone and then he has to read it. And some words that he still does not understand. And then, 'Mommy, how do you say here?' I have to go back to see what the correct word is like to be able to pronounce it, because it is not the same for me to say it as I understand it, what the word is like, because I confuse him more.*]

These mothers have found non-traditional ways to support their children. The internet, through cell phones, has become an important resource for them. Yet, even after making huge physical and financial investments, these mothers still questioned their role and/or expressed a belief that they were not very engaged. This failure to see their engagement is the subject of the next section.

'No que digamos mucho': Mothers assess their engagement

More often than not, the mothers in this study internalized the school's definition of engagement, and as such they perceived engagement as participating in activities that take place at the school. In response to a question from me, Elodia describes how she perceives her engagement as 'no mucho' and 'poco tiempo', even though, as we have seen, these mothers devote a great deal of time to their children at home.

> No mucho. [...] Es que como yo trabajo, nada más cuando yo llego, les dedico un poco de tiempo. [El trabajar limita las maneras que lo puedo apoyar] en lo de la escuela. Participar con ellos. [Estar físicamente en la escuela] Sí. En [casa en] las tardes, sí. Yo les ayudo con su tarea y a leer.

> [*Not much [...] It's just that since I work, when I arrive, I dedicate a little time to them [Working limits the ways I can support him] in the school. Participate with them [Being physically at school] Yes. At [home in] the afternoons, yes. I help them with their homework and to read.*]

Likewise, Nancy responds with a 'no mucho', even though she proceeds to explain how it is that she is engaged with her child's schoolwork:

> No que digamos mucho, ¿verdad?, pero trato. [...] Bueno, solamente diciéndole, 'Haz la tarea'. A veces, él me dice, 'Mami, yo no lo entiendo'. Le digo, 'Pero, ¿cómo dice en español para yo decirte?'. Lo único que sí, como yo le dije, 'Yo voy a mirar si yo puedo ayudarte, solo en Matemáticas. Porque ya si es leer, y entenderlo, todo está en inglés, ahí te toca a ti, yo no', le digo, 'Pero hazlo'. Sí. Motivándolo a hacer la tarea. [...] Porque digamos, yo no me relaciono mucho. No me relaciono, así que digamos–, como que dicen, 'Vengan para ser voluntarios de [inglés] PTA o algo así'. Eso es en lo único que no me relaciono. Pero en el trabajo de los niños, sí.

> [*I guess you can say not much, right?, but I try [...] Well, just saying, 'Do the homework'. Sometimes, he tells me, 'Mommy, I do not understand'. I say, 'But how does it say in Spanish for me to tell you?' The only thing I did, as I said, 'I'm going to look if I can help you, only in Mathematics. Because if it is reading, and understanding, everything is in English, then it's your turn, I cannot', I say, 'But do it. 'Yes. Motivating him to*

do the homework. [...] Because let's say, I do not interact much. I do not interact, so let's say–, like they say, 'Come to volunteer for PTA or something like that'. That's the only thing I do not relate to. But in the children's work, yes.]

Both Elodia and Nancy present themselves as disengaged. It is only after being pressed that they identify ways in which they support their child's learning. Nancy also alludes to the fact that the school only calls upon her to participate in parent teacher association (PTA) meetings and on-site activities, which further contributes to the mothers' understanding of academic participation being based on what takes place at school only. This instinct to discount one's efforts is not unique to them. Paty also questioned her engagement even after explicitly describing how she sought out and hired a tutor for her child as a way to meet her child's needs:

No. Yo la verdad a [Dan] desde que entró a la escuela nunca lo he mandado al afterschool [sic]. Porque como ahorita le toca a las escuelas lejos, entonces no puedo ir a traerlo. [...] Nos han recomendado. [Dan] califica para after-school. Pero luego le digo: 'Hijo, ¿y si te pongo?', 'No, mamá', dice él, él dice que no. Pero a veces digo: 'Bueno, creo que sí le hace falta, porque necesita ayuda', ¿verdad?. Pero a veces digo: 'En el tiempo del verano uno sale tarde, vamos a tren, nos venimos caminando, cualquier cosa'. Pero como ahorita en el invierno, mucha nieve, mucho frío [...] a veces yo les explico: 'No puede venir [Dan] porque la verdad yo vivo lejos. Hasta allá, hasta acá' [...] Entonces a veces digo: 'No'. A veces yo por eso les digo a los maestros: 'Dígame qué es lo que necesita'. Por decir, como ahorita que usted me dicen que ayuda, por eso luego me dicen: 'Es que [Dan] necesitaria ayuda en esto', 'Okay', dice: 'Es recomendable el after-school', 'La verdad no puedo. Pero dígame y yo le busco la persona quien le ayude'. [...] Entonces por eso yo busco a esa persona a modo de que él no se atrase. Yo siento que es una forma de recompensarle eso. Pero a veces digo yo: 'No sé si esté bien o esté mal'.

[No. I the truth is [Dan] since he entered the school I have never sent him to afterschool. Because now since his school is far away, so I can not go and bring him. [...] They have recommended us. [Dan] qualifies for after-school. But then I say: 'Son, what if I put you?', 'No, mom', he says, he says no. But sometimes I say: 'Well, I think he does need it, because he needs help', right? But sometimes I say: 'In the summer time one leaves late, we go to train, we come walking, anything'. But like now in the winter, a lot of snow, a lot of cold [...] sometimes I explain to them: '[Dan] cannot come because the truth is that I live far away, go there, go here' [...] So sometimes I say: ' No'. Sometimes that's why I tell teachers: 'Tell me what he needs'. To say, like right now you tell me what help, that's

why they say to me: 'It's that [Dan] would need help in this', 'Okay', he says: 'After-school is recommended', 'I really can not. But tell me and I'll find the person who will help him. '[...] So that's why I look for that person so that he does not fall behind. I feel that it is a way of making up for it. But sometimes I say: 'I do not know if it's right or wrong'.]

Some of this disconnect originates from the mothers feeling that they have to engage in the ways that the schools say they should engage: 'Vengan a ser voluntatios del PTA' [come volunteer for PTA] or '[Dan] califica para after-school' [[Dan] qualifies for afterschool]. The mothers have legitimate reasons as to why they don't engage in those ways: 'Yo vivo lejos' [I live far away] or 'yo trabajo' [I work]. Yet, they feel an innate sense of failing: 'dedico un poco de tiempo' [I dedicate a little time], 'yo no me relaciono mucho' [I do not interact much], 'no sé si esté bien o esté mal' [I do not know if it's right or wrong], and discount their participation. The mothers in this study exhibited many ways in which they supported their children's academic development and the ways in which they have internalized deficit perspectives regarding their engagement. What they did not instinctively volunteer was the fact that they were doing so while facing a myriad of challenges.

Conclusion

Mothers view a mother's role as being the first teacher. As such, they teach their children, support them, help them and provide for them. However, disability labels take many aspects of this role away from MoEBLADs because they present a myriad of unknowns. As such, mothers are frustrated by the ways that disability labels and English-only placements shift all of the 'power' from them to the teachers, doctors and service providers; the experts – 'los que le dieron la etiqueta' [the ones who assigned the label], leaving the mothers feeling 'impotente' [powerless]. This shift also adds to their labor given the investment in time that they make in order to support their children in traditional ways (e.g. homework and reading) and in having to find other ways to push back on the diagnosis and stay present in their children's lives as learners (e.g. finding tutors, teaching them Spanish).

As a result, the mothers do not know what to do – how to help, support and teach their children. Thus, they step away from the academic realm (the place where the disability 'lives') and find other ways to still be the child's mother: doubling down on sacrifices, doubling down on external support. All of this is a form of mothering by proxy: teaching them about God, teaching them self-care and fostering caring relationships with their other children. Ultimately, these acts are a way for the mothers to maintain their relevance in their children's growth and development, something that is often challenged by schools, and sometimes even by their children. Still, while they may defer to formal educators outside of their home, they are acutely aware of their responsibilities to their children. As such, they find subversive ways to support their children's learning, even if their children don't notice, or actively discount, them.

Note

(1) PAZ is a free afterschool program offered at the child's school.

Reference

Ishimaru, A.M., Torres, K.E., Salvador, J.E., Lott, J., Williams, D.M.C. and Tran, C. (2016) Reinforcing deficit, journeying toward equity: Cultural brokering in family engagement initiatives. *American Educational Research Journal* 53 (4), 850–882. https://doi.org/10.3102/0002831216657178

10 Broken Spirits: Challenges Faced by MoEBLADs

Throughout the interview process, the mothers would often hint at the ways in which they were constantly being pulled in multiple directions. In response, I set up a series of interviews that would allow us to dive deeply and explicitly discuss the complexities of motherhood. During this interview, the three focal mothers were asked to list their responsibilities and any other concerns or pressing issues that they found taxing. In every case, the child with the disability was often last or missing from the list. The reason for this is that the mothers were managing much larger issues than their child's disability: they needed to support the needs of their other children – some of whom lived in other countries, had chronic health problems, were abusing drugs and alcohol or were recovering from sexual assault. Additionally, the mothers were also caring for their aging and ailing parents as well as serving as surrogate mothers for their own siblings. Unfortunately, the mothers were unable to turn to their partners for support because all of them were involved in abusive spousal relationships. While the impact that these factors have on mothers has been studied, they have not been positioned in relation to disability; in other words, existing studies tend to focus on one of the aforementioned issues or on disability as maternal stressors rather than a combination of all (Fusco *et al.*, 2016; Garcini *et al.*, 2016; Heward-Belle, 2017; Levendosky *et al.*, 2000; Ramirez & Monk, 2017; Zadnik *et al.*, 2016). This chapter highlights how all of these pressures, combined with social isolation, resulted in the mothers feeling overwhelmed and incredibly lonely.

Fractured Roles: A Mother to More than One

When asked where Dan's disability falls in her list of concerns, Paty indicates that 'ahorita no es tan importante, por que él esta estable' [right now it's not that important, because he's stable]. She is much more concerned about her other child, Carlos Santo, who lives in Mexico and 'está consumiendo drogas' [is using drugs]:

Pues ahorita, pues sí, es una preocupación de que él no se empeore. Y a la misma vez como que ahorita no es tan importante, porque él está estable. Sí, me preocupan sus estudios, como de Tanya también, no sé. Pero ahorita lo que a veces está en mi cabeza ahorita para mí es mi hijo Carlos Antonio, es eso lo que a veces me está preocupando ahorita más. Que [Dan y Tanya] me tienen aquí, claro, no las 24 horas porque yo también trabajo, pero ellos también van a la escuela. Pero todo el tiempo posible yo puedo estar con ellos, y sin embargo con mi hijo no, con los dos, porque solamente son por teléfono.

[*Well, right now, it's a concern that he does not get worse. And at the same time, like right now, it's not that important, because he's stable. Yes, I'm worried about his studies, and [Tanya]'s too, I do not know. But now what is sometimes in my head right now for me is my son Carlos Antonio, that is what sometimes worries me more now. That [Dan and Tanya] have me here, of course, not 24 hours because I also work, but they also go to school. But I can be with them as long as possible, and yet with my son I can't, with both, because they are only on the phone.*]

For Paty, Dan's needs were not as pressing as the needs of her other two children whom she had left in Mexico at the ages of 3 and 5, and hasn't seen in over a decade. Her participation in transnational parenting (Boehm, 2012; Lahaie *et al.*, 2009; Poeze, 2019) caused Paty great distress; Dan and Tanya have her 'todo el tiempo posible' [as long as possible] but her other two children only have her 'por teléfono' [on the phone].

Thinking about her children in Mexico and worrying about them was the only way she could mother them from afar, and, in some ways, assuage her guilt for getting pregnant with both Dan and Tanya and subsequently leaving them for so long:

Yo y mi esposo habíamos planeado que dos años. Le digo '¿Cómo en qué tiempo hacemos la casa?' Dice 'Si tú llegas y trabajas y yo trabajo, en dos años ya hicimos la casa'. Y yo estuve de acuerdo, dije 'Sí'. Y sí, llegamos a los tres meses empecé a trabajar, él casi luego empezó a trabajar [...] y si, empezamos a trabajar el empezó a construir, él estuvo construyendo, al año yo salgo embarazada o antes del año salgo embarazada de [Dan].

[*Me and my husband had planned that [it would be for] two years. I said to him 'In about how long do we build the house?' He says 'If you arrive and work and I work, in two years we will have already made the house'. And I agreed, I said 'Yes'. And yes, we arrived, after three months I started to work, he later started working [...] and yes, we started to work, he started to build, he was building, a year later I get pregnant or before the year, I was pregnant with [Dan].*]

Paty had never intended to be apart from her older children indefinitely. The original plan was to come to the United States, work for 'dos años' [two years] – just long enough to buy land and 'construir' [build] a house – and then go back. Her separation from her children was meant to be temporary, but then 'salgo embarazada' [she got pregnant].

Cuando nació [Dan] de plano deje de trabajar un tiempo, entonces yo estaba con [Dan] y más desde ese momento cuando me dijeron de su problema, yo me sentía más, como que más tenía que estar con él.

[*When [Dan] was born, I stopped working for a while, so I was with [Dan] and more from that moment when they told me about his problem, I felt more, like, I had to be with him even more.*]

After learning of Dan's 'problema' [problem], Paty decides to stay home, sacrificing her earning potential to care for him and extending the amount of time that she would need to stay in the United States.

[E]ntonces yo ya era un año, no trabajaba, estaba dedicada a [Dan]. Pero [...] la construcción de allá y los gastos de acá y me decía [mi esposo], 'es que no me alcanza'.

[*Then it was already a year, I did not work, I was dedicated to [Dan]. But [...] the construction there and the expenses here and [my husband] told me, 'its just that I can't cover it all'.*]

Wanting to return to her children back in Mexico and faced with the reality of mounting expenses due to the ongoing cost of 'construcción de allá' [construction over there] coupled with 'los gastos de acá' [the expenses here], Paty returns to work. She pays her sister, who is pregnant with her first child, to take care of Dan, but a year or so later, she's pregnant again.

Entonces fue como empecé nuevamente a trabajar, porque [mi hermana] en lo que estaba [embarazada], ella cuidaba a [Dan], o sea nos ayudábamos, y después este ella pues ya tuvo a su niño, no lo siguió viendo, yo estaba trabajando y luego al año, seis meses yo me embazo de Tanya, seguíamos así trabajando, ella mi hermana me ayudaba, yo la ayudaba y así estábamos. Pero después llegó el momento que Tanya iba a nacer y pues deje de nuevo de trabajar, deje de trabajar y también, de Tanya un año no trabaje, no trabaje.

[*So that's how I started working again, because [my sister] while she was [pregnant], she took care of [Dan], that is, we helped each other, and after that she had her child, she did not keep caring for him. I was working and then, after a year... six months, I was pregnant with Tanya, we were still working, she helped me, I helped her, and that's how we were.*]

But then the time came that Tanya was going to be born and I stopped
working again, stop working and I was also with Tanya for one year. I
didn't work, I didn't work.]

Paty was so desperate to return to her children that she continued
working through her fourth pregnancy, but 'despues llegó el momento
de que Tanya iba a nacer' [then the time came that Tanya was going to
be born] and she stopped working 'de nuevo' [once again]. Paty's sense
of guilt is palpable as she cried while repeating the phrase 'no trabajé' [I
didn't work].

This experience of raising children in two separate countries, intentionally or not, was also true for other mothers. Carlota, Nancy and
Carmela found themselves in the same situation, raising children back
in Mexico. Carlota sent her oldest child to Mexico when her marriage
became abusive:

Sí, el mayor es de otra relación, que yo le había comentado que él no
[vive] conmigo [...] lo que yo hice fue agarrar al niño y mandarlo a mi
país [para protejerlo].

[Yes, the oldest is from another relationship, I mentioned that he does
not [live] with me [...] what I did was grab the child and send him to my
country [to protect him].]

Nancy's oldest children initially stayed in Mexico, then came to the
United States, returning to Mexico for university:

Sí, [los mayores] dos años estuvieron en México [mientras yo estuve
aquí] y después los mandé a traer. Estuvieron aquí conmigo hasta que
la niña cumplió 18 años, y se regresó a estudiar. Ahora está estudiando
en México.

[Yes, [the older ones] two years were in Mexico [while I was here] and
then I sent for them. They were here with me until the girl turned 18, and
went back to school. Now she is studying in Mexico.]

Of Carmela's five children, two were born in Mexico and three were born
in the United States. So the older two have not always been with her in
the United States, and one is still in Mexico:

Dos [hijos] nacieron en México. Y, tres nacieron acá en Estados Unidos
[...] No. No siempre [han vivido conmigo]. Los más grandes no han
vivido todo el tiempo conmigo. [... Todavia,] uno está en México.

[Two [children] were born in Mexico. And, three were born here in the
United States [...] No. [They have] not always [lived with me]. The older
ones have not lived with me all the time. [...] One is [still] in Mexico.]

In the end, the mothers are more worried about those they left behind or sent away than the emergent bilinguals labeled as dis/abled (EBLADs) who remain by their side.

This sense of stability in their children's lives was influenced by the needs of children living abroad and by the needs of their in-country children and other relatives. Many of these mothers served as the primary caregiver for their parents and other siblings.

In addition to caring for their children in Mexico, the mothers were also caring for other children in the United States, some of whom were also enduring major challenges. María worries about her younger son, Jayden, who suffers from asthma and is often hospitalized:

> [Me preocupa la] enfermedad de Jayden, porque como él tiene asma me está faltando mucho a la escuela por lo mismo del asma. Entonces seguido se me está enfermando. Tiene también como dos semana que estuvo tres días internado en el hospital. Salió y todavía estuvo una semana con la tos. Parece que ya se había compuesto, y apenas el viernes volvió otra vez con la tos. Entonces ahorita está con tos. [...] [E]l viernes no fue a la escuela porque tenía tos, estaba frío, entonces el frío es lo que le hace daño.

> [[I worry about] Jayden's illness, because as he has asthma, he's missing a lot of school because of asthma. Then he's getting sick. Also like two weeks ago he was in the hospital for three days. He left and still had a cough for a week. It seems that he had already feeling like himself, and just on Friday he started coughing again. So right now he's coughing. [...] Friday he did not go to school because he had a cough, it was cold, so the cold is bad for him.]

Paty worries about her youngest daughter, Tanya, who suffered sexual abuse at the hands of a family member:

> Pero a veces siento que no sé, siento que como madre a veces fallo, y mucho. [Tanya] cuando cumplió los siete años, pasó por un malo. No fue algo–, pero sí la tocaron. El dolor más grande que yo misma lo–, no, no. Fue, fue mi familia, que a veces se–, le digo yo no sé si fuera más duro. Es que yo no pude hacer nada. Es que no, no sé. A veces me sigo arrepintiendo, a veces les digo, se lo dejan en manos de Dios. Porque él sabe lo que pasó. Y además fue mi sobrino que tiene él 14 años, tenía 14. Él la tocaba a mi hija. Cuando yo le dije a mi hermana, y mi cuñado dice... Mi hermana no, se agachó la cabeza y lloraba. Y mi cuñado me contestaba, y yo le decía que por qué su hijo hacía eso, que si no le llamaba la atención. Él me dio a entender que mi hija fue la que lo provocó. Y yo le dije, '¿Cómo va a hacer una niña de siete años a uno de 14?'. Le dije, 'Bueno, tengo para que mi hija no vuelva a venir acá. Y si va a venir, o pueden ir ustedes a la casa', porque tampoco le puedo cerrar a mi

hermana las puertas, le digo, ella va a ser recibida. 'También tus hijos, lo único que voy a hacer es yo nada más tengo que cuidar a mi hija. Tengo que estar más al pendiente a ella'.

[*But sometimes I feel that, I do not know, I feel that as a mother I sometimes fail, and a lot. [Tanya] when she turned seven, she went through something bad. It was not something–, but they did touch her. The greatest pain, that I myself– no, no. It was, it was my family, that sometimes I … I tell you I do not know if it is harder. It's just that I could not do anything. No, I do not know. Sometimes I keep repeating, sometimes I tell them, leave it in the hands of God. Because he knows what happened. And, it was also my nephew who is 14 years old, he was 14. He touched my daughter. When I told my sister, and my brother-in-law said … My sister no, she bent her head and cried. And my brother-in-law answered me, and I told him why did his son do that, that if he did not call his attention. He gave me to understand that my daughter was the one who provoked him. And I said, 'How is a seven-year-old girl going to do a 14-year-old boy?' I said, 'Well, I have it so that my daughter will not come here again, and if she will come, or you can go to the house', because I cannot close my doors to my sister either, I tell her, she's going to be received, 'and also your children, the only thing I'm going to do is I just have to take care of my daughter, I have to be more aware of her'.*]

In this situation, Paty must deal with the trauma her daughter has been through, reconciling the fact that it was her nephew who 'tocaba mi hija' [touched my daughter], that her daughter was blamed for the assault: 'me dio a entender que fue mi hija fue la que lo provocó' [He gave me to understand that my daughter was the one who provoked him], while also trying to maintain a relationship with her sister.

Even when the issues or situations are not as extreme, mothers are constantly being pulled in multiple directions. During one of the observations, I witnessed how Ana had to stop helping María Teresa with her homework in order to enroll David in preschool:

- María Teresa returns to her homework and resets fingers without prompting – looks at mom, as mom looks over answer, she says 'quince' [fifteen]
- Mom gets a phone call – her neighbor is heading to a school to sign her son up for school in the event that he doesn't get into the local pre-k.
- After nearly 50 minutes, there are 3 problems remaining on the half of the page. [Ana] begins packing up, putting the homework into a neat pile on the table and cleaning up the snack. They must all go – there is no one else for the kids to stay with. Homework will have to wait until they return. Ana directs her kids to get ready. They continue eating snack at the table.

- Mom instructs María Teresa to get ready while she puts shoes on David.

(Ana, Observation #1)

Ana was in the middle of helping María Teresa with her math homework when they were interrupted by a phone call. This phone call, focused on the pre-kindergarten enrollment process, shifted Ana's attention from María Teresa to David, her three year old. This is a small glimpse into the ways in which mothers are constantly negotiating each child's needs.

However, it is not only their children they must care for. María shares her home with her father and is also his default caregiver. While her mother is helpful when she is here, she holds a traveling visa so she 'va y viene' [comes and goes]. At the time of the study, her mother was in New York so María was not tasked with her father's care, but she knew it was just a matter of time before 'se vaya mi mamá' [my mom leaves] and she would need to take over once again.

Ahorita lo que me preocupa es mi papá. Él es diabético, él vive con nosotros, pero ahora no tiene mucho, tendrá como tres, cuatro semanas más o menos que le salió una ámpula en la pierna, entonces se le está haciendo feo, ya fue al doctor, le dieron antibióticos, parece que ya estaba mejorando, pero volvió otra vez. Entonces por su diabetes tengo miedo de que se le vaya a a infectar más y pueda tener operación o algo así. Eso es lo que me preocupa más ahorita de él. Porque también como mi mamá tiene visa, va y viene. Ahorita que está mi mamá, pues es lo que lo está apoyando a él, pero cuando se vaya mi mamá, pues no sé qué va a pasar con él si él no se compone.

[*Right now, what worries me is my dad. He is diabetic, he lives with us, but it hasn't been that long, he will have like three, four weeks or so that he got an ampulla on his leg, and it is getting ugly. He went to the doctor, he was given antibiotics, it seemed like it was already improving, but it came back again. So because of his diabetes I am afraid that it will become more infected and he may need an operation or something like that. That's what worries me most about him right now. Because also since my mom has a visa, she comes and goes. Now that my mom is here, that's what is supporting him, but when my mom leaves, I do not know what will happen to him if he does not make up.*]

Paty also has to look after her brothers with whom she shares her home:

Porque mis papás no están acá y cuando yo hablo, que soy la que hablo más seguido con mi mamá, me pregunta siempre por ellos, '¿Cómo está mi hijo este? y ¿Cómo está mi hija esta? ¿Cómo está?' Y [por] todos sus hijos preguntan.

[*Because my parents are not here and when I speak, I am the one that talks most often with my mother, she always asks me about them, 'How is my son doing?', and 'how is my daughter doing? 'How are they?' She ask [about] all her children.*]

Paty feels this sense of obligation to look after her siblings in part because her mother is the one who looks after her own children back in Mexico.

Unfortunately, the mothers are unable to receive support from their partners. In most cases, the spouse was another source of stress. The Testimonialistas all shared multiple ways in which their husbands abused them. These experiences are presented in the next section.

Bound in Broken Marriages: Tomaba, insultaba, amenazaba, presionaba, lastimaba

The women dealt with a variety of abuses from spouses. Some were direct, such as verbal abuse; others, however, were indirect, such as the neglect that was a by-product of alcoholism.

María was not only dealing with needing to provide care for her aging father and her other child's health, but she was also dealing with the fact that her husband 'toma mucho' [drinks a lot]; to the point that the children notice.

Y ya de mi esposo es de que él toma mucho, y ese es el problema que ahorita tenemos, de que él quiere estar con dos, tres cervezas todos los días, todos los días. Y ya no puedo más con él de decirle que ya deje de tomar. Porque ya Justin se da cuenta de las cosas, y luego él se molesta, él dice que ya no quiere ver a su papi tomando. Y ya Justin ya habló con él y le dijo, 'Papi, ya no más cervezas', pero él dijo, 'Sí, sí, ya no más cervezas', pero él sigue haciendo lo mismo.

[*And then with my husband it is that he drinks a lot, and that is the problem we now have, that he wants to have two, three beers every day, every day. And I can't tell him to stop drinking any longer. Because Justin already realizes things, and then he gets upset, he says he does not want to see his daddy drinking anymore. And Justin already talked to him and said, 'Daddy, no more beers', but he said, 'Yes, yes, no more beers', but he just keeps doing the same.*]

Her oldest son, Justin, even proclaims that he 'no quiere ver a su papi tomando' [does not want to see his daddy drinking anymore] and even says to him, 'Papi, ya no más cervezas' [daddy, no more beers], but to no avail.

Alcohol abuse was a common theme with the three Testimonialistas. In the lives of these women, their partners' alcohol abuse often led to their abuse. Carlota was afraid of her child's father:

Por miedo de que el papá me insultaba y me amenazaba.

[*Out of fear because the dad would insult me and threaten me.*]

María was pressured by her partner, 'tanta y tanta presión', because she could not get pregnant. She was repeatedly told she was a failure as a woman:

Y él me presionaba mucho, porque él quería tener un hijo, y yo no me podía embarazar. Pero yo pienso que fue el estrés el que no me podía yo embarazar, porque él siempre me decía, 'No, que tú no sirves para mujer, no puedes darme un hijo', y ya tanta y tanta presión que yo sentí, que ya no podía yo más.

[*And he pressured me a lot, because he wanted to have a son, and I could not get pregnant. But I think it was the stress that I could not get pregnant, because he always said to me, 'No, you are a good for nothing woman, you cannot give me a son', and already so much and so much pressure that I felt, that I could not go on.*]

Paty felt abused by her children's father as she recounted his problems with alcoholism as he drank 'más, más' [more, more]. She described how his behavior made her feel 'lastimaban' [injured], 'dolía' [hurt].

Él cuando llegamos a este país empezó a tomar más, más. Había días que no venía dos días. Se iba con sus hermanos. Y yo siempre le hablaba por teléfono '¿Dónde estás?' a veces ni me contestaba. Entonces yo siempre le decía a Diosito, 'Dios, endurece mi corazón. Haz que no sienta lo que yo siento ahora. Porque él no viene. Yo lo espero y él no viene'. Quedé embarazada de [Dan] y seguía. Entonces pues ya no me sentí tan mal porque estaba [Dan]. Pero siempre yo le decía a Dios que endureciera mucho mi corazón, porque había palabras que me lastimaban. No me golpeaba, pero sí dolía cuando él me decía.

[*When he arrived in this country, he started drinking more, more. There were days that he did not come for two days. He left with his brothers. And I always talked to him on the phone 'Where are you?' sometimes he did not answer me. Then I always said to God, 'God, harden my heart, make me not feel what I feel now, because he does not come, I wait for him and he does not come'. I got pregnant with [Dan] and it continued. Well then I did not feel so bad because I had [Dan]. But I always told God to harden my heart, because there were words that hurt me. He did not hit me, but it hurt when he said those things to me.*]

In some cases, the mothers were trying to find ways to deal with spousal infidelity while maintaining the 'happy marriage' façade for their children. Ana tell us that story:

Bueno, es que cuando yo vi esos mensajes, yo lo que hice esa noche, como estaban los niños, cuando el primer mensaje que yo lo vi, que pude ver la lista, estaba la niña ahí al lado mío, entonces como que algo tenía aquí y no podía, lo que hice fue es irme a la cocina y tomar agua y [unintelligible]. Estaba la niña ahi conmigo.

Al otro día cuando él vino lo que yo hice fue es que, me dijo que por qué estaba yo así. Yo le dije que no me pasaba nada, 'No sé tú qué te pasa'. Y me dice, '¿Es por las amigas?', le digo, 'Es que no me pasa nada, no sé tú, porque siempre dices tus amigas, los mensajes, siempre estás ahí', y yo le dije que por qué me había hecho eso, qué es lo que le hizo falta aquí en nuestro hogar, que si el teléfono le daba todo. Y lo que hice pues yo fue abrazarlo. Y ahí estuvimos hablando así abrazados, pero así pasó.

[*Well, it's that when I saw those messages, what I did that night, since I was with the children, when I saw the first message, that I could see the list, the girl [, my daughter] was there next to me, then like I had something here and could not, what I did was to go to the kitchen and drink water and [unintelligible]. The girl [my daughter] was there with me. The next day when he came what I did was, he told me why I was like that. I told him that nothing was wrong with me, 'I do not know what's wrong with you'. And he says, 'Is it because of the friends?' I say, 'It's just that nothings wrong with me, I do not know about you, because you always say your friends, the messages, you're always there', and I told him why he had done that to me, what was it that was lacking in our home, if the phone gave him everything. And what I did then was hug him. And there we were talking like that, holding each other, but that's how it happened.*]

When Ana learned of her husband's affair, she continued to act as if 'no me pasaba nada' [nothing was wrong with me] because 'estaba la niña ahí' [the girl [her daughter] was there]. Her role as a mother is so all-consuming that she even denies her own feelings as a woman and as a wife.

These mothers know that 'esas son muchas preocupaciones' [these are too many worries] for one person. But like Paty says, they accept it as part and parcel of their motherhood: 'es nuestro cargo, ¿verdad?, de ser mamases' [our load, right?, to be moms].

What makes this load heavier to carry and these struggles even more difficult to manage is the fact that these women are isolated from their families and their communities. Many of these women identified feelings of solitude as part not only of their immigrant experiences, but also their experiences as mothers, as discussed in the following section.

Sola, vacía, desesperada: Buried Feelings

As first-generation immigrants, many of the women lacked local family: 'sola, sin ayuda de nadie' [alone, with help from no one]. Even those who had family nearby led solitary lives: 'cada quien por su lado' [to each their own].

María discusses how isolated she feels:

> A veces me siento tan desesperada, cuando yo tengo un problema en la escuela, y no sé a quién recurrir. No sé en quién apoyarme, para que me asesore qué puedo hacer. A veces me siento sola.

> [*Sometimes I feel so desperate, when I have a problem at school, and I do not know who to turn to. I do not know who to lean on, so they can advise me what I can do. Sometimes I feel alone.*]

Ana, who has a sister in New Jersey, reveals that the loneliness is not remedied simply by having family nearby:

> [Mi hermana] vive en New Jersey. Casi no nos vemos. Y tengo otro hermano que tiene dos hijos, ya son de 15 años, pero no están, casi no nos vemos. O sea que cada quien aquí, cada quien por su lado.

> [*[My sister] lives in New Jersey. We almost never see each other. And I have another brother who has two children, they are already 15 years old, but they are not here, we almost do not see each other. That is, each person here, to each his own.*]

Paty mentions how the loneliness makes her feel empty. She also acknowledges the fact that here, in the United States, she feels more alone than anything else.

> A pesar de todo lo que yo hacía, dentro de mí, al menos yo me sentía, dentro de mí, no sé si era del corazón, en la mente, me sentía sola, me sentía vacía, que quería llenarlo con algo, que no sabía ni qué era. [...] Yo estoy más sola acá que otra cosa.

> [*In spite of everything I did, inside me, at least I felt, inside me, I do not know if it was of the heart, in the mind, I felt alone, I felt empty, I wanted to fill it with something, I did not know what it was ... [...] I am more alone here than anything else.*]

Lastly, Rosa indicates how social programs allow these women and their children to survive without the support of a community:

> Entonces, al tiempo, cuando andaba así sola, sin ayuda de nadie, decidí coger una ayuda, asistencia pública, que lo llaman.

> [*Then, at the time, when I was alone, without anyone's help, I decided to get help, public assistance, they call it.*]

Not having someone to 'apoyarme' [lean on] leads these women to feel extremely 'sola' [alone], 'vacía' [empty] and 'desesperada' [desperate]. Given all of these stressors, including the fact that they are enduring the same struggles that other immigrants deal with – particularly around the fear that has stemmed from the 2016 presidential election and their undocumented status – not a single mother has the capacity to focus solely on her qualifying child's needs. They were responsible for mothering not only these children, but also their other children, their parents and their spouses. Often, this was done at the expense of their own self-care. All of these challenges have a serious impact on these women's ability to effectively care for their children and their own mental health:

Paty feels like she is constantly failing as a mother:

Pero a veces siento que no sé, siento que como madre a veces fallo, y mucho.

[*But sometimes I feel that I do not know, I feel that as a mother I sometimes fail, and a lot.*]

María admits that she often feels so overwhelmed and pressured that she falls into a deep depressive state:

Como que a veces me entra depresión, a veces me siento tan presionada de todas las cosas que están pasando, todas las preocupaciones que tengo, ay, que a veces ya digo, 'No quiero hacer nada, no quiero pensar en nada', y a veces como que me desanimo y como que entro en depresión. [...] Porque a veces [...] estoy con– tensa, frustrada [...] Cuando no está mi mamá, yo siento que quiero explotar, y a veces lo único que hago es llorar, llorar, llorar y ya.

[*Because sometimes I get depressed, sometimes I feel so depressed about all the things that are happening, all the worries I have, oh, that sometimes I say, 'I do not want to do anything, I do not want to think about anything', and sometimes I get discouraged and like I go into depression. [...] Because sometimes I [...] am tense, frustrated [...] When my mom is not there, I feel that I want to explode, and sometimes all I do is cry, cry, cry and then.*]

Through María's story, one is able to understand that these women are not mothers in a vacuum and that they have to meet the needs of multiple people. They experience incredible amounts of internal and external pressure with minimal support. As a result, they end up quietly suffering from 'depression' [depression] to the point that they 'quiero explotar' [want to explode] and are so overwhelmed that 'lo único que hago es llorar, llorar, llorar y ya' [all I do is cry, cry, cry and that's it]. Still, these mothers push forward and persevere because for them motherhood is not only an important source of joy, but it is also at the core of their identity.

References

Boehm, D.A. (2012) *Intimate Migrations: Gender, Family, and Illegality Among Transnational Mexicans*. New York: New York University Press.

Fusco, R.A., Jung, N. and Newhill, C.E. (2016) Maternal victimization and child trauma: The mediating role of mothers' affect. *Children and Youth Services Review* 67, 247–253. https://doi.org/10.1016/j.childyouth.2016.06.020

Garcini, L.M., Murray, K.E., Zhou, A., Klonoff, E.A., Myers, M.G. and Elder, J.P. (2016) Mental health of undocumented immigrant adults in the United States: A systematic review of methodology and findings. *Journal of Immigrant & Refugee Studies* 14 (1), 1–25. https://doi.org/10.1080/15562948.2014.998849

Heward-Belle, S. (2017) Exploiting the 'good mother' as a tactic of coercive control: Domestically violent men's assaults on women as mothers. *Affilia* 32 (3), 374–389. https://doi.org/10.1177/0886109917706935

Lahaie, C., Hayes, J.A., Piper, T.M. and Heymann, J. (2009) Work and family divided across borders: The impact of parental migration on Mexican children in transnational families. *Community, Work & Family* 12 (3), 299–312. https://doi.org/10.1080/13668800902966315

Levendosky, A., Lynch, S.M. and Graham-Bermann, S.A. (2000) Mothers' perceptions of the impact of woman abuse on their parenting. *Violence Against Women* 6 (3), 247–271. https://doi.org/10.1177/10778010022181831

Poeze, M. (2019) Beyond breadwinning: Ghanaian transnational fathering in the Netherlands. *Journal of Ethnic and Migration Studies* 45 (16), 3065–3084. https://doi.org/10.1080/1369183X.2018.1547019

Ramirez, N. and Monk, G. (2017) Crossing borders: Narrative therapy with undocumented Mexican women on a journey beyond abuse and violence. *Journal of Systemic Therapies* 36 (2), 27–38. https://doi.org/10.1521/jsyt.2017.36.2.27

Zadnik, E., Sabina, C. and Cuevas, C.A. (2016) Violence against Latinas: The effects of undocumented status on rates of victimization and help-seeking. *Journal of Interpersonal Violence* 31 (6), 1141–1153. https://doi.org/10.1177/0886260514564062

11 Motherhood as Purpose

The issues and tensions that the mothers encounter were never readily volunteered. In most cases, the strife was alluded to but never centered. It is possible that the mothers did not readily volunteer information about the burdens they bear because for them motherhood is not a duty, it is a blessing. While previous research on motherhood as a blessing exists, most of the literature related to mothering children with disabilities focuses on the struggle (Al-Yagon, 2015; Apple, 1995; Burke & Hodapp, 2014; Dykens *et al.*, 2014; Elliott *et al.*, 2015) rather than the nuances, and often without recognition of how external factors, especially related to school, shape the maternal experience (Burke & Hodapp, 2014; Findler *et al.*, 2016; Lalvani, 2019). For the women in this book, 'mother' was in many cases their most valued title. Nonetheless, the mothers recognized that their relationships with their children were multifaceted – filled not only with mutual love and admiration, but also with tensions, power struggles and countless sacrifices.

'Una mamá muy feliz': The Joy of Motherhood

Mothers overwhelmingly feel 'feliz' [happy] and 'bien' [good]. They also consider their children 'una bendición' [a blessing].

Ana feels incredibly happy about the fact not only that she was able to have a child, but also that the child was a daughter, something she had always wanted:

> Yo me sentí feliz, porque yo siempre, desde un principio, antes que naciera ella yo siempre quise niña. El papá quería niño, pero pues yo digo, 'Yo, lo que Dios me regale, mientras que nazca bien, no importa'. Porque como yo estaba enferma de la tiroides, el doctor me dijo que por nada me podía embarazar hasta cierto tiempo, porque el bebé podría salir con defectos. [...] Sí, siempre, porque yo siempre quise una niña, siempre. Yo la quiero bastante. Bueno, igual al niño. A los dos los quiero. Pero bueno, yo siempre, siempre, siempre quise una niña. Al principio, una niña.

[*I felt happy, because I always, from the beginning, before she was born, I always wanted a girl. The father wanted a boy, but I say, 'I, what God gives me, as long as it is born well, does not matter'. Because I was ill with my thyroid, the doctor told me that I could not get pregnant for a long time, because the baby could come out with defects. [...] Yes, always, because I always wanted a girl, always. I love her very much. Well, like the boy. I love them both. But well, I always, always, always wanted a girl. At first, a girl.*]

Sara finds that her child is 'una bendición' [a blessing]; she loves him not only because it is her duty as a mother but also because of who he is:

[Robert] es una bendición. [...] Porque todas las mamás queremos a los niños, son nuestros hijos. Es un niño muy cariñoso.

[*[Robert] is a blessing [...] Because all mothers love children, they are our children. He is a very affectionate child.*]

Nancy also discusses her son's personality when she expands on how happy she is to be his mother:

Soy una mamá muy feliz con él. Bien amoroso, cariñoso, él conmigo, me anda abrazando, me anda besando y todo. Yo me siento bien. Sí.

[*I'm a very happy mom with him. Very loving, affectionate, him with me, hugging me, kissing me and everything. I feel good. Yes.*]

When speaking about their children, most of the mothers would use words such as affectionate, kind, loving and sweet to describe their child. They would mention the difficulties of parenting their children, but overwhelmingly they spoke about their children using positive descriptors such as 'amoroso' [loving], 'cariñoso' [affectionate], 'bueno' [good], 'ordenado' [orderly] and 'sentimental' [sentimental].

Nancy made a point to list all of the qualities she valued in her child, particularly the fact that he 'es apegado' [is very attached] to her, which she mentions twice:

Él es un niño muy amoroso, bueno, tiene sus dificultades como todos [...]. [risas]. Muy ordenado, sí, mas muy responsable. Pero, pues, conforme van de etapa en etapa, usted sabe que ya van haciendo sus diferencias. Pero, un niño muy bueno, muy amoroso, cariñoso, y le gusta estar pegado a mí. Que no le importa si el papá no está, pero la mamá siempre tiene que estar. Es que no es que no le importe el papá, pero, ciertamente, más es apegado a mí. [...] Soy una mamá feliz de él, pues, por este, porque no me puedo quejar, ¿verdad?

[*He is a very loving child, well, he has his difficulties like everyone [...]. [laughs] Very neat, yes, but very responsible. But, as they go from stage to stage, you know that they are already making their differences. But, a very good child, very loving, affectionate, and likes to be attached to me. That he does not care if the dad is not there, but the mom always has to be. It's not that he does not care about dad, but, certainly, more is attached to me. [...] I am a happy mom of him, well, because of this, because I can not complain, right?]*

When María shares the characteristics that make her child loveable, she also includes the fact that he is this way with other people too, which makes him endearing not just to her, but to everyone with whom he interacts socially. She elaborates on his loving nature as a way to juxtapose his behavior when 'se pone en su crisis' [he has a crisis]:

Justin es un niño muy cariñoso. Muy amoroso. Pero cuando sí se pone en sus crisis, a veces me da tristeza de verlo así. [...] Cualquier persona se va a querer con él, porque él es muy cariñoso. [...]. Y él se da a querer, porque él los abraza, a los señores también. Y con nosotros también. Él es cariñoso, pero cuando yo quiero abrazarlo, casi no se deja. [...] Pero en sí, casi no se deja abrazar. Y es lo que tiene él, que es muy cariñoso. Muy también sentimental. Le gusta convivir ...

[Justin is a very affectionate child. Very loving. But when he does get in its crisis, sometimes I feel sad to see him like that. [...] Anyone is going to love him, because he is very affectionate. [...] And he gives himself to love, because he embraces them, to men too. And with us too. He is affectionate, but when I want to hug him, he hardly lets himself. [...] But, he almost does not allow himself to be embraced. And that is what he has, that he is very affectionate. Very also sentimental. He likes to share with other ...]

It is possible that María does this as a way to counter the school's framing of Justin as an antisocial child – an assertion that María vehemently denies.

Like María, Ana also describes María Teresa as caring toward others. In this way, she showcases that the way her child behaves with her is not the exception but the rule:

Es bien dulce, bien tierna, bien alegre, que todo el tiempo me anda diciendo, 'Mamá, mamá, te quiero', o así, con el papá, o con el niño.

[She is very sweet, very tender, very happy, that all the time she is saying to me, 'Mom, mom, I love you', or so, with the father, or with the boy.]

Paty, on the other hand, is the only mother who makes any mention of a potential weakness among the list of Dan's positive characteristics, although 'sensitive' is not a negative characteristic either:

[Dan] es muy bueno, es tierno, pero a veces es muy sensible.

[*[Dan] is very good, he is tender, but sometimes he is very sensitive.*]

The mothers often talked a lot about how they felt loved by their children; given the unhealthy relationships with their spouses, it is very likely that these mother–child relationships were the most nurturing and caring relationship in their lives. The mothers often spoke of the ways in which their children 'se siente orgulloso' [feel proud], appreciate, support and care for them. María beamed when she recounted how Justin had acknowledged the fact that 'tú me cuidas mucho' [you take care of me a lot]:

'Mami, tú me cuidas mucho', le digo, 'Sí, hijo, yo siempre te voy a cuidar'.

[*'Mom, you take care of me a lot', I say, 'Yes, son, I'm always going to take care of you'.*]

María also assures him, and in some ways me, that she will always take care of him.

One of Carlota's greatest joys as a mother is that her son prefers her to anyone else:

[É]l se siente orgulloso de que no a todos los niños su mamá los va a recoger. Por lo mismo de que trabajan. Y él se siente orgullosísimo cuando va su mamá. Cuando va su papá, o cuando va su hermano no le gusta. Prefiere a su mamá [...] Nos sentimos bien, sí me siento bien en ese momento.

[*He is proud that not all the children are picked up by their mother. For the same reason that they work. And he feels very proud when his mom goes. When his dad goes, or when his brother goes, he does not like it. He prefers his mother [...] We feel good, yes I feel good at that moment.*]

She is also moved by the fact that he feels proud that his mom still picks him up from school, a rare experience (and sentiment) for his peers. These feelings of mutual love and admiration are not only based on the mothers' perceptions, but also on the actual words of the children during their interviews. In the next section, the children are given an opportunity to share the way they feel about their mother.

'Es mi mejor amiga': Emergent Bilinguals Labeled as Dis/abled (EBLADs) Talk about Their Mothers

Just like their mothers, the children also spoke warmly about their mothers and employed multiple superlatives to support their feelings.

They used words like 'nice', 'helpful' and 'best' to describe them. Justin not only shares the fact that he thinks that his mother is 'nice' and 'helpful', but he also supports this assertion with evidence:

> She is nice. She is helpful. [...]Because she can help make things that we need [...] Like like papers, like books, like toys, like games – [...]Yes [my mom gets me all those things]. [...My mom is nice b]ecause she's because – My mama says she is nice because she can be my best mother. [...] My mom help me to learn. [...] By working my homework. [...] Because if I don't [under]stand that, my mommy help me. If I got it, then I do it by myself. [...] You know, when we eat foot when we come back from school, what we'll eat, my mommy gets me food, food. [...] Because she always want to work to me. [...] Because if I don't [under]stand that, my mommy help me. If I got it, then I do it by myself. [...] If something [sic] that is mistake, mommy will help me erase, and we'll try again to write it. [...] He can [sic] talk Spanish a little and mommy can think and write on the board. He can use the phone to write, and the [sic] white does then say what looks in the book.[1]

Even at his young age, Justin acknowledges all the ways in which his mother supports him: she helps him with homework, she makes sure he understands what he is learning and she prepares his food. He recognizes all of these acts as acts of love and caring.

María Teresa, on the other hand, speaks openly about the ways in which her mother shows her love and why 'ella es [su] major amiga' [she is [her] best friend]: 'me abraza' [hugs me], 'me acaricia' [caresses me], 'se sienta conmigo' [sits with me] and 'me ayuda' [helps me].

> Ella es una buena mamá. [...] Porque ella siempre me quiere. [...] Me abraza. [...] [Yo me siento b]ien. [...] Porque ella es mi mejor amiga. [Me hace sentir] Feliz. [...] Porque me acaricia. [Ella es una mama] Buena. [...] Porque ella siempre me ayuda en la tarea. [...] Tal vez ella se sienta contimo o me ayuda a leer.
>
> *[She is a good mom [...] Because she always loves me [...] She hugs me [...] [I feel] good [...] Because she is my best friend. [It makes me feel] Happy. [...] Because she caresses me. [She's a [good mom]. [...] Because she always helps me with the homework [...] Maybe she sits with me or helps me read.]*

Meanwhile, Dan is aware not only of the sacrifices his mother makes, but also the reasons why. In addition to appreciating and recognizing his mother's efforts, he thinks of ways in which he can use his education to help her:

Because I feel like she's like the best mom and I'm lucky to have her.

[She is the best mom] Because I know she just wants me to get a good future, she wants me to have a bright future, she also makes me go to school. And I should come to [Saturday] academy which is I chose by myself and I said, 'yes'. She wants me to have a good future because she hasn't go to school, she start to go, she stopped going to school on fifth grade, and I thought and say if I could go to middle school I could teach her stuff. [...To help me learn] Sometimes she asks some questions and I understand the text. [...] Sometimes she tells me words, she asks me these words, if I understand them. So then I could put them in a pad, in my notebook and put in my vocabulary. And that's it.

While all three of the Testimonialistas' children were able to iden-tify ways in which their mothers showed them love and supported their learning, they were also able to identify barriers to greater support. When asked 'What things do you think make it hard for your mom to help you learn?', all three children identified English as the primary impediment. First, Dan makes it clear that it is not just his mother's limited English but also his limited Spanish that creates problems in their household:

The language. [...] Because the language, I only get a lot of words of Eng-lish and it's harder for me to explain it. [...] Because sometimes I can't explain it that well, and she wants me to say in more easy words but I can't because I don't really get her. [It's hard for my mom to help me], a little bit English she does speak, [and I speak only a little bit of Spanish] so it's a little harder for me.

While Justin states that his mother is still able to help him, he identi-fies the fact that the process is longer and more complicated when the homework assignments are in English. He is also able to identify the strategies his mom uses to mediate the language gap that exists between the home and the school: using the phone, Google and English/Spanish glossaries to translate the work.

[I] can talk Spanish a little and mommy can think and write on the board. [She] can use the phone to write, and then write what it say, what goggle says, in the book.

Since María Teresa is in a bilingual class, she is able to identify the support that her mother is able to provide as being linguistically bound: 'Las tareas que ella no puede hacer son las de inglés' [The homeworks that she cannot do are the ones in English].

Nomás ella me ayuda a hacer la tarea en la casa. [...] Las tareas que ella no puede hacer son las de inglés. [...] Porque ella no entiende inglés ahorita. [Eso me hace sentir] Triste. Quisiera [mas ayuda] para que yo haga toda la tarea.

[She only helps me to do the homework at home [...] The homeworks that she can not do are the ones in English [...] Because she does not understand English right now. [That makes me feel] Sad. I would like [more help] so that I could do all the homework.]

All of the children and all of the mothers talked extensively about homework. This focus on homework represents the central role that homework plays in the mother–child relationship. Homework was the source of a great deal of stress for the mothers and frustration for the child. As a result, homework often created more distance than unity between the mother and the child. This is explored further in the following section.

'Las tareas': Ostracized by Homework

As noted previously, homework for the children was the primary indication that their mothers were not able to fully support their school-based education. 'Tarea' was one of the most recurring topics discussed throughout the study. Homework was the greatest source of 'dificultades' [difficulties] for mothers.

Nancy struggled with getting her son to complete tasks:

Solo, pues, en las tareas. Él conmigo [se molesta], porque–. O, yo con él, ¿cómo le puedo decir? En las tareas, luego yo–. O en los avisos. Algunas veces, no revisé lo de las hojas. No mandé–, que eso lo quería español. Entonces, ahí vienen las dificultades para mí, ¿verdad? Porque no le entiendo. Solo adonde le entiendo. Y ahí me voy imaginando lo que dice.

[Well, in the homework. He is [bothered] with me, because– Or, me with him, how can I tell you? In the homework, then I– Or in the notices. Sometimes, I did not check the sheets. I did not send–, I wanted that in Spanish. So, there come the difficulties for me, right? Because I do not understand. Only where I understand. And then I am imagining what it says.]

This left both Nancy and her son feeling frustrated. Nancy is frustrated because she is unable to understand the school's correspondence, and her son is frustrated because he doesn't feel supported by her.

Rosa was unable to support her child when he asked for help, which left her feeling defeated:

Es porque–, en las tareas, ayudarles, ya cuando yo no puedo, entonces digo, 'Lo siento, pero no voy a poder ese día'.

[It's because ..., in the homework, helping them, when I can not, then I say, 'I'm sorry, but I'm not going to be able to do that day'.]

Carmela, on the other hand, acknowledges her struggles with English and expands on the ways in which she tries to support her child even when she cannot actively engage in the task at hand:

Sí, porque–, ¿cómo dicen ellos?, la discapacidad que tiene, yo trato de hacer la tarea con él, de sentarme con él a escuchar para ver cómo está leyendo, y aunque yo no sé inglés, yo lo escucho para ver si él está leyendo.

[*Yes, because ..., how do they say ?, the disability that he has, I try to do the homework with him, to sit down with him to listen to see how he is reading, and although I do not know English, I listen to him to see if he is reading.*]

Through Carmela's example, we can see that even when language interferes with their ability to actively engage with their children in the homework, the mothers still stay connected by encouraging their children to do the work, by sitting with them and listening to them as they read. It is important to note that while a mother with a more privileged social positioning might be able to look at the homework load and reject it, for these mothers homework was a way for them to exert agency, for them to stay engaged and present in their children's learning, for them to stay connected to the life their children lead at school. It is for this reason that they so willingly invested so much time and attention to tasks that some might consider inappropriate or inconsequential (Figueroa, 2011; Fitzmaurice *et al.*, 2020; Hutchison, 2012). On the other hand, homework also hurt the mothers by affirming existing power structures around particular languages and even while in the lower grades, EBLAD children are able to identify and assign more power to English than to Spanish. As we will see in the next section, this can lead to children assigning more power to one speaker over another, regardless of age or family title.

'Tú no sabes inglés': Language as Power

Already at a young age, children are starting to understand the power dynamics associated with linguistic policies and with linguistic abilities. In some cases, this also creates power imbalances between the mother and child.

In Dan's experience, English makes him 'feel' smarter, but this hegemonic understanding of language constructs his mother as less than:

[I feel a] little kind of intelligent than everybody in the family, only here, in the house. Because I'm the only one that really working hard to get a bright future.

We see this recounted in Nancy's experience when her children laugh at her attempts to decode materials that are sent home in English:

Ellos se ríen conmigo, 'Mami, pero tú no entiendes inglés, ¿cómo puedes decir que eso dice?'. Le digo, 'Papi, yo entiendo dos o tres palabras, lo demás solo me lo imagino'. Y me dice el niño grande, 'Mami, pero eso es lo que está diciendo'. Dice, 'Y tú no sabes inglés, ¿cómo me estás explicando lo que dice aquí?'. Le digo, 'Es que salteado sí lo entiendo, pero no lo entiendo todo'. [...] para ellos le encuentran chiste que cómo puedo decir que yo no sé inglés, y que luego ya estoy diciendo lo que dice. Le digo, 'Pero no en todo me va a pasar eso, porque hay mucho que no entiendo' [...]. Le digo, 'Papi, no creas que yo no más–, no creas que yo estoy jugando o mintiendo que yo no lo entiendo, pero si yo entiendo dos o tres palabras así, entonces yo lo demás me imagino'. Y ellos se ríen, me dice, 'Ay, mami, qué imaginación'.

[*They laugh at me, 'Mommy, but you do not understand English, how can you say what that says?' I say, 'Honey, I understand two or three words, the rest I just imagine'. And the older boy says to me, 'Mommy, but that's what he's saying'. He says, 'And you do not know English, how are you explaining what it says here?' I tell him, 'It's just that I understand pieces of it, but I do not understand everything' [...] for them they find it a joke that how can I say that I do not know English, and then I am already saying what it says. I say, 'But that wont happen for me with, because there is a lot that I do not understand' [...]. I say, 'Honey, do not think that I am just... do not think I'm playing or lying that I do not understand, but if I understand two or three words like that, then I imagine everything else'. And they laugh, he says, 'Oh, Mommy, what imagination'.*]

Several mothers shared stories or vignettes that highlighted the power struggles taking place in the home as a result of disparate language practices at home and at school. Given the emphasis that mothers place on schooling, it is not surprising that this high regard would transfer to English since for many of these students the bulk of their educational experience is enacted in English. Ultimately, while these mothers make great efforts to stay engaged in their children's academic development, they are unable to mitigate the deficits that are embedded in their Spanish monolingual practices as a by-product of school-based English-mostly language practices.

Nonetheless, as schools continue to implement language policies that ultimately push out parents, the mothers continue to make sacrifices that they believe will result in high returns for their children even when these are not in the women's own best interest. These mothers are using limited resources in order to support their children These mothers do not have a lot of money for themselves; they do not get a manicure, they do not purchase cups of coffee, and yet their children have $15 and $20 per hour tutors.

'No voy a sacrificar a mi hijo': The Children's Needs Come First

Aside from limited resources, the most sacrificed commodity among mothers of EBLADs was time – time with their EBLAD child, time with their other children, time with family, time to run errands, time for self-care, etc. The time that they have available to them is used to support the needs of their children. This is substantiated throughout the different sections of this book. On Saturday mornings, they are doing laundry but they are also taking their children to Saturday enrichment and/or remedial programs, staying at the school and waiting for their children and then bringing them home. All the while they are also caring for their other children.

Even though Darius' disability needs required that he attend services, this did not absolve Carlota of her responsibilities to her other children.

[La evaluadora] tomo la decisión de que tuviéramos las terapias, que yo llevara al niño a sus terapias. Era muy fuerte todo eso, tenía que tomar trenes. Y no solo lo tenía yo a él, si no, a los otros dos también. Tenía yo que atenderlos.

[[The evaluator] made the decision that we had the therapies, that I would take the child to his therapies. It was very taxing, I had to take trains. And not only I had him, but also, the other two also. I had to take care of them.]

Paty also shares how the need to shuttle a child to and from services was complicated by needing to care for an even younger child:

De cuando para él entró a la escuela, pues fue difícil porque yo tenía que cargar a [Tanya] en la cangurera. Porque fue en tiempos–, me acuerdo que cuando le hicieron la evaluación había mucho nieve por Chapel St., entonces metía a [Tanya] en la cangurera y [Dan] la agarraba de la mano porque ni con la carriola podía uno pasar la nieve. Entonces a veces salía del subway o cogía un taxi para que me llevara cuatro o cinco calles para que le hicieran la evaluación. Yo le decía a mi esposo: 'Yo tengo que buscar de una manera u otra forma'. Tampoco puedo dejar a mi hijo, como tampoco dejarla a ella.

[From when he went to school, it was difficult because I had to carry [Tanya] in the carrier. Because it was in times–, I remember that when they did the evaluation there was a lot of snow on Chapel St., then I put [Tanya] in the carrier and grabbed [Dan's] hand because even with the stroller one could not pass the snow. Then sometimes I got out of the *subway or took a taxi to take me four or five streets to do the evaluation. I said to my husband: 'I have to look one way or another way'. Neither can I leave my son, nor can I leave her.*]

Paty not only had to deal with managing two children, but she also had to do so in the winter using public transport. All of which amounted to increased levels of stress.

María was one of the few mothers who explicitly discussed the ways in which caring for her child with a disability had directly impacted her own ability to participate in social engagements:

A veces, a mí me pasa lo mismo, porque yo no puedo ir a una fiesta, yo no puedo ir a un lugar, al cine, porque mi niño no soporta estar allí. Y yo, le digo, yo a veces me siento aislada de la gente por lo mismo, por mi hijo, pero tampoco yo no voy a sacrificar a mi hijo, porque yo quiera estar en un lugar, que yo quisiera estar.

[*Sometimes, the same thing happens to me, because I can not go to a party, I can not go to a place, to the cinema, because my child can not stand being there. And I, I say, I sometimes feel isolated from people for the same reason, because of my son, but I am going to sacrifice my son, because I want to be in a place, that I would like to be.*]

But the mothers weren't just unable to partake in social activities, they were also unable to partake in any self-care.

Many of the mothers spoke about how time-consuming it was to have an EBLAD child – the countless 'reunions' [meetings], regular 'citas médicas' [doctor's appointments], 'todos los servicios' [the services] – yet they always found the time to tend to the needs of their child and those of their other children, spouses and parents. On the other hand, when it came to their own needs for self-care, they were noticeably restrained. While none of the Testimonialistas' children had missed a single doctor's appointment in the last year, none of the Testimonialistas had found the time (or money) to visit an OB/GYN. As a matter of fact, none of the mothers had visited any doctor since the birth of their youngest child; for one mother that meant that it had been three years since her last doctor's visit, for another it meant nine. However, the greatest sacrifice that these women have made and continue to make is to remain in less than ideal living situations, as Ana explains here:

No. Ya diremos ya hasta cuando como por julio, a finales de julio, cuando salieron los niños de la escuela, julio, agosto, pues nomás yo lo sabía; entre yo y él. Y ya al final cuando él me dijo que si quería yo irme, que me fuera, pero los niños se le iban a quedar a él, porque él estaba seguro que me los iban a quitar. Entonces yo tuve un poco de miedo, porque como a mí me da epilepsia, y yo tuve miedo que me los iba a quitar. Entonces yo no me fui a ningún lado. Así con todo lo que estaba pasando yo dije, 'Me quedo, porque yo no voy a dejar a los niños'. Y en ese momento pues yo quería irme a algún lado para donde él no supiera de mí, por lo menos una semana, si de verdad él no nos quería o no valoraba a su familia. Pero pues digo, '¿A dónde me voy a ir? No tengo otro lado'.

[*No. We'll already say until about, like July, at the end of July, when the children left school, July, August, because I only knew it; between me and him. And at the end when he told me that if I wanted to leave, I would leave, but the children would stay with him, because he was sure that they would take them away. Then I had a little fear, because like I have epilepsy, and I was afraid that they would take them away. So I did not go anywhere. So with everything that was happening I said, 'I'm staying, because I'm not going to leave the children'. And at that moment, I wanted to go somewhere where he did not know about me, at least a week, to see if he really did not love us or value his family. But I said, 'Where am I going to go? I have no other option'.*]

Ana would never leave her children, so when confronted with the possibility of losing them if she were to leave her husband, she decided to remain with her cheating spouse.

Similarly, the other Testimonialistas were very clear about the fact that they not only stayed in unhealthy marriages but also in the United States because it was in the best interest of their children. All three women shared that life would be better for them in Mexico, where they could return to their families and communities and where they knew the culture and had maximum linguistic access. However, since most of the mothers came from families and communities in rural locations with limited means, a better life in Mexico was not possible for the EBLAD child. For many of these children, limited resources and rural communities would have resulted in inadequate schooling experiences and no special education services.

Whereas one may be inclined when reading about these sacrifices to deem them extreme and really burdensome, it is important to view them in context. It is critical to understand that for these women being a mother is a major source of pride. As such, everything that they do, every minute that is spent, every dollar that is set aside, emboldens their capacity to be a mother. Ultimately, they are willing to withstand so many difficult situations because it is in the best interest of their children. These women not only make sacrifices to uphold their maternal identity, they also gain strength from them:

Pues sí, dice uno, 'De mover el cielo'. Pues sí, sí por mi hijo, sí muevo lo que tenga que mover. Porque no, no me gustaría–. [...] Pues no [tengo acceso a] todos los recursos, pero a veces uno, por los hijos, o por ayudarlos, por el bienestar de ellos, uno pelea por ellos. Porque le digo que, cuando empezó este cambio de escuelas, yo decía, 'Creo que lo voy a dejar, creo que voy a tomar eso de volver a regresarlo a esa escuela'. Pero yo decía, 'Pero, ¿por qué? ¿Por qué lo voy a dejar a mi hijo, si es algo que yo no veo que está bien en él? Yo tengo que pelear, debo de ser fuerte para él, para que él sea también fuerte'. [...] Sí [haber tenido éxito en el pasado con Dan], sí me hace sentirme más segura de mí misma, que puedo hacerlo. Que a veces es un poquito difícil, pero sí se puede. Yo no sé si sea esa su pregunta. [risas] Sí se puede.

[*Well yes, like the saying goes, 'To move the sky'. Yes, yes for my son, I do move what I have to move. Because no, I would not like – [...] Well, I do not [have access to] all the resources, but sometimes one, for the children, or for helping them, for their welfare, one fights for them. Because I say that when this school change began, I would say, 'I think I'm going to leave it, I think I'm going to go back to that school again'. But I said, 'But, why, why am I going to leave my son there, if it is something that I do not see that is right for him? I have to fight, I must be strong for him, so that he can be strong too. '[...] Yes [having been successful in the past with Dan], it does make me feel more confident about myself, that I can do it. That sometimes is a bit difficult, but you can. I do not know if that is your question. [laughs] Yes you can.*]

In this testimony, Paty shares a primal truth of each mother in this study – that she is willing to move heaven and earth to make sure that her children are safe, healthy and well.

These mothers are not disengaged, and their experiences are not reflective of women who are unable to advocate for themselves or their children. Rather, these experiences prove how engaged and how strong they really are. Ultimately, they do not make these sacrifices because they are weak or powerless, but rather because they are strong. They are strong because their children need them to be. They are strong because they are mothers.

Note

(1) For the child interviews, the child was allowed to choose the language in which the interview would be conducted. Justin and Dan opted for an English interview and María Teresa chose Spanish.

References

Al-Yagon, M. (2015) Fathers and mothers of children with learning disabilities: Links between emotional and coping resources. *Learning Disability Quarterly* 38 (2), 112–128. https://doi.org/10.1177/0731948713520556

Apple, R.D. (1995) Constructing mothers: Scientific motherhood in the nineteenth and twentieth centuries. *Social History of Medicine* 8 (2), 161–178. https://doi.org/10.1093/shm/8.2.161

Burke, M.M. and Hodapp, R.M. (2014) Relating stress of mothers of children with developmental disabilities to family–school partnerships. *Intellectual and Developmental Disabilities* 52 (1), 13–23. https://doi.org/10.1352/1934-9556-52.1.13

Dykens, E.M., Fisher, M.H., Taylor, J.L., Lambert, W. and Miodrag, N. (2014) Reducing distress in mothers of children with autism and other disabilities: A randomized trial. *Pediatrics* 134 (2), e454–e463. https://doi.org/10.1542/peds.2013-3164

Elliott, S., Powell, R. and Brenton, J. (2015) Being a good mom: Low-income, Black single mothers negotiate intensive mothering. *Journal of Family Issues* 36 (3), 351–370. https://doi.org/10.1177/0192513X13490279

Figueroa, A.M. (2011) Citizenship and education in the homework completion routine. *Anthropology & Education Quarterly* 42 (3), 263–280. https://doi.org/10.1111/j.1548-1492.2011.01131.x

Findler, L., Klein Jacoby, A. and Gabis, L. (2016) Subjective happiness among mothers of children with disabilities: The role of stress, attachment, guilt and social support. *Research in Developmental Disabilities* 55, 44–54. https://doi.org/10.1016/j.ridd.2016.03.006

Fitzmaurice, H., Flynn, M. and Hanafin, J. (2020) Parental involvement in homework: A qualitative Bourdieusian study of class, privilege, and social reproduction. *International Studies in Sociology of Education* 0 (0), 1–22. https://doi.org/10.1080/09620214.2020.1789490

Hutchison, K. (2012) A labour of love: Mothers, emotional capital and homework. *Gender and Education* 24 (2), 195–212. https://doi.org/10.1080/09540253.2011.602329

Lalvani, P. (2019) *Constructing the (M)Other: Narratives of Disability, Motherhood, and the Politics of Normal*. New York: Peter Lang.

Part 3
Making Room for Mothers: Visions of Radical Possibilities

12 Repairing Broken Systems

The experiences of mothers raising emergent bilinguals labeled as dis/abled (EBLADs) are fraught with challenges, but equally defined by tenacity, love and commitment. These women experience many hardships, yet they do not allow such hardships to define them or to limit their children or their capacity to mother. Similarly, their values, perspectives and ideologies are as complicated, intertwined and, at times, contradictory as the concepts of dis/abilities and bilingualism. Yet, these mothers make great efforts to sort through their feelings, their ideas and the information that is thrust upon them by schools in order to facilitate successful learning for their children. The catalyst for all of this effort lies in the fact that the women in this book view a mother's role as that of being the first teacher. As such, they are eager to teach their children, support them, help them and provide for them. However, disability labels take many aspects of this role away from mothers of emergent bilinguals labeled as dis/abled (MoEBLADs) because they present a myriad of unknowns. They shift all of the 'power' from mothers to the teachers, doctors and service providers; the experts – 'los que le dieron la etiqueta' [the ones who assigned the label], leaving the mothers feeling 'impotente' [powerless].

As a result, the mothers do not know what to do – how to help, support and teach their children; therefore, they step away from the academic realm (the place where the disability 'lives') and find other ways to still be the child's mother: doubling down on sacrifices, doubling down on external support. All of this is a form of mothering by proxy: teaching them about God, teaching them self-care and fostering caring relationships with their other children.

In addition, the one area where they still feel in charge is *in* Spanish. Spanish is the one part of their child's life where they, and not the school, are still the authority: 'español es la lengua maternal' [Spanish is the mother tongue], 'el inglés es el lenguaje de este país' [English is the language of this country], 'yo le enseño español' [I will teach him Spanish], 'yo le puedo enseñar' [I can teach him], 'yo le ayudo' [I can help]. When students are placed in bilingual programs, the mothers feel empowered because they feel they can support their children, assess what they know and what they are being taught in school. However, when schools remove children from bilingual settings and place them in monolingual settings, they take away some of the mother's power and authority. Yet, these mothers find their roles as mothers to be so central to their identity and to their child's advancement that they recoup some of this power by engaging in other parts of their children's lives.

However, most educators do not have a full grasp of this multiplicity of roles. Additionally, a mother's perception of herself and of her role is often unnecessarily challenged by the systems with which she must interact. While the hope is that the narratives shared in this book have brought those issues to light, it is also important to consider how the theories and processes used to gather these stories can be used to create more inviting, inclusive and compassionate educational spaces. What follows are my visions for radical possibilities starting from changes that can be made to policies and teacher education programs, and ending with changes that can be enacted in schools tomorrow.

Putting Theory into Practice

In Part 1 of this book, I outlined the theories that shaped this study: intersectionality, language access as a human right, dis/ability as social construction and testimonios as tools of empowerment. While these theories were integral to the design and analysis of this study, it is my hope that through the remaining chapters it has become evident that the perspectives of MoEBLADs must be at the center in order to understand and best meet the needs of EBLADs.

Intersectionality allows stakeholders to view mothers as the complex human beings they are – taking into account not only the different systems of oppression with which they interact, but also the different people/entities to whom they are beholden. This lens also allows for a deeper understanding of the range of social experiences that students have both inside and outside of the school. In many ways, being the child of an intersectional mother is an identity marker in and of itself because a mother's experiences greatly influence the way in which she raises her child. Access to bilingual education is a human right that should be given to all students, not only those who are deemed as befitting or able to acquire the benefits that come with being bilingual. Access to bilingual learning environments should be granted to all emergent bilingual students in order for them to be able to maintain healthy, supportive and loving relationships with their mothers and transnational siblings.

Additionally, access to bilingual education in the current age of mass deportation is critical to students being able to maintain their independence, as well as have access to an education in the event that their families are forcibly removed from their communities in the United States. By placing students in monolingual settings, schools are not aptly preparing students for their present or their future given that neither of these is bound to English-dominant nations. Instead, these children, their present and their future, are inalienably tied to their Spanish-speaking mothers.

An approach to special education through a dis/ability studies in education framework allows educators and schools to implement special education services in a way that is compatible with the mothers' understandings of special education and dis/ability labels as temporary. Alternatively, there should be more transparent conversations with parents that address the actual educational experiences and trajectories of students who are labeled as dis/abled as being more permanent than not. The mothers in this study made it very clear that they view increased services as an effort to remedy the dis/ability faster, yet this is not necessarily reflective of the intentions or values of the school. However, by adopting a dis/ability as social construction model, schools would need to consider the student and family's social experiences when developing individual education plans (IEPs). Many of the mothers' views regarding dis/ability as human variety were influenced by their experiences with diversity in ability in their country of origin. As such, this model is also supportive of a family's transnational experiences. Additionally, by adopting a special education model that is grounded in dis/ability as social construction, schools can be better equipped to meet the needs of EBLADs in least restrictive environments.

Viewing a woman's narrative as an intentional and political act could transform parent and school relationships from one in which school representatives are privileged and mothers seen as needy into one in which both parties are viewed as valuable and active participants and contributors. By creating space in which mothers are allowed to share their experiences, their needs and their strengths, schools have the capacity to redistribute and repurpose their resources in such a way that they are providing the child and family with the supports that they themselves identify as needing and wanting. This increases the probability of successful educational and social-emotional outcomes.

Each chapter that has been dedicated to the mothers' narratives outlines how their own ideologies align with these aforementioned theories. The mothers viewed their children as 'normal' but limited by their schools' practices and disability labels; they understood that their children were bilingual regardless of how schools classified them; they understood that bilingualism was not a benefit, it was a need and a right; they viewed and valued their children as whole people, not as the sum of their labels. In sharing their stories, the mothers also understood the power in their experiences, the power in their narrative and their capacity to impart change. These theories are not academic jargon, they are ways to explain experiences, to contextualize the individual within the systemic, to name *abstract* feelings and intuitions. Theory allows us to make concrete what is often deemed fleeting or ethereal. As such, it is important that educators, researchers and policymakers take up these theories not just to acknowledge the experiences of the marginalized but also to reduce inequality and increase inclusion.

Intersectional Educational Policies

While policies exist to address the learning needs of students labeled as disabled separate from the learning needs of emergent bilinguals, there remains a major demand for educational policies that address the needs of EBLADs and their families. Singular policies have the potential to create great harm because they do not fully address the needs of the learner, often relegating them to one 'specialty' over another. Additionally, these singular policies do not fully consider the needs of the family. While dis/ability-centered policies like the Individuals with Disabilities Education Act (IDEA) are heavily focused on parent and student rights, these issues are discussed exclusively in English, with information often disseminated only in English as well. On the other hand, other policies, like New York State's Commissioner's Regulations Part 154, that address the linguistic needs of emergent bilinguals and acknowledge the existence of a home language, are primarily accessible by teachers and only use the terms 'disabled' and 'disability' when speaking about the evaluation process. Again, the focus of these policies is not how best to serve the needs of EBLAD students as much as it is how to make sure emergent bilinguals are not inappropriately referred and evaluated. Once under the care of special education providers, these students' multilingual needs are whitewashed and the focus on English acquisition intensifies.

However, this study has highlighted the ways in which educational and social-emotional issues around language and dis/ability are intimately connected. Whereas all the mothers were much more concerned with remedying the dis/ability before developing their child's bilingualism, one could argue that the development of bilingualism and biliteracy is in many ways an equally pressing need. If a student has a dis/ability but they are only getting services in English rather than in both English and the home language, then the child's opportunities to practice the skills learned in those settings are limited to the school, as is the child's academic support network. However, by incorporating the child's home language into the services, the child's learning environment broadens and the opportunities for their parents to support their academic development at home increase. Current educational policies only partially address the needs of these students. These issues can be remedied by amending existing separatist policies in order to be more inclusive of all minoritized students and/or by enacting new policies specifically developed for this population. The most important task is to ensure that EBLAD students are being properly serviced and that parents are adequately informed and included. In order to do this, holistic policies that address their unique needs and build on their cultural, communal and linguistic strengths must be established.

Correcting the Literature

Many emerging scholars write about the need to reframe pre-existing scholarships, but the truth is that the existing literature does not need to be reframed, it needs to be corrected. The findings of this study support previous studies, which revealed parental engagement strategies within Latinx communities that vary from, but are no less critical than, traditional methods of engagement. However, this study also highlights the ways in which mothers attempt to support their children in traditional ways. Much of the existing literature focuses on redefining engagement to include tasks such as encouraging the child to go to school and teaching good manners. While those remain valuable forms of engagement, this study indicates that MoEBLADs have also adopted very traditional modes of academic engagement such as reading with their children, helping them with homework, taking them to the library and finding tutors. Additionally, the mothers in this study are emblematic of the great lengths to which mothers go in order to support their children's academic growth in more traditional ways. It is important for future scholarship to acknowledge these acts, given that they have the capacity to counter biased anecdotal evidence that is often cited by school representatives in order to disparage and discount parental participation. Even while being highly engaged and making considerable financial and timely investments, these mothers often viewed themselves as disengaged because they have internalized the school's definition of engagement as participating in acts that take place at school. Scholarship has not just the capacity but ultimately the responsibility to validate all forms of academic engagement inside and outside of schools. It is of critical importance that research be inclusive of all experiences rather than continuing to support hegemonic systems of power and perception.

This study confirms that regardless of school-based English monolingual language policies and programming, EBLADs are bilingual children. As such, more research needs to be dedicated to the actual linguistic practices of EBLADs. As previously stated, a great deal of the literature surrounding this population focuses heavily on English language development rather than bilingualism/biliteracy support and development. Additionally, by focusing primarily on the economic and cognitive benefits of bilingualism, bilingual education researchers are contributing to the cooption of bilingual education as a gifted and talented program that excludes socioeconomically, culturally, linguistically and neurodiverse learners. The kind of research presented in this study is needed in order to counter and ultimately destroy unfounded beliefs of bilingualism as confusing for children labeled as dis/abled. In order to push this conversation on true inclusion forward, we must begin to make greater use of the term 'neurodiversity'. Neurodiversity, unlike disability or special education, is not a term rooted in medical ideology but rather a term that is grounded on scientific research. As such, neurodiversity is a term that describes the fact that thinking differently is within the definition of normal – it represents human variation. Thinking differently is not just a reflection of cultural diversity. The struggles that these students encounter are not just cultural misunderstandings. As a matter of fact, this idea of 'cultural misunderstandings' can be a dangerous idea to introduce because it can quickly and easily lead to the idea of cultural deficiency. These erroneous beliefs about the linguistic and neurological needs of EBLADs are inadvertently upheld by bilingual education researchers' ongoing disregard for neurodiversity and special education researchers' continued dismissiveness of multilingualism. EBLADs' capacity to communicate in Spanish at home and in English at school is indicative of the ways in which bilingualism is not a limitation for students labeled as dis/abled. Once again, research has to take the lead in eradicating inaccurate statements that are based on perception rather than actual data. There remains a need to address the exclusion of neurodiverse students from bilingual education programs. Additionally, the bilingual education community needs to examine the ways in which its pursuits of self-preservation contribute to the othering and exclusion of EBLAD students and their families, not only from bilingual learning spaces but also from bilingual education discourse as a whole. Similarly, the special education community needs to consider the ways in which monolingual placements, be they inclusive or not, contribute to the ongoing isolation of EBLAD children within their homes and of their mothers within their schools. It is important to consider how the linguistic decisions that are made for children lead not only to segregation within families, but also to the segregation of families within schools.

The final way in which the current literature needs to be corrected is in the way it frames culturally and linguistically diverse parents. Similarly to the ways in which they are framed in discourse surrounding parental engagement, parents of emergent bilinguals labeled as dis/abled (PoE-BLADs) are often discussed within the special education and dis/abilities advocacy literature as absent and/or disengaged. This is often blamed on issues of class, race and language. However, there is little or no discussion of the ways in which schools contribute to parents being uninformed as well as misinformed. This study presented the ways in which MoE-BLADs viewed and valued teachers' perceptions as superior due to their positionality. While a great deal of the literature surrounding a parent's role in the special education process focuses heavily on their advocacy practices, very little of it discusses the ways in which educational disparities between parents and teachers contribute to unequal power dynamics.

The MoEBLADs in this study were often unaware of their rights as parents; additionally, whenever they tried to advocate for their child they were often met with walls of resistance. Because these mothers have limited resources, their capacity to fight back is greatly restricted. If the expectation is on parents to be more engaged, then future research must explore the ways in which schools facilitate and/or hinder engagement. For example, what message is communicated to a parent when they are never given an IEP in their preferred language? What about when no independent translators are made available for IEP meetings? How is a parent's capacity to advocate for their child impacted by only being given the parental rights guide in English or only in written form, and often without explanation or discussion? Do parents genuinely view teacher statements during IEP meetings as suggestions? Lastly, does a 45-minute IEP meeting during which multiple educators need to speak foster feelings of equal partnership with parents? For far too long, scholarship has placed the burden of participation on the mothers without analyzing the ways in which schools hinder access. As such, future research needs to be conducted in order to properly contextualize existing levels of maternal advocacy within spaces in which power is not equally distributed, oftentimes intentionally.

Start with Collaboration in Mind: Preparing the Next Generation of Teachers

Although a great deal of the changes needed within education are grounded in policies and practices that take place in schools, there are also several ways in which teacher education programs can change in order to improve the social and academic outcomes for EBLADs and their families. A list of suggestions that can serve as a starting point follows.

Demystifying language learning and multilingual education for students labeled as dis/abled

There is still a lot of misinformation regarding students labeled as dis/abled's capacity and ability to learn multiple languages. This misinformation is based on outdated data that is not reflective of students' actual linguistic practices. In order to ensure that students labeled as dis/abled have equal access to bilingual learning spaces, pre-service and in-service teachers in bilingual and special education programs should be presented with the current research which indicates cognitive and social-emotional gains for students labeled as dis/abled who are educated bilingually. This is of particular importance for educators who seek to be inclusive. If we aim to create truly inclusive classrooms, schools and societies, then we must also make sure that all students have access to multilingual education and/or bilingual learning spaces. This is particularly important for students who are emergent bilinguals. These students are already bilingual, regardless of the school's classification. As such, teacher candidates need to be educated about the linguistic human rights of all students with the same fervor that they are educated about other civil rights, including but not limited to dis/ability rights and racial equity.

Develop strategies that allow families who speak languages other than English to support their EBLAD learners

Teacher preparation programs that prepare teachers to work with multilingual learners – whether that be in monolingual settings or not – need to help teacher candidates develop strategies that will allow non-English-speaking families to participate in the learning of their children. These strategies must extend beyond holidays and cultural celebrations into collaborative practices that can be sustained throughout the academic year. Additionally, teachers need to be prepared to make more concrete and clear use of the existing relationship between home and school as well as ways in which to change these relationships if they are not constructive and mutually beneficial. Some in-school strategies could include inviting mothers to be classroom parents – during this time they can lead read aloud with the class or a small group in the home language or give a community tour in the home language.

At home, strategies can include sending books home in the home language that the parent can read to the child; providing parents with home language guides for academic tasks; sending home bilingual newsletters that let mothers know what the class is currently working on and examples of how the mothers can support this work that are not linguistically bound. It would behoove teacher training programs that teach about lesson plan and curricula development to incorporate a parent connection section into their teaching models and teacher expectations.

Consider home language practices when developing curriculum and units of study

Unless it is specifically geared toward bilingual certification, most teacher preparation programs focused on the education of culturally and linguistically diverse students lean heavily toward English teaching methods. As such, the home language practices are not given as much consideration as English language teaching. In many cases, the so-called language gap is used as a way to validate this omission of the home language (Angrist et al., 2008; Hirsch & Moats, 2001; Rich, 2013). However, this focus on English not only excludes EBLADs from bilingual learning programs, but it also critically impacts the ways in which home languages are valued by children and their families. Beyond supporting bilingualism and biliteracy, considering home language practices can support students' social and emotional development. By incorporating the home language into lessons and units of study, teachers communicate value for the home language to their students. As such, the child is encouraged to value the home language. The home language shifts from a language barrier to a source of pride and potential growth. Current presentations of English as central can result in a loss of linguistic and cultural identity for the child and in a disruption of the parent–child relationship by placing speakers of languages other than English as inferior, including parents.

In order to avoid contributing to this, teacher education programs should teach all teachers to consider the language practices of each student in the home and encourage teachers to find ways to incorporate the home language into the classroom in ways that are culturally responsive and socially sustainable.

Extend special education teacher preparation beyond English as a second language

One way to support the inclusion of home languages in school is by expanding teacher language training beyond English-only teaching. While sitting in on professional development training, one often hears someone proclaiming that all teachers are language teachers. While this is absolutely true, it is important to consider the unspoken yet implicit and impactful assertions that this statement makes about language. Whenever a teacher makes this claim, the language they are talking about is English. However, that is not the only language that students speak. These students are not living in English-only worlds and so their education must not be solely focused on English only. In order to address the linguistic needs of EBLADs, it is necessary for special education teachers to think about the student's linguistic practices in the same way that they consider learning styles/modalities. In order to do this, teacher candidates must be taught strategies that will help them support their students' bilingualism and biliteracy even if they are not necessarily bilingual and biliterate. Just as special education teacher candidates are taught to incorporate teaching methods such as universal design for learning (UDL) in order to make their lessons accessible to all learners, they should also be trained on multilingual theories such as translanguaging. Just like UDL, translanguaging aims to meet the needs of all learners while viewing their current linguistic practices as points of strength rather than weakness. Translanguaging should not be considered a modification or accommodation, but rather a theoretical stance and an intentional pedagogical approach that creates space for students to learn and express themselves using all of the linguistic and multimodal resources at their disposal, rather than simply a named language like English or Spanish that is a sociocultural construction.

Additionally, any college course can influence how students view culturally and linguistically diverse people by exposing them to multilingual texts and expanding the cannon to include more writers of color. The needs and strengths of individuals with varying home language practices should be integrated into all teaching courses through the use of intersectional texts, literature with people of color as the central characters and studies that center the experiences of individuals of diverse backgrounds. Pre-service teachers should be encouraged to learn about their students' lives and experiences outside of school. They should also be encouraged to get to know their students' communities in addition to the communities where they work. Information like this will help pre-service (and in-service) teachers develop pedagogical practices that complement students' and families' lives at home. This will allow teacher candidates to have a greater understanding of these populations' lived experiences, which could lead to more socially just teaching practices.

Reframing the way we talk about (and to) parents

Teachers often make a lot of assumptions about special education parents, their goals and their intentions. This is particularly true regarding parental rights. Many teachers believe that parents are acutely aware of their rights about due process and about being able to be advocates for their children. However, that is not necessarily always true. Oftentimes, PoEBLADs are viewed as either disengaged when they behave in passive ways or confrontational when they act assertively. It is important for teachers to understand and be aware of the assumptions that they make about the ways in which parents act and the decisions that parents make. These are often influenced by a teacher's positionality in the world.

It is also important to understand that when we perceive parents in these diametrically opposed ways (as either meek or overbearing), we are privileging White, middle-class standards and reinforcing the status quo of structural inequality. In many ways, society expects teachers to behave as gatekeepers of the status quo; as a result, we further alienate parents, disadvantage students and make our tasks as educators much more laborious. As such, it is critically important that pre-service and in-service teacher candidates engage in social justice curricula that force them to unpack their own perceptions and understandings of minoritized people and minoritizing systems, as well as their expected and actual roles within these systems.

Additionally, teacher candidates should be taught more concrete ways to engage and connect with parents as well as ways to build effective partnerships. Beyond this, they must be informed about the ways in which parents should be talked to and talked about in order to disrupt unequal distributions of power and collaboration between the home and the school, both in the eyes of the child and in the eyes of society. As such, teacher education programs should ensure that they do not solely present PoEBLADs through deficit narratives that focus solely on their needs while disregarding their contributions.

Recollecting Together: Communal Learning through Collective Inquiry

Another aspect of this study that was very fruitful was the use of the descriptive processes. The stories that were gathered through the processes highlight the potential for community building that is created when educational researchers incorporate pedagogical practices and inquiry tools from other fields into their work with parents. This is particularly true for the use of recollections, descriptive observations and participatory rank methodology. These methods allowed for the complexity of the mothers' lives to come to the forefront. The mothers were able to share that they value bilingualism for their children, the ways in which bilingualism will benefit their children in the future, along with the ways that dis/ability labels increase their children's access to services while also increasing the strains on the women. Additionally, narrative questions allowed the mothers to steer the conversations/interviews in directions that were not anticipated. As such, they revealed the ways in which linguistic and cognitive labels impact the lives of other family members; the ways in which the mothers feel isolated from their communities as a result of the labels; and the emotional and individual sacrifices that the mothers make in the interests of their EBLAD children.

The recollections were critical to this study because they not only allowed the mothers to share more of their experiences without interruption, but they also allowed them control over what they shared as well as expanding their audience to include other mothers like them. While all the women had been tasked with sharing a memory in which they had a difficult time supporting their child's learning, their stories were not reflective of educational barriers – nor barriers related to the child's linguistic placement or dis/ability label. Instead, the mothers shared about the ways in which their lives are already strained and the ways in which their own monolingualism, their marriages and their struggles with their other children make it difficult for them to be more engaged. While many of the stories shared during the recollection session had been introduced in the one-to-one interviews, the recollections allowed the women to hear their experiences alongside each other, to notice the ways in which they were not alone, in which their stressors were not a reflection of an innate failure, but rather of a shared experience and ultimately a strength. The fact that the participants shared such intimate stories with each other, in their first meeting, is indicative of the need these women have for community, for open discourse and for support. In addition to continuing to make space for recollections in research as a way to create space for participant voices and community, it would also be very beneficial to use recollections with parents in schools. Recollections could be used during parent–teacher association meetings; they could be used at the beginning of parent trainings, etc. With regard to the needs of EBLAD families, recollections could be used during IEP meetings and during triennials – here the prompt could center on sharing a memory of the child as a way to build a collective awareness of each individual's experience with that child. This practice could greatly increase parental participation during these meetings; it would also allow the mothers some control over how their child is discussed, and it would give the school representatives a glimpse of the mother–child relationship and the child's life outside of school.

Family Observations as Pedagogical Practice: Resurrecting the Home Visit

There was a time when home visits were conducted as part of a child's educational record. Multiple studies have shown the benefits that can arise from teachers engaging in home visits (Auerbach, 2009; Mann, 2014; Meyer & Mann, 2006; Weiss, 1993). However, in the late 1990s, one prominent study stated that '[t]here is no evidence that providing case management by means of home visits is an effective way to improve social, educational, or health outcomes for adults or children' (St Pierre & Layzer, 1999). This study focused primarily on the role of home visits on the outcomes of children and families from low socioeconomic backgrounds. Findings like this have contributed to the drastic reduction in home visits within public schools, particularly in urban environments. Nonetheless, the St Pierre and Layzer study did not address the impact of home visits on parental engagement or community building. Whereas home visits associated with comprehensive child development programs were found to have low impact in relation to their high costs, perhaps it is time to revisit the role that home visits can play in the lives of minoritized families. One way to reduce costs is to engage in teacher-directed home visits that focus primarily on observation rather than service delivery. In addition to being cost-effective, descriptive observations allow for a more complete understanding of the child's social and linguistic practices. However, it is important that these observations be descriptive observations intended to understand and document what is, rather than to qualify it. All of the mothers in this study offered their home as a research site and/or interview location. Many invited me into their home for the very first interview and most others after one or two interviews. Even those who did not initially offer up their home were welcoming once they were presented with the purpose of the observations and the role I, as the researcher, would play. It was made explicitly clear that the observations were to serve as an additional data set with which to understand the child, the family dynamic and the family's linguistic practices. The mothers were also given access to all notes and recordings that were made during and/ or as a result of the observations. This level of transparency established trust and allowed the participants to understand why the observations were important. As such, it would be useful for schools to first train their educators in descriptive observations and then make home observations a central component of the parent–school relationship. Likewise, parents can be invited into the classroom to observe their child in order to build mutual levels of exposure, trust and vulnerability. In addition, by giving the mothers an opportunity to watch their children in school, they can develop a greater understanding of their child's linguistic practices as well as the ways in which their dis/ability impacts their school-based learning.

Disability? Language? Family?: Putting Needs in Context

Similar to the observations and recollections, the participatory rank method (PRM) could also be used to strengthen parent–school relationships. In this study, the PRM revealed the urgency and/or lack thereof that a mother feels about their child's bilingualism and/or dis/ability by putting these needs alongside the other needs that the mothers were managing. During the PRM, the three Testimonialistas disclosed the factors that impact their ability to be more active in their children's education. This exercise exposed the varying stressors that mothers must manage as well as the financial, physical and emotional tolls these took on them. As previously mentioned, the PRM is a method that is typically used in public health research; given the impact that education has on these families and that public (physical and mental) health matters have on educational outcomes, it is wise to incorporate more field-based methods into educational research. The PRM could also serve as a tool for schools. Through the use of the PRM, schools would be better equipped to meet the actual needs of the parents in their schools, which would be reflected in the services and workshops they provide, thus not only increasing participation but also outcomes.

During the recollections, all of the mothers expressed an interest in mental health supports as well as child-rearing workshops from their schools in lieu of workshops focused on teaching the latest math strategies or those explaining reading levels. This revelation is particularly important when one takes into account the disparate linguistic practices between the school and the home. What use is an academically focused parent workshop if the child is only bringing home English materials, thereby eliminating the mother's capacity to support her child? These mothers have shown themselves to be incredibly industrious and have found creative ways to support their children academically and linguistically. Unlike a survey, PRMs' use of conversation and reflection allows for the speaker to discuss their needs as they relate to their life rather than the needs that relate to the listener (surveyor). Engaging in a PRM with parents would allow schools to identify the non-traditional ways in which parents are supporting their children's development and the ways in which schools can facilitate greater parental involvement both at home and at school.

Supporting Families at Home

The mothers in this study did not readily identify school practices that were supportive of them. More often, when asked 'In which ways does your child's school support you and your family's needs?', the mothers often answered with general references to sending books home, providing meals at school, hosting afterschool programs, providing school-based services, etc. However, when asked for ways that they could be supported, mothers often asked for specifics like workshops on how to support their child with a disability at home (i.e. behavior management and homework support) and they wanted to know about the expectations regarding their level of engagement with the school and with their child's academic lives. In addition to these recommendations, I believe that as educators we must reconsider the purpose of homework. The mothers in this study have indicated the immense amount of familial stress that is brought about by homework. Thus, teachers should strongly consider the amount of homework they assign; they should send home translated copies of homework assignments which could easily be done by setting up a weekly homework schedule (e.g. Mondays 30 minutes of reading, Tuesday 30 minutes of writing using a prompt, and so on), thereby reducing the load on teachers as well as parents. Providing translated homework is particularly important for homework assignments that require parental support and guidance. Along that vein, students should be allowed to complete academic tasks in their home language. In this way, parents can gain insight into their child's learning as well as support their home language development while staying connected to content. With regard to afterschool programs, schools that have emergent bilinguals placed in monolingual programs should prioritize offering language enrichment, homework support and tutoring to these students during afterschool programming. These programs should be offered at no cost or through a sliding scale.

Supporting Mothers

As an educator, and mother, finalizing this book in the midst of a pandemic when schools are being tasked with the financial and public health safety of the world, I recognize that for too long we have asked schools to take on more and more responsibilities as social systems, including schools, are stripped of their budgets (Giroux, 2018; Leachman *et al.*, 2017). To date, schools are responsible for offering meals, child-care, welfare checks and mental and physical healthcare, in addition to education. Some schools have been able to meet their communities needs through the development of full-service community schools (Royston & Madkins, 2019), but most of the time schools are left to their own devices (e.g. apply for grants and find community partners). As such, I hesitate to make recommendations that would ask schools to take on more. And yet, I also recognize that families, and society at large, view schools as central to the health and sustainability of their communities. Schools are a source of community and information. Thus, my first recommendation is that we restore school funding and allocate money for the services we know parents and students need. Some of those services fit within the scope of traditional perspectives on education such as at-home technology access for all students, dedicated school translators and interpreters, an increase in bilingual teachers and programs and small group tutoring. Other services, such as parenting workshops, adult English as a new language classes and family counseling, do not fit within traditional conceptualizations of schooling but are no less impactful on children's academic success. Knowing that there are other mothers in the world who are susceptible to domestic violence, who are raising children across multiple states and countries, it is important that we consider supports that are parent focused. The purpose of naming these needs is, again, not to ask more of schools but to share supports that mothers have identified. These are needs that have to be foregrounded at the district, state and federal level.

References

Angrist, J., Chin, A. and Godoy, R. (2008) Is Spanish-only schooling responsible for the Puerto Rican language gap? *Journal of Development Economics* 85 (1–2), 105–128. https://doi.org/10.1016/j.jdeveco.2006.06.004

Auerbach, S. (2009) Walking the walk: Portraits in leadership for family engagement in urban schools. *School Community Journal; Lincoln* 19 (1), 9–31.

Giroux, H.A. (2018) When schools become dead zones of the imagination. In K.J. Saltman and A.J. Means (eds) *The Wiley Handbook of Global Educational Reform* (pp. 503–515). Hoboken, NJ: John Wiley & Sons, Ltd. https://doi.org/10.1002/9781119082316.ch24

Hirsch, E.D. and Moats, L.C. (2001) Overcoming the language gap. *American Educator* 25 (2), 4–9.

Leachman, M., Masterson, K. and Figueroa, E. (2017) A Punishing Decade for School Funding. Center on Budget and Policy Priorities. See https://www.cbpp.org/research/state-budget-and-tax/a-punishing-decade-for-school-funding (accessed 16 September 2020).

Mann, V. (2014) Spanish-language home visitation to disadvantaged Latino preschoolers: A means of promoting language development and English school readiness. *Creative Education* 5 (6), 411–426. https://doi.org/10.4236/ce.2014.56051

Meyer, J.A. and Mann, M.B. (2006) Teachers' perceptions of the benefits of home visits for early elementary children. *Early Childhood Education Journal* 34 (1), 93–97. https://doi.org/10.1007/s10643-006-0113-z

Rich, M. (2013) Language-gap study bolsters a push for pre-K. *The New York Times*, 21 October. See https://www.nytimes.com/2013/10/22/us/language-gap-study-bolsters-a-push-for-pre-k.html (accessed 10 December 2020).

Royston, M.M. de and Madkins, T.C. (2019) A question of necessity or of equity? Full-service community schools and the (mis)education of Black youth. *Journal of Education for Students Placed at Risk (JESPAR)* 24 (3), 244–271. https://doi.org/10.1080/1 0824669.2019.1615920

St Pierre, R.G. and Layzer, J.I. (1999) Using home visits for multiple purposes: The comprehensive child development program. *The Future of Children* 9 (1), 134–151. https://doi.org/10.2307/1602725

Weiss, H.B. (1993) Home visits: Necessary but not sufficient. *The Future of Children* 3 (3), 113–128. https://doi.org/10.2307/1602545

13 Moving Forward Together

The first time that I saw the mothers together was also the last time.

Throughout my years working with descriptive inquiry, I had seen all of the ways in which shared storytelling turned individual strangers into a community. Sometimes, the connections made during those recollections would develop into lifelong friendships and sometimes they would fizzle out after a week. Still, regardless of the longevity of the resulting relationship, there was always something so powerful about that day – the day when the stories were told; the day when you learned to take up space and to give up space; the day you shared a part of yourself without context, without addendums, and connected with a room full of strangers around stories about entry or play. I wanted this for Paty, María and Ana.

I, like others, have known the loneliness of suffering in silence and the immense comfort of a supportive ear. In listening to their stories, I saw myself, my mother, my aunts, my former students' mothers. I understood both the specificity of their experience and the universality of their feelings. I also understood that while we would remain connected, the level of intimacy that had developed over months of conversation was not sustainable. Eventually, I had to write about what had been shared in order to report on the studies outcomes but, more importantly, as a way to honor the lives and stories that had been shared with me. I was also on the verge of becoming a mother for the second time. Ultimately, the relationship we had developed would change. I want to make it clear that I do not have any delusions of grandeur nor believe that merely talking to me had changed these women's lives. However, I do know that the power of storytelling, of friendship, of community and participating in this study did offer that. Still, I knew that the most significant thing that I could give them was a moment to feel what I felt during my summers in Vermont, a moment to feel a part of a community, and with that in mind the four of us gathered on a Sunday afternoon in my home to share a recollection and a meal.

We all prepared stories to share around one prompt:

Think back to times when you felt connected to your child's learning and schooling experience, yet were also unclear as to how to support them. This can be a moment in which you ultimately felt successful, ineffective, frustrated, confused or overwhelmed.

Surprisingly, to me, none of the mothers really spoke to this question; instead, they reflected on the things that get in the way of their support of their children's academic careers. They talked not only about language, but also about their own education levels. But the longest and strongest topic from the recollections that day tied together the suffering and stress that these mothers were enduring. Once again, a room of women who had never met before, took the anonymity, of sorts, as an opportunity for release.

Paty talked about Carlos Santo's drug abuse; María expounded on her husband's alcoholism; and Ana recounted her husband's affair. As each woman talked, the others nodded not just in support, but also in agreement: they had been there, they knew this pain. After they were all done sharing, they began to talk openly about the similarities in their experiences: María revealed that her husband had also had an online affair, so had Paty's. Ana and María talked about how frustrated they felt by their Spanish monolingualism; Paty shared how frustrating it was to have access to classes but lack availability. But they also talked about how much they loved their children, how much joy they found in motherhood – even if it was all-consuming and exhausting. They went on like this for three hours.

That afternoon, we gathered for nearly five hours. While sharing a meal, we shared our testimonios. We laughed. We cried. We came together and found comfort in each other. We recounted the moments that tried to break us and in doing so showed our whole selves. If only for one day.[1]

This book is a culmination of the relationships that were built, of the stories that were told and the moments that were shared. I have made every attempt to present these women as complex beings; I do not want them to be reduced to tropes: they are neither strong nor broken, they are not fragile or resilient. They are Paty, Ana, María, Carmela, Carlota, Nancy, Rosa, Sara, Rosario and Elodia. These 10 mothers are complex women who are living their lives to the best of their abilities, putting the needs of their children at the forefront time and time again. Yet, the experiences that they have with their spouses, other children, parents, friends and other public systems, heavily influence the choices they make and how they make sense of their children's academic experiences. Thus, I see this book not as a presentation or a revelation but rather as an invitation for teachers, administrators and researchers to dig deeper, to act intentionally, to connect with mothers. They have a lot they want to share.

I want to close by acknowledging that throughout this book, I often hesitated to compare these mothers' experiences to those gathered in other studies, in large part because this study was unique, it happened in a very particular moment in time, in a particular community. However, the biggest motivator was that I wanted to stay true to the process of descriptive inquiry which is grounded in describing what is before you without comparison to others. Throughout the study and throughout the writing of this book, I have returned to Carini's words in 'Meditation: On Description':

> Describing I pause, and pausing attend. Describing requires that I stand back and consider. Describing requires that I not rush to judgment or conclude before I have looked. Describing makes room for something to be fully present. Describing is slow, particular work. I have to set aside familiar categories for classifying or generalizing. I have to stay with the subject of my attention. I have to give it time to speak, to show itself.

> I have to trust that what I am attending to makes sense; that it isn't a merely accidental or chance event. [...] To describe teaches me that the subject of my attention always exceeds what I can see. [...] To describe requires and instills respect.

> [...]

> To describe is to value. (Carini, 2001: 163–164)

As such, I wanted to share these women's stories without tying them to others, I wanted to give them 'time to speak'. I knew that their experiences were not 'merely accidental or chance event[s]' and I understood that their experiences alone are worthy and have a lot to teach us. I wanted to make 'room for [these mothers] to be fully present'. It is my hope that as you read this book, you feel like I have done that. I hope that you see that you now carry with you the stories of these mothers. I hope that you can appreciate the complexity of it all, why I chose to describe rather than compare; I was instilling respect, I was valuing.

Note

(1) At the end of the collective session, all of the Testimonialistas traded contact information. In order to respect their privacy, any contact I have had with the Testimonialistas since has primarily revolved around our families (my daughter was born six weeks after the study concluded) and/or follow up studies. Unless, of course, the mother brought up a different topic. Nonetheless, to date I am not aware of them gathering again.

Reference

Carini, P.F. (2001) Meditation: On description. In P.F. Carini (ed.) *Starting Strong: A Different Look at Children, Schools, and Standards* (pp. 163–164). New York: Teachers College Press.

Making Personal, Professional and Global Connections: An Afterword

David J. Connor

Parents who are sometimes seen, but rarely heard. Stereotyped as passive, meek, neglectful of attending parent–teacher conferences and other school events.

Children who are emergent bilinguals labeled as dis/abled (EBLAD), prompting confusion in schools – vulnerable to falling between the many cracks created by a fragmented and confusing educational system.

Teachers who are insufficiently prepared in their own life experiences and within education certification programs to best prioritize pedagogical approaches to meet EBLADs' needs.

School psychologists who emphasize monolingualism in education programs, reflecting society's devaluing of languages other than English.

These are the actors in the world that Dr María Cioè-Peña shares with readers – a place currently seething in a hostile political climate where undocumented people fear for themselves and their children. In *(M)othering Labeled Children: Bilingualism and Disability in the Lives of Latinx Mothers*, María deftly guides us through this complex world, at best partially known, and usually unseen by most readers. As a mother, as a Latina, as a woman of color, as a bilingual person, as an immigrant, as a former working-class child who recalls the urban, public school experience, María brings these aspects of her identity to bear on interpreting the lives of mothers who are some of the most marginalized people in our society.

There is so much to be said about this book, but due to space limitations, I have selected three broad realms to comment upon, with each realm containing several elements to discuss. For this purpose, I used a pedagogical device that begins with an assumption – every reader makes connections with the text as they engage in the ongoing process of reading. These connections are categorized as: text-to-self (igniting personal associations), text-to-text (linking to other literature, both similar and different) and text-to-world (corresponding to issues of life in general). I always liked teaching this method as it encourages every reader to engage with the text in a highly personalized manner. At the same time, making these connections generates diverse points that are taken up in discussions that are complex, layered and worth exploring.

'Complex' and 'layered' are words to describe the world that María explores and the portrayals of mothers in this book. As I progressed through the chapters, I found myself having internal conversations about many thoughts triggered by her writing. Even after putting down the manuscript, vivid descriptions of mothers' experiences lingered in my mind as I walked along busy avenues or waited to meet friends for coffee. As a member of María's dissertation committee, I recall the study's first incarnation, and telling colleagues how interesting I was finding the study. In reading the initial manuscript, I was brought close to the lives of these mothers, and their words had an emotional impact upon me, making an indelible impression. In the remainder of this afterword, I share some of the thoughts that went through my mind as I read both the initial draft and the current book.

The Personal

On a personal level, I had two main connections. The first was thinking about Roberto (pseudonym), a Mexican-American friend I've known for over three decades. As I read the accounts of mothers' lives, they reminded me of tales Roberto shared over the years about his single mother who had immigrated in the late 1950s to the United States from Mexico. She worked non-stop in low-wage sweatshops to provide for her two sons, believing they'd have a better life than herself. Roberto would tell me about his responsibilities as a seven-year-old translator for his mother, when she negotiated all kinds of systems in a society in which she never felt a true sense of belonging. Arriving with little education, raising two boys and working long hours, his mother found learning English simply too much to handle. Her situation reminds me of when people make comments along the lines of, 'If you live here you should learn the language'. In an ideal world, perhaps. But, in some cases, it is neither easy nor simple (and raises the question of, given what we know of the benefit of bilingualism, how many Americans born in the United States take it upon themselves to learn another language?). Moreover, being unable to learn the dominant language knowingly circumscribes the lives of those who already struggle on many fronts. The idea of *sacrificio* (Cuevas, 2019), the notion of Latinx mothers placing all others before themselves, even to their own detriment, is exemplified in this book.

The second personal connection was of recalling experiences I had as a teacher with monolingual Spanish-speaking mothers of bilingual high schoolers labeled learning disabled (LD) or emotionally disturbed

(ED). My students, too, acted as translators for their parents. It made for memorable situations for several reasons. Students, who were sometimes challenging with larger-than-life personalities, seemed to shrink as they stood next to their mother. I interpreted their behavior as being respectful toward their mother, mixed with a level of anxiety in case I shared information that made them look bad. In these situations, I could see a qualitative change in my students, who were often characterized in special education textbooks as having learned helplessness and were generally stereotyped as unmotivated. In those moments at parent–teacher conferences, they were adult-like, an active facilitator of conversations, responsible for giving their mother access to an English-speaking world and hear news about their own academic performance. I also sensed their internal tug-of-war. On the one hand, students were proud that their mother came to school, demonstrating an interest in them, clearly symbolizing love and care. On the other hand, students also possessed diametrically opposed feelings including, at times, visible shame. They were embarrassed that their mother could not speak English, thereby explicitly marking her status as a member of the social underclass, complete with associations of undereducation and underemployment. It was painful to witness.

The Professional

At the professional level, I think there has always been significant conceptual confusion within the fields of bilingual education about disability, and in the field of special education about bilingualism. For many years in schools, children were traditionally divided into one group or the other, separated into self-contained programs, and known as the 'sped kids' and the 'ESL kids'. Rarely were there bilingual special education programs, and those existing struck me as being hyper-segregated. The growth of inclusive education changed the landscape somewhat, requiring educators to be more flexible in differentiating instruction to meet the needs of a recognized diverse student body, and to have ongoing collaborations with other professionals. That said, when recently teaching pre-service and in-service teachers, I noticed that a general sense of apprehension remains about how best to support students identified as disabled *and/or* bilingual learners. In my own teacher-certifying institution, special educators are required to take only one course in teaching emergent bilinguals, and general educators take only one course in inclusive education. While well intended, these single courses are insufficient, suggesting tokenism by foregrounding important issues as if they are exceptions to the norm. Instead, the norm for teachers should be to always center diversity, as it exists in all classrooms throughout New York City and around the country. In my experience, unfortunately, only a minority of professors take this approach. One of them is Dr Bob Gyles, a colleague who, in every university class he teaches, asks potential educators to relate whatever concept or method he is teaching them to (a) an emergent bilingual student, (b) a student with learning disabilities, and (c) an 'advanced' child. It is a simple but strong message for educators to cultivate a disposition that always centers learners with diverse abilities and needs, providing them access to our lessons.

In switching the focus from teacher education programs to educational research, I was once again struck by the incredible power of *testimonios*. As a methodological choice, they go to the heart of capturing life experiences at the intersections of markers of identity. Using them as a tool, researchers access forms of truth that rarely see the light of day and are featured in the hallowed pages of education journals. A beauty of testimonios is the dignity they bring to speakers, providing an opportunity to be listened to in a world that usually devalues and disregards them. The testimonios in this text reveal how the mothers bear witness to the material effects of how policies and politics illustrate systemic, interlocking issues of racism, ableism, classism and sexism in ways that most people do not experience. Positioned at their own particular interstices of race, class, gender and ability (linguistic and otherwise), these mothers' *testimonios* reveal their recognition of how power manifests and circulates within their lives. As such, María's work joins a body of research that purposefully centers diverse parents who have traditionally been denied space to share their words and their worlds (see e.g. Harry & Ocasio-Stoutenberg, 2020; Lalvani, 2019; Sauer & Rosetti, 2020; Valle, 2009).

The Global

At the global level, I contemplated historical issues of immigration central to these mothers' stories, including the courage to take risks and chances when entering a different country and culture. All of these narratives reinforce our knowledge of the fundamental desire of mothers to create better lives for their children, even if they themselves never quite feel that they 'fit in' to society like they do in their place of birth. While María writes of mothers in New York City, the setting could be anywhere in the United States, or in urban centers around the world such as London or Paris, Frankfurt or Sydney, where immigrants – both documented and undocumented – strive to adapt and provide for their children.

Perhaps one of the most lasting impressions I have as a reader of this book is the power of maternal love, and its outweighing of spousal love. The strength of connection between mother and child, and how much – for the women in this study – the mother tongue equates with expressing her love and care. We witness mothers becoming language teachers, by necessity, in their own homes, engaging in their developing children's oral bilingualism, teaching Spanish through religion and customs. At the same time, mothers worry about losing the powerful connections they have with their children who are increasingly translanguaging between home and school, their place of learning representing the mainstream world. As previously mentioned, the mothers' sense of *sacrificio* is astounding, including believing English is more important than Spanish for their children to know. Keenly aware how their offspring's bilingualism will be an invaluable asset, they also know that an important part of their child's life – the world in English – will be out of reach for them. Mindful of not wanting the connections to their children lost entirely to English, the mothers must navigate their own highly complex existence that also involves social isolation, domestic violence, caring for multiple generations of family members and transnational parenting, while living in constant fear of the threat of deportation. Because of these multiple responsibilities, mothers put themselves last and watch as teachers, service providers and doctors assert their power and influence over their children, including pushing for monolingual settings. Mothers comply with what school professionals say and want, while steadfastly nurturing their children's language development in Spanish at home. As María notes, schools are sadly a major factor in the distribution of misinformation regarding bilingualism and disability. That has to change.

Connections Taken Together

I am assuming that if you've arrived at this point in the text, you've had a similar experience to me – making various connections to your personal experiences, to other sources of professional knowledge, to global issues and even universal ones, such as how motherhood manifests in human societies. These connections have engaged us, stimulated our thinking and expanded our knowledge. What stays with me the most by far, however, are the featured mothers. I have never met them, but feel like I know them – at least in part. There's something about when a person shares their existence that makes us more knowledgeable of being human in general. The mothers trusted María, opening up about experiencing joy and happiness through the relationships with their children, while also feeling overwhelmed and lonely, pulled in all directions, expected to be the glue in ensuring all family members' needs were met at the expense of their own. They are all but erased in the power dynamics of our society, including by the patriarchy within their own homes. And yet, they are still standing, quietly claiming the knowledge they possess. As María observes, 'none of the mothers identified a deficit in their child until an individual whom they viewed as an expert told them so'. They don't see their child with a deficit lens, or agree with the disability labels, but they accept these things as an inevitable part of the system. The mothers also understand that their children *are* bilingual, and it is their child's right to be so. Bilingualism, they recognize is a strength, not a hindrance. Finally, the mothers are also highly aware of the forces that impede their own agency, including language, gender, race and disability, recognizing they rarely have places to publicly acknowledge what limits them.

In *(M)othering Labeled Children: Bilingualism and Disability in the Lives of Latinx Mothers*, we have been taken into the world of 'parents who are sometimes seen, but rarely heard'. When engaging with the book, our own worlds were paused as we entered those of the mothers. As readers, we contemplated their lives, thoughts and perspectives in an intimate space that made us mindful of our shared humanity. This is the beauty of María's work. Within a world that seems indifferent at best, and hostile at worst, these Latinx mothers shared who they are, in their own way, in their own words. Not only do their *testimonios* stand alone, but they are also a collective testimony to the power of thoughtful, respectful, reflective research that can be achieved from a position of both cultural closeness and humility (Nomikoudis & Starr, 2016). As such, this work exemplifies how researchers should follow their instincts and explore areas we care deeply about, *and know about*, that are not represented sufficiently or accurately in the scholarly literature of our fields and, by extension, society at large. *Sigamos adelante*/Let's continue forward.

References

Cuevas, S. (2019) '*Con much sacrificio*, we give them everything we can': The strategic day-to-day sacrifices of undocumented latino/a parents. *Harvard Educational Review* 89 (3), 473–496.

Harry, B. and Ocasio-Stoutenberg, L. (2020) *Meeting Families Where They Are: Building Equity through Advocacy with Diverse Schools and Communities*. New York: Teachers College Press.

Lalvani, P. (ed.) (2019) *Constructing the (M)other: Narratives of Resistance at the Intersection of Motherhood and the Politics of Normal*. New York: Peter Lang.

Nomikoudis M. and Starr M. (2016) Cultural humility in education and work: A valuable approach for teachers, learners and professionals. In J. Arvanitakis and D.J. Hornsby (eds) *Universities, the Citizen Scholar and the Future of Higher Education* (pp. 69–84). Basingstoke: Palgrave.

Sauer, J.S. and Rossetti, Z. (2020) *Affirming Disability: Strengths-Based Portraits of Culturally Diverse Families*. New York: Teachers College Press.

Valle, J. (2009) *What Mothers Say about Special Education: From 1960s to the Present*. New York: Palgrave.

Index

Note: References in *italics* are to figures, those in **bold** to tables; "n" refers to chapter notes.

able bendiciones xi–xiii
Aceves, T.C. 106
Ana (*Testimonialista*) 47, *47*, 48–9
  broken marriage 138–9
  buried feelings 140
  children's needs 153–4
  disability as secret 73–4
  disability as social construction 69–70
  home 53–6, *55*
  joy of motherhood 143–4, 145
  language as disability marker 98–9
  language learning at home 108–9
  María Teresa's view 147, 148–9
  minimizing of disability 71
  monolingual ideologies 101–3
  mother to more than one 135–6
  mother's efforts to learn English 110, 111, 112
  origin of disability 68
  the physical toll 84–5
  seeking external support 121–2
  using technology 123, 124
Annamma, S.A. *et al.* 10n
Anzaldúa, G. 35
assimilation 19–20

Baglieri, S. *et al.* 21, 27n16
Bernal, D.D. *et al.* 35
bilingual education 4, 9, 160–1, 164
bilingual special education 8, 98
bilingualism 3–4, 18
  from daughter to teacher 4–5
  education settings *96*, 96–8, *97*

false dichotomy 98–103
  importance of xii–xiii
  perceptions of 9
  as strength 164, 182–3
bilingualism: multilayered meanings and purposes 89
  me puedan deportar: in case of deportation 93–6
  mi hermano, ¿le contestó?: binational siblings 92–3
  mi idioma: linguistic identity 89–90
  oportunidad: financial security 90–2
Black, Cathleen 5
#BlackLivesMatter 16, 25n4

Carini, P.F. 33, 37, 39, 41n3, 46, 48, 177
Carlota (mother) 46, *47*, 152
  broken marriage 137–8
  diagnosis as information 77
  joy of motherhood 146
  label as resource 76
  language learning at home 108, 113
  linguistic identity 90
  minimizing of disability 71, 72
  monolingual ideologies 101
  mother to more than one 133
  origin of disability 69
  using technology 123, 125
Carmela (mother) *47*, 47–8
  diagnosis as information 77
  homework 150
  impact of disability label 80
  linguistic identity 90

mother to more than one 133
mothering by proxy 120
opportunity 90–1
origin of disability 70
using technology 123–4
Chuck, E. 26n12
Civil Rights Movement 27n17
Cohen, S.R. 13, 14
communal learning through collective
   inquiry 169–70
community education xii–xiii, 173
Connor, D.J. *et al.* 17, 27n17, 178–83
Crenshaw, K. 15–17, 25n1
culturally and linguistically diverse (CLD)
   students 98

Davis, Angela 25n1
deportation 93–6
descriptive inquiry (DI) 36, 37–9, 41n3,
   177
descriptive review (DR) 38
dis/ability
   minority (group) model 27n17
   social interpretation(s) of 21, 27n17,
      67–8
   see also social construction model
      (SCM) of dis/ability
dis/ability classifications 96, *97*
dis/ability critical race studies (DisCrit) 23
dis/abled by proxy 16, 25n3
disability, defined 27n18
disability labels and mothering 67–8
   bendita herencia: origins of disability
      68–9
   disability as social construct 67
   entre menos sepan, mejor: disabilities as
      closely guarded secrets 73–4
   pequeñitos problemitas: minimizing of
      disability 71–3
   una niña normal: disability as social
      construction 69–71
disability labels: functions of 74–5
   más: label as resource 75–7
   no le entendía: label as relief 78–9
   yo no sabía: diagnosis as information
      77–8
disability labels' impact on lives of
   MoEBLADs 7, 79–80
   impotente: emotional toll 80–1

me cansaba: physical toll 84–6
me sentí mal: labels as source of sadness
   81
no me daban respuesta: worrying
   through evaluation process 82
por eso no puedo . . .: labels as
   confinement 83–4
¿qué puedo hacer?: psychological toll
   82–3
conclusion 86–7
disability studies (DS) 21, 22, 26–7n15
disability studies in education (DSE)
   23–4, 26–7n15
DisCrit (dis/ability critical race studies) 23
DR (descriptive review) 38
Duncan, Isadora 3
Durán, L.K. 13, 107
Durand, T.M. 7

EBLADS (emergent bilinguals labeled as
   dis/abled) 24, 53
   bilingual programs 98
   dis/ability classifications 96, *97*
   education settings 96, *96*
   linguistic genocide 20
   schools 44
   talking about their mothers 146–9
   terminology 8, 9, 103n1
   see also false dichotomy: remedy
      disability/develop bilingualism
education xii–xiii
   intersectional policies 162–3
   settings *96*, 96–8, *97*
Elodia (mother) 47, 47, 75, 101, 126, 127
#EqualPayForEqualWork 16, 25n4
exclusion 10

false dichotomy: remedy disability/develop
   bilingualism 98–103
   dificultades en decirlo bien: language as
      disability marker 98–100
   ellas me dijeron . . .: monolingual
      ideologies 100–3
family observations as pedagogical practice
   170–1
family support 166, 172–3
feminism and intersectionality 25n5
feminist disability studies 23
financial security 90–2

Finkelstein, V. 27n17
Fishman, J.A. 51n1

Gage, N.A. *et al.* 97
Gallo, S. 45
García, O. 51n1
Garland-Thomson, R. 22
global connections 181–2
goals of this book 36
Gyles, Bob 180–1

Hague Recommendations 19, 26n9
Hankivsky, O. 15
Harry, B. 17, 67
Himley, M. 33, 35, 38
home language 5, 18–19, 26n6–7, 166–7
home visits 170–1
homework 149–50, 172
hooks, bell 25n1
Huber, L.P. 35
Hugo, Victor 3

ICT (integrated co-teaching classes) 8,
      10n3
IDEA *see* Individuals with Disabilities
      Education Act
identity xiv, 6, 89–90
IEP *see* individual education plans
Ijalba, E. 106
impairment, defined 27n18
inclusion 5–6
inclusive learning spaces/classrooms 5,
      10n3
individual education plans (IEPs) 5, 13,
      99, 103n1, 120–1, 161, 165, 170
Individuals with Disabilities Education Act
      (IDEA) *96*, 162
Individuals with Disabilities Education
      Improvement Act (2004) *96*
inequities 15
integrated co-teaching classes (ICT) 8,
      10n3
intentions 9–10
interpreters 21, 106, 107
intersectionality 6, 9, 15–18, 23, 25n1,
      25n5, 160, 162–3

Klingner, J. 67
Kurth, J.A. *et al.* 97

labeled as dis/abled (LAD) 5, 10n1
labels xii, xiv–xv, 10, 18–21, 22, 27n20
      see also disability labels and mothering;
         disability labels: functions of;
         disability labels' impact on lives of
         MoEBLADs
language as disability marker 98–100
language as power 150–2
language-based harassment 19–20, 26n12
language learning at home 108–15
language policies 19–21
Latinx, defined 10n7
Latinx families xv
Latinx mothers 7
      see also MoEBLADS (mothers of
         emergent bilinguals labeled as dis/
         abled)
Layzer, J.I. 170
linguistic genocide 19, 20–1, 26n8
linguistic human rights (LHR) 18–21,
      26n14, 166
linguistic identity 89–90
Long Island University (LIU) 37
Loren, Sophia 3
Lynch, J. 26n12

María (*Testimonialista*) 46, 47, 49–50
      broken marriage 137, 138
      buried feelings 140, 141
      in case of deportation 94
      children's needs come first 153
      diagnosis as information 77–8
      disability as social construction 70
      home 56–9, *57*
      impact of disability label 81
      joy of motherhood 145, 146
      Justin's view 147, 148
      label as confinement 83–4
      label as relief 78–9
      language as disability marker 99–100
      linguistic identity 89, 90
      minimizing of disability 71
      mother as teacher 118, 119
      mother to more than one 134
      mother's efforts to learn English
         110–12, 113
      the physical toll 86
      seeking external support 122
      using technology 124, 125

McCall, L. 16, 17
Menken, K. 43–4
Mexico 20, 26n13
minoritizing labels xii, xiv–xv, 10, 22, 27n20
minority (group) model 27n17
MoEBLADS (mothers of emergent bilinguals labeled as dis/abled) 13–15, 36
   disability 21–4
   intersectionality 15–18, 23, 25n1, 25n5, 160
   labeling language, silencing people 18–21
   Latinx mothers 13
   linguistic practices and perceptions 106–8
   rights as parents 165, 168–9
   theoretical framework 15–25
   from theory to reality 24–5
MoEBLADS as language brokers 106–8
   el catecismo en español: teaching Spanish through God 109
   es así en inglés ¿okay?: reciprocal learning 114–15
   language learning at home 108–15
   uno tiene que aprender el idioma: Mothers' efforts to learn English 109–14
   yo le enseño: home language education 108–9
   conclusion 115–16
MoEBLADS' challenges 130
   broken marriages: *tomaga, insultaba, amenazaba, presionaba, lastimaba* 137–9
   fractured roles: mother to more than one 130–7
   sola, vacía, desesperada: buried feelings 139–42
MoEBLADS' involvement in academic development 118
   el traductor del teléfono: using technology 123–6
   mi hija me ayuda: mothering by proxy 120–1
   no que digamos mucho: mothers assess their engagement 126–8

trato, en lo que puedo. . .: mothers as teachers 118–20
yo busco a una persona: seeking external support 121–3
conclusion 128–9
monolingual ideologies among school professionals 100–3
monolingual inclusion classes 6, 10n4
Montelongo, A. 14, 108
mother tongue(s) 18–19, 26n6, 181
motherhood as purpose 143
   es mi mejor amiga: EBLADs talk about their mothers 146–9
   las tareas: ostracized by homework 149–50
   no voy a sacrificar a mi hijo: children's needs come first 152–5, 182
   tú no sabes inglés: language as power 150–2
   una mamá muy feliz: joy of motherhood 143–6
mothers xi–xiii, xiv–xv, 3–4, 181–2
   and bilingualism 4–5
   a desire to center mothers 8–9, 182–3
   as equal partners 14
   Latinx mothers 7
   Mexican–Americans 7
   mothering at the margins 6–7
   supporting mothers 172–3
   in this study 46–51, 47
   see also MoEBLADS (mothers of emergent bilinguals labeled as dis/abled); *Testimonialistas*
moving forward together 175–7
multilingual education 165–6

Nancy (mother) 47, 47
   binational siblings 93
   in case of deportation 94
   diagnosis as information 77, 78
   engagement 126–7
   homework 149
   joy of motherhood 144–5
   language as disability marker 99
   language as power 151
   minimizing of disability 71
   mother to more than one 133
   origin of disability 68

reciprocal learning 114, 115
Nash, J.C. 15
nationalism 19–20
needs in context 171–2
neurodiversity 69, 87n1, 164
New York City
    Department of Education (NYCDOE)
        5, *96*, 97, *97*
    Shared Pathways to Success (SPtS) 5
    Sunset Park 8, 44–5
    'The Multilingual Apple' 43–4, 51n1
New York State's Commissioner's
    Regulations 162
normal/normalcy 22, 27n19

other people's stories 33
    descriptive inquiry 36, 37–9, 41n3, 177
    gathering of stories 39–41, *40*
    testimonios 33–7, 41n1, 48, 181, 183

parental involvement 6–7, 10n8, 14, 164,
    170–1
parental rights 165, 168–9
participatory rank method (PRM) 171–2
Partlow, J. 26n13
Paty (*Testimonialista*) 46, 47, 50–1
    assesses her engagement 127
    binational siblings 92
    broken marriage 138, 139
    buried feelings 140, 141
    in case of deportation 94–5
    children's needs come first 152–3,
        154–5
    Dan's view 147–8, 150
    diagnosis as information 77
    home 59–64, *63*
    impact of disability label 80–1
    joy of motherhood 145–6
    label as confinement 84
    label as resource 75–6
    language learning at home 108
    monolingual ideologies 100–1
    mother as teacher 119
    mother to more than one 130–3,
        134–5, 136–7
    mother's efforts to learn English 110,
        111, 112, 113–14, 115
    psychological toll 82–3

seeking external support 122–3
personal, professional and global
    connections 178–9
    connections taken together 182–3
    global 181–2
    personal 179–80
    professional 180–1
Pew Research Center 20
place and time 43
    the mothers 46–51, *47*
    New York City 43–4
    Sunset Park 8, 44–5
    time: 2016 election 45–6
positionality xiv–xvi
PRM (participatory rank method) 171–2
professional connections 180–1

reciprocal education xii–xiii, 114–15
recollections 38–9, 169–70
religion 67, 109
repairing broken systems 159–60
    correcting the literature 163–5
    disability? language? family?: putting
        needs in context 171–2
    intersectional educational policies
        162–3
    putting theory into practice 160–2
    recollecting together: communal
        learning through collective inquiry
        169–70
    resurrecting the home visit 170–1
    start with collaboration in mind 165–9
    supporting families at home 172
    supporting mothers 172–3
Robinson, J.E. 87n1
Rodriguez, R.J. *et al.* 108
Rosa (mother) 47, *47*
    buried feelings 140
    diagnosis as information 77
    homework 149
    minimizing of disability 71
    mothering by proxy 120
    mother's efforts to learn English
        109–10
    source of sadness 81
    uncertainty 82
Rosario (mother) 47, 48, 71, 75, 91,
    118–19

Sara (mother) 47, 48, 70, 82–3, 90, 120, 121, 144

#SayHerName 25n4

school-to-parent communication 107–8

SCM *see* social construction model (SCM) of dis/ability

segregation 23, 27n21

self-contained classes 5, 10n2

Shared Pathways to Success (SPtS) 5, 6

Skutnabb-Kangas, T. 18–19, 20–1, 26n6–8

social construction model (SCM) of dis/ability 21–4, 27n17, 27n18, 69–71, 161

social justice 9, 168

Society for Disability Studies 27n17

Spanish language xii, 20

Spanish-speaking homes/complicated classrooms 96–8

special education 9
  bilingual programs 8, 98
  culturally and linguistically diverse (CLD) students 98
  dis/ability classifications 96, *97*
  English-only programs 97–8
  parental rights 165, 168–9
  settings 96, *96*
  teacher preparation 167–9

Spivak, G.C. 35

SPtS *see* Shared Pathways to Success

St Pierre, R.G. 170

Stokes, B. 20, 26n14

story gathering 39–41, *40*

Sunset Park 8, 44–5

Taylor, S.J. 24

teacher preparation programs 165
  consider home language practices 166–7
  demystifying language learning and multilingual education 165–6
  develop strategies for family support 166
  extend special education teacher preparation beyond ESL 167–8
  reframe the way we talk about/to parents 168–9

technology use 123–6

Testimonialistas 35, 40, 41n2, 48, 53
  gathering of stories 39–41, *40*
  see also Ana; María; Paty

testimonios 33–7, 41n1, 48, 181, 183

Title I schools 44, 51n2

translanguaging 61, 167, 182

translators 106, 107

Traugh, C. 37

Trump, D. 20, 93

Truth, Sojourner 25n1

universal design for learning (UDL) 167

values 6, 10n5

Vickstrom, E. 43

Wolfe, K. 13, 107

women of color (WoC) 15–16

Women's March on Washington 25–6n5

Yuval-Davis, N. 25n2